Room 4.1.3

PENN STUDIES IN LANDSCAPE ARCHITECTURE
John Dixon Hunt, Series Editor

This series is dedicated to the study and promotion of a wide variety of approaches to landscape architecture, with special emphasis on connections between theory and practice. It includes monographs on key topics in history and theory, descriptions of projects by both established and rising designers, translations of major foreign-language texts, anthologies of theoretical and historical writings on classic issues, and critical writing by members of the profession of landscape architecture.

This is how it should be done: lodge yourself on a stratum, experiment with the opportunities it offers, find an advantageous place on it, find potential movements of deterritorialization, possible lines of flight, experience them, produce new flow conjunctions here and there, try out continuums of intensities segment by segment, have a small plot of new land at all times.

—*Gilles Deleuze and Félix Guattari,* A Thousand Plateaus

ROOM 4.1.3

INNOVATIONS IN LANDSCAPE ARCHITECTURE

RICHARD WELLER

WITH ESSAYS BY

ROD BARNETT

JACKY BOWRING

PAUL CARTER

PETER CONNOLLY

DENIS COSGROVE

GAVIN KEENEY

JULIAN RAXWORTHY

PENN

University of Pennsylvania Press

Philadelphia

Publication of this volume was assisted by a grant from the Getty
Grant Program.

Text copyright © 2005 University of Pennsylvania Press
Illustrations copyright © 2005 Room 4.1.3

Published by
University of Pennsylvania Press
Philadelphia, Pennsylvania 19104-4011

Library of Congress Cataloging-in-Publication Data

Room 4.1.3 : innovations in landscape architecture / Richard
Weller.

    p.   cm - (Penn studies in landscape architecture)
    Includes bibliographical references and index.
    ISBN 0-8122-3784-6 (alk. paper)
1.Landscape Architecture. I. Title II. Series.
SB472.W45 2004
712—dc22   2003070549
CIP

Contents

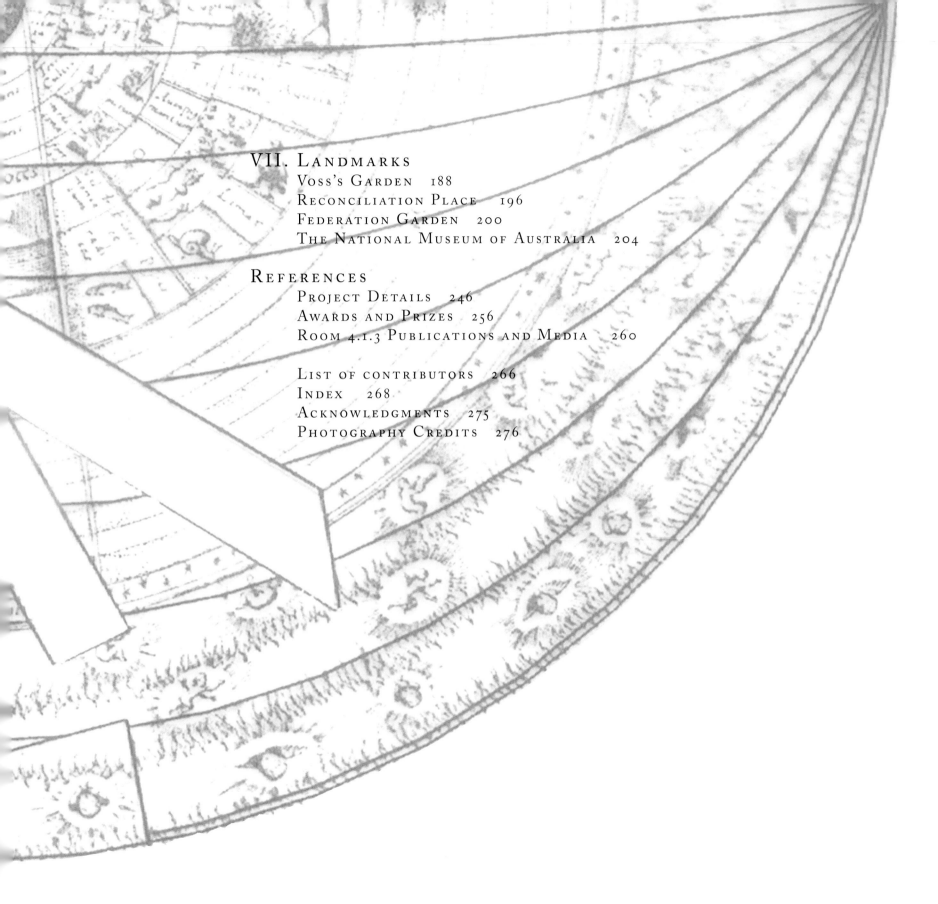

A professor of mine who advised me that I was unemployable suggested that I meet Vladimir Sitta, an immigrant from Czechoslovakia who washed up in Sydney in 1981. Sitta is now co-director of Room 4.1.3, and the same professor subsequently employed me in 1994 to help him construct a new landscape architecture program in the Faculty of Architecture, Landscape, and Visual Arts at the University of Western Australia from where I now pen this introduction. When we met, Vladimir and I did not discuss jobs, but we did exchange drawings, some of which had helped him win the prestigious Lenne Preis, not once but twice, a fact somewhat lost on Australian landscape architecture.

At the time of completing my studies I was more interested in painting than design, and I had organized my life around it. Intellectually and financially unable to sustain this difficult romance, I found landscape architecture and urban design competitions to be an acceptable compromise of the ideal and the real, the private and the commercial. Design competitions are the *arte povera* of the periphery, offering exaltation and exotica. By virtue of anonymity, competitions allow one to transcend rank.

From our position, competitions were the only chance of manufacturing a landscape of ideas, and even if we lost expensively, we developed intellectual property and therefore won, honorably. As well as doing competitions (quite often with a modicum of success) in the mid-eighties, Vladimir and I connected up with a businessman-guru-creative director who flew into Sydney to redesign the city and tether the gossamer of his global web at that end of the Pacific rim.

His company, Creative Design and Technology (CDT), not only recognized Sydney's global potential, but he had personally visited the future and reported back that it was a theme park. He and his elaborate entourage of producers, writers, animators, and model makers invented their own projects and traded ideas and drawings for yen. Although troubled by a themed future, we saw an opportunity for our own interests and fulfilled our bizarre brief to imagineer fantastic and unlikely structures, sometimes drawing new cities in a matter of days. In many places around the world, from Coney Island to unmapped terrain in Kalimantan, Borneo, sometimes with clients and sometimes without, we invented mega projects and new societies to sustain them. Much of this work was so "fantastic" that it is inappropriate to this volume, although one project for Singapore is included.

Exhausted by the cyclic unemployment and capriciousness of the global market that made CDT's projects impossible, we headed off in different directions in 1990. A builder and a sculptor, Vladimir wanted to return to the fine art and craft of the garden, an acclaimed practice that he maintains, in addition to Room 4.1.3, to this day. Alternatively, I wanted a practice that would face up to cultural studies and test theory's mounting pretenses. I wanted a landscape architecture that would emerge from grittier soil, and at the time this meant one had to be right where the Wall suddenly was not–Berlin 1990.

Captivated by No-Man's-Land, that extraordinary fault line through the twentieth century, I set myself the task of completing a set of drawings concerning ideas for its future. In order to do so, at the behest of the staff at the offices of the great magazine *Daidalos,* I began collaborating with the reputable local landscape design firm Müller Knippschild Wehberg (MKW) on local competitions. With Jan Wehberg and Cornelia Müller (now trading as Lutzow 7), I enjoyed a range of ideas competitions, adamant about an anti-aesthetic and programmatic invention which, fortunately, a German audience appreciated. Jan and Cornelia also introduced me to Daniel Libeskind, whose influence endures.

In the early 1990s Berlin seemed remarkably open to speculation, but as its new city center emerged from the sublime dereliction of the Potsdamer Platz, the twenty-first century looked, in plan at least, not very different from the nineteenth. Consequently, Berlin became predictable, and I accepted an offer to construct a new design course in Perth, the world's most isolated city and a place I had never been. Being back in Australia's deep time allowed me the space in which to focus on a range of nationally symbolic projects on offer as the mirage of Australia's centenary of Federation (1900-2000) shimmered on the horizon. With Vladimir in Sydney and myself in Perth, we established Room 4.1.3 as a virtual office so as to span the three thousand kilometers of desert in between and in so doing formalized a fifteen-year friendship securely based on a mutual disdain for landscape architecture's innocuous complicity in society's glib postmodern prospectus.

Among many projects, in 1997 we won the National Museum of Australia with Australia's most inventive architects, Ashton Raggatt McDougall. The museum has triggered considerable international debate, and we are pleased to have ensured that the museum's landscape architecture is a complex exegesis on both Australian conditions and the artifice of landscape design. We took the opportunity in this book to contextualize that project's high profile and glaring surfaces within our larger body of diverse work. Now, anchored in the University of Western Australia at one end and inner-city Sydney at the other, Room 4.1.3 divides its daily labors among project management, documentation, education, and research. Taken together this amounts to a real and an ideal effort to think and build critical landscape architecture.

Motivated by a lack of imagination in the form and content of contemporary cities, the projects in this book claim to be allegorical topographies that retain their political and poetic integrity. To invoke such integrity through the agency of landscape design implies that this is a practice of resistance. Not only is this politically incorrect, reeking of a sulking Marxism, but it is also far too heroic. The work does, however, concern a quest for alternative spaces and places of intensity, places where meanings cluster and reconfigure, where new myths might entwine and take root. If this proceeds by negation, then it is only to make space for optimistic alternatives. In order to open up to alternatives we have utilized and sustained a play of signification, not as a style but rather as a quest for lucid moments in the white noise miasma of the contemporary city.

If not sites of resistance, then certainly these projects are motivated by a romantic disposition. None of the work, however, claims to express intuitive truth or falls prey to vainglorious old quests for access to nature as "other" through art. Similarly, if not sites of resistance, the projects are the sites of our genuine efforts to avoid the decorative subservience and complicity of mainstream practice and make something significant in its absence. We are, however, motivated not so much by a disdain for orthodoxy as by a passion for the discipline. Whether mainstream practice can retrieve much from this work is not a question we have worried

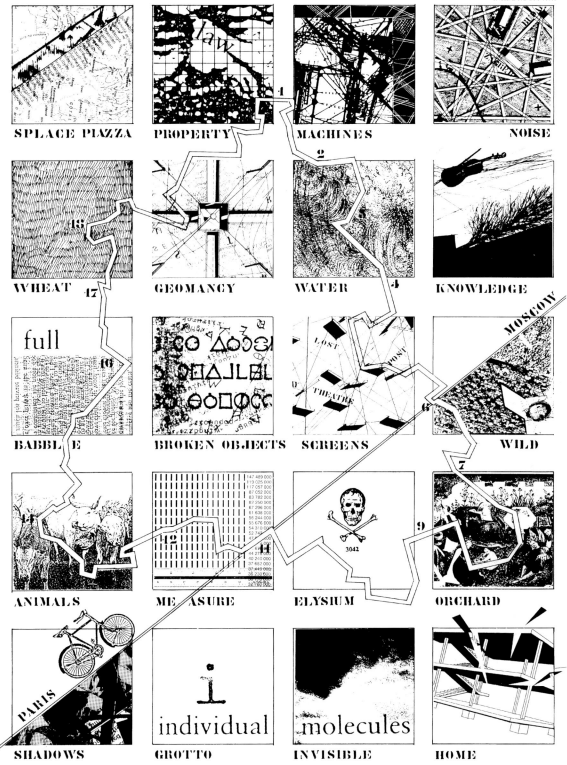

SPLACE PIAZZA   PROPERTY   MACHINES   NOISE

WHEAT   GEOMANCY   WATER   KNOWLEDGE

BABBLE   BROKEN OBJECTS   SCREENS   WILD

ANIMALS   MEASURE   ELYSIUM   ORCHARD

SHADOWS   GROTTO   INVISIBLE   HOME

over, and no doubt some will dismiss this work as the frustrated ranting of a belated avant-garde and assign it to the coast of arcane symbology.

This collection of work is more than just a gathering of curious flotsam and jetsam; this body of work takes shape by trying to avoid dissolution into landscape architecture's doldrums or evaporation into its broad dusty plains. By the same token, in refusing a consistent methodology and remaining open to every project initially on its terms, we try to avoid entrapment in our own oases. Rather than allow landscape architecture's postmodern identity crisis to lead us into a debilitating schizophrenia, we have tried to make a virtue of landscape architecture's (almost impossible) breadth.

Typically, the thinking landscape architect is fostered out to cultural studies, art, and architecture—makes a go of it, suffers paranoia, then attempts a return. It is the return that matters, and it is this that is traced in this volume. Of course, some paths in this body of work lead nowhere, so to map them here is not only to save other explorers some time but also to illustrate fulsomely the nature of the labyrinth in which postmodern landscape architecture finds itself.

This book assumes its place as part of a more general development by which landscape architecture is emerging from academic isolation, intellectual slothfulness, socioecological Calvinism, and aesthetic naiveté, which prevailed in the early 1970s and 1980s when Vladimir Sitta and I were educated. Most notably this emergence sees the gaps between theory/praxis and design/planning closing down. Theory and praxis conduct a complex dance, and to separate them for long is perilous, a point that partially explains landscape architecture's relative dearth of critical writing and designing.

Although this might be once again a time for unambiguous manifestos, this book's diversity of words and images does not move toward a singular thesis for contemporary landscape architecture. Rather than being seen as merely a pluralistic catalogue, our hope is that the book sets up refractions through theory and practice, making it possible for the reader to find ways in which theory circumscribes design's conceits and how praxis, by sheer invention and proposition, leaps across theory's tendency toward ponderous, circuitous neatness.

Certainly much humble, dogged work is being done in landscape architecture to rehabilitate, revegetate, and reconcile, but our work is more about the direct contestation and perpetuation of meanings in the city. Meaning is the immaterial infrastructure of the city and its society, its superstructure. Accordingly, these projects are crafted as interventions in the symbolic order of things as much as they are intended for the quotidian landscape. As opposed to apologia for development, didactic incantations of the loss of a sense of place, or phony re-creations of the prelapsarian, our work chips away at the contemporary edifices of Culture and Nature and seeks interconnection with broader postmodern cultural concerns.

Since meanings are at stake in our work, language dominates a project's development. Projects emerge from information overload, editing, wordplays, associations, and the rigors of writing. Projects are pushed to the threshold where meaning effaces itself and left to teeter, a precipice of maximum hermeneutic valency. We do worry that such acrobatics are contained to the garden theater, yet it is in that marvelous domain that the panoply of landscape architecture's representational potential can be brought into play.

Just as you do not expect theater to do social work but you rightly expect it to be about society, our work is largely about socioecological drama. We are not interested in landscape's lullabies or comforting an audience over its losses, although we would utilize nostalgia, sentiment, kitsch, and Arcadia as soon they were seen fit to perform in larger rhetorical productions. We aim to produce volatile, interactive sets, and open-ended yet structured scripts, what Baudelaire might have meant when in 1859 he urged the formation of useful illusions, not naturalism, in set design.

Not only is the work theatrical, but quite obviously it would not be as it is had we not so sharply felt the influence of environmental art practices. These practices embarrassed landscape architecture into aesthetic experimentation and in turn encouraged reflection on landscape's representational traditions. Landscape architecture is now somewhat superficially reconnected with its muses, but there remains much in twentieth-century art which it needs to work through so that it might better arrive at a truly relevant contemporary way of seeing—an ecological vision, perhaps.

James Corner's writings in the early 1990s on hermeneutics, ecology, and representation have resonated through our drawings, and now, as a collection, the work can be taken as one answer to his recent call for more design experimentation, more sophisticated forms of representation, and greater critical foresight and cultural knowledge in landscape architecture. But, if we are to read Corner's recent writing seriously, we encounter discrepancies between his words and our designs. That is, our projects often trade exclusively in rarefied sites, places he pejoratively names "semantic reserves." In short, Corner's use of the pejorative is designed to turn landscape architecture away from its paltry postmodern spate of symbolizing culture and nature and direct it onto more substantive and efficacious modes of production. Through arguments that privilege *landschaft* (working place), not *landskip* (contrived scene), Corner now turns into the harsh light and away from the grotto wall to face the real, not its representation.

In the broader course of postmodern landscape architecture's direction, Corner is, in principle, right. Although we could not be accused of creating facile scenery, our practice has allowed itself to retreat into ivory towers, bunkers, gardens, and the semiotic alleys of the city–places somewhat removed from the instrumentalities Corner now urges landscape architecture to take creative control of. Perhaps, then, this book demonstrates the failings as well as the fruits of an indulgence in "semantic reserves" and recognizes that work such as ours is part of postmodern landscape architecture's aesthetic rite of passage, a passage that, if one were to follow Corner, might lead us beyond the garden fence.

But surely the profligacy of meanings and promiscuity of form evident in our work need not be diametrically opposed to instrumentality. At best, some of our projects set coordinates toward what we would call an art of instrumentality, precisely because landscape is a field in which such stereotypical dualisms as art and science, culture and nature, design and planning can commingle and blur. An art of landscape architecture would need to be about the world and its socioecological dramas, but it would also need to be, as John Dixon Hunt insists, about landscape architecture, which is, in turn, largely about the intellectual and formal laboratory of the garden and its history. But Hunt is not only speaking of gardens as isolated and rarefied "semantic reserves" (although by definition this remains their particular strength); rather, they also contain clues for the meaning and making of whole places, suggesting again, by a different route, that landscape architecture is at best an art of instrumentality.

Admittedly closer to art than instrumentality or amenity, we do nonetheless attempt to provide inspirational public infrastructure through the agency of design. Mainly in the absence of tight-fisted clients and often under the aegis of open-ended competition briefs, we have, insofar as possible, attempted to turn away from images toward strategies of programmatic invention and novel interventions. Not to be confused with local practices of empowering communities to make their own neighborhoods, our practice remains one of authorial assertion and intervention for which we make no apologies.

To varying degrees, interventions are crafted as catalysts for people to then self-organize and colonize the actual and symbolic contours of public space. In that regard, the work is not unaware of its naiveté in regard to the instrumentalities of democratic urban place-making, and much can be lost in trying to translate conceptual and idealistic design into forms and things that could partake of the brazen contradictions of public space on the occasion of its extinction. In every instance, however, we have produced these projects with the intention and proviso that they be built. This work is not a detached conceptual project, even though some of the graphics are more concerned with tracing ideation than conventions.

Each project is intimately of its site. However, "site" is now a stretched and ambiguous device of orientation. Sites are local and global, particular and general, fact and fiction. With the partiality of knowledge as a rule, our work makes no claim to the essence, or even an accurate tapping of a site's particular heart, soul, and memory. Each project does, however, arise more than less from the specific locale in which it takes place, but any "place" is, for us, as much cultural ether as biophysical matter. Locked into both, we then send out tendrils, rhizomatically connecting with larger sociopolitical, ecological, and representational possibilities. The work is then about relationality, and each project is a crystallization within a web. This is not to say that the projects do not seek more profound orientation than that of surface networks. On the contrary, we have been preoccupied with the tensions between place and placelessness.

The work we do can also be situated as something in between architecture, art, and landscape design, since it combines aspects of these disciplines in an effort to overcome their stricter predeterminations and representational limits. This confluence could be signified by the twentieth-century term *field* as opposed to the eighteenth-century term *landscape*. The inclusive conception of landscape as field can be understood as interdisciplinary and ecological, merging binary distinctions between landscape and object, within the general milieu of the denatured and the cyborgian.

Many of the projects confront the increasingly common challenge of what to do with denatured, postindustrial, postdialectical spaces. Landscape architecture is often mocked for its specious and ultimately contradictory and impossible romance with unmediated Nature. Indeed landscape architects have failed to apprehend the (delightful) conceit of naturalism as only one of many aesthetic possibilities; they have failed to acknowledge that naturalism is, in fact, a manufactured contrivance. Compounding the problem, such naturalism is often presented with the vague notion that nature and culture will reach some kind of harmony, an unbelievable, all-too-easy, static synthesis that does more to reiterate a fallacious nature/culture divide than to reimagine it. Focusing more on biophysical systems than cultural systems, landscape architecture has had a different twentieth century than the arts. Landscape architecture, somewhat zealously, met the late twentieth century with what it thought to be the true language of nature. But the true language of nature is something of an oxymoron, for we always put words in its mouth.

Here, then, is our alphabet.

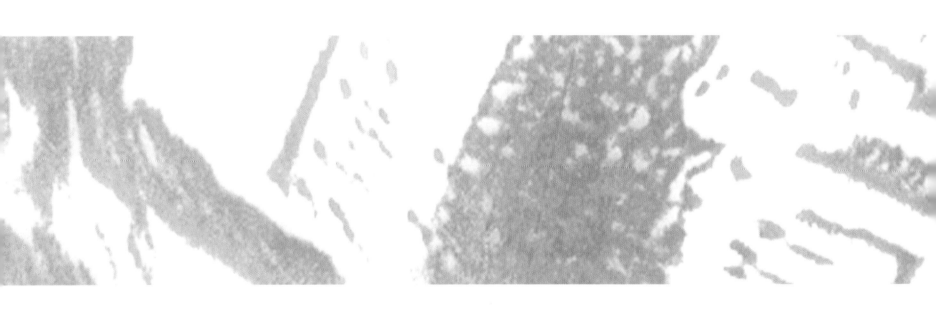

I. DIALECTICAL GEOGRAPHIES

The Satellite's Garden and the Vertigorium

Berlin 1990

Landscape architecture is, among other things, an art of orientation. Pagan inscriptions on the earth's surface oriented the clan to the creation of the world. The orthogonal axes of archaic urban form mirrored the cosmos, alignments that gardens, inside the city walls and free from the demands of food production, repeated amidst signs of abundance. The garden's manifold delights and deities came to signify a Golden Age, one lost and one desired, and it is this fraught longing that then motivates the narrative structures of monotheism which reduced the garden to the setting for the fall and something to die for.

The same orthogonal diagram that structured cities, located the *axis mundi* (world axis) in the heart of medieval fortifications and monasteries, rendered that which was once pagan, Christian or Islamic. A central font marked the waters of ablution, the Edenic source of the World Rivers, and aligned the soul to Purgatory. As the mind's eye of the Renaissance opened, the mechanics of vision sliced through the walls of the *hortus conclusus* reaching in vain for baroque infinitude. Modernity, substituting Man for God, ruled up the empirical world into an endless graticule.

The existential geometry of the twentieth century sees the enlightened grid buckle, warp, and fractalize through the protean space-time fields of relativity. Somewhere there, the postmodern self now struggles to make a place for itself–somewhere between the natural and the denatured, the real and the virtual, between the social horror of history and an ecologically imperiled future.

This first project, the Vertigorium, named as such by combining Roman *vomitoria* with the modern desire for flight, literally falls into landscape architecture's history of orientation. It does so in the quintessential twentieth-century city, Berlin. It begins by flying across that city, then attempts a landing. On the ground and in the labyrinth of the city it seeks to pick a significant line and secure a center. There it marks a place and builds a grotto.

Not so much a designed object as a map, the Vertigorium draws a connection between the two main topographic features of an otherwise flat city: the Hill of the Devil (Teufelsberg) and the Hill of the Cross (Kreuzberg). The former is created from Berlin's war-torn fabric, a place where people now like to fly kites, a place crowned by an American satellite surveillance center. The latter is a natural landform featuring a large monument to Prussian military campaigns by Karl-Friedrich Schinkel, a landscaped waterfall and a large wooden cross.

The metaphoric fall that we make into this dialectical situation between the two hills is recorded in a series of nine simple images beginning with the heights of a satellite photo of the city. Via successive enlargements of this original image, a fall is figured, but, as opposed to just landing on the surface of the city, we enter the pixels of the image. By continuing to enlarge the pixels the image darkens until we reach blackness–void, Nietzsche's godhead.

In reality, it is proposed that these images are engraved and imprinted on metal plates set in monumental stone tablets placed evenly across the city, with the first and the ninth placed on the Kreuzberg and the Teufelsberg, respectively.

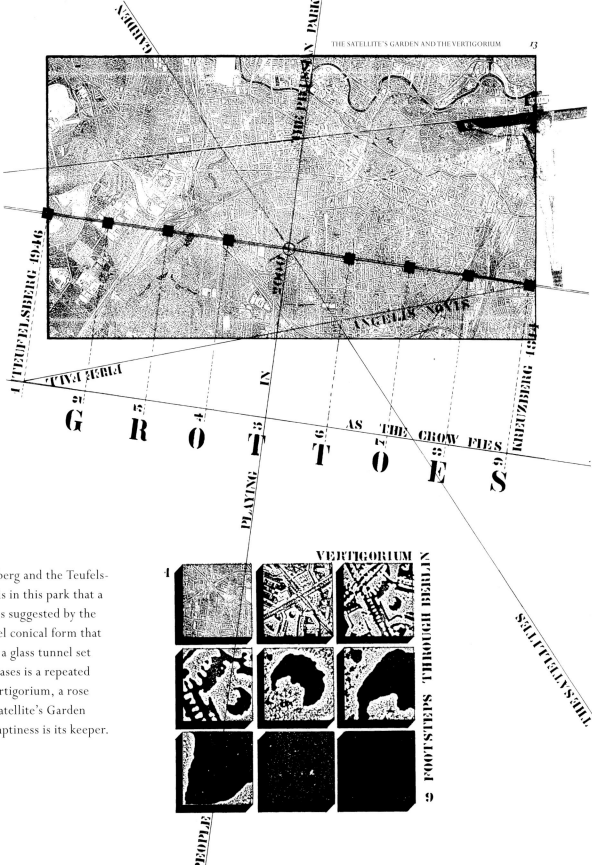

At the exact center of the axis linking the Kreuzberg and the Teufelsberg on the Fehrbelliner Platz is a small park. It is in this park that a grotto entitled the Satellite's Garden is dug in. As suggested by the sketches, the grotto is either a dark glass and steel conical form that straddles its negative imprint cut below grade or a glass tunnel set over an amphitheater. Set into the glass in both cases is a repeated version of the images recording the fall in the Vertigorium, a rose window of the fall. The volume encased by the Satellite's Garden could become a small performance space, but emptiness is its keeper.

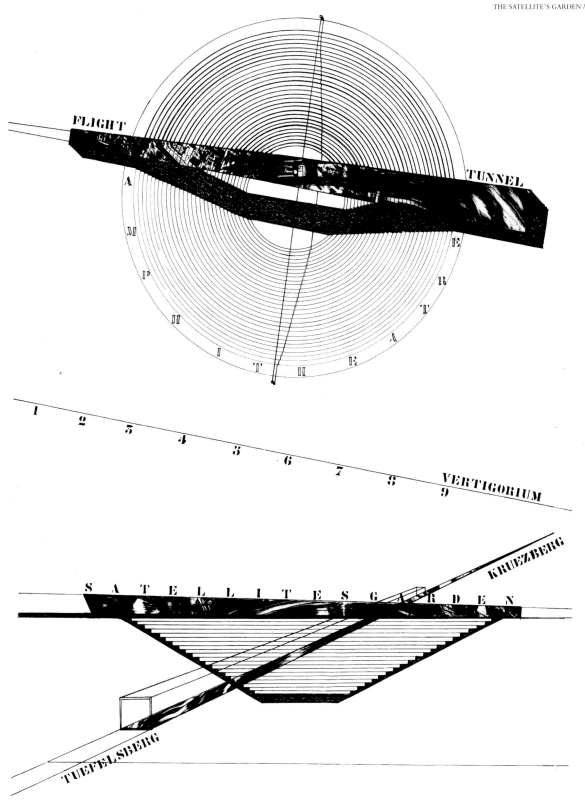

No-Man's-Land

Berlin 1990–1994

Defined by two concrete walls (which became known in the singular as the Berlin Wall) No-Man's-Land was, and in part still is, a zone 160 kilometers (102.5 miles) long and on average 50-100 meters wide. The space of No-Man's-Land is a jagged rift formed in haste when Berlin bifurcated under the pressure of cold war stalemate.

No-Man's-Land was the missing piece between Paradise (the West) and Utopia (the East), the larger and older dialectic into which the cold war fits. Now, after almost half a century of cold war machinations, no longer the symbolic edge of two worlds worth fighting for, No-Man's-Land is just scar tissue across a postmodern, postdialectical metropolis. No-Man's-Land exudes a raw poetry of Germany's wounds, resounding with an emptiness and sublime dereliction that every city stands against. The peculiar beauty of No-Man's-Land is the mnemonic resonance and semiotic density of its emptiness, a modern space par excellence. Its great irony is that No-Man's-Land is now everyone's land, but not for long. Capital as well as nature hates a void.

For West Berlin, caged inside East Germany, the Wall became the longest mural in the world, a neat edge to a subsidized and hedonistic lifestyle officially condoned as the front line of liberty. Easterners had the Wall explained to them as an antifascist and anticapital barrier, a protective device for their own good. They were told that should they attempt to dash across and taste of the "free" world, they would be shot in the legs, depending on a guard's virtuosity with an old Russian rifle.

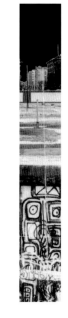

In the center of Berlin adjacent to Peter Lenne's Teirgarten, No-Man's-Land was a thin, weedy crust through which one could just make out the trace of the city's great prewar plazas, the Leipziger Platz and the Potsdamer Platz, the latter often noted as Europe's most vibrant prewar urban center. In a heavy rain, fragments of the bricks and tiles of Berlin's old heart are revealed. To scratch the surface somewhat deeper is to reach Hitler's bunkers, which burrow to the Reichstag and beyond.

The strategic cold war geomancy of No-Man's-Land is now meaningless. But if an old orientation is gone, then this begs the question, where are we now? This is a question landscape architecture is historically adept at negotiating, even if now we are more concerned with notions of disorientation than orthogonal simplicities and superstitions. It is also a poetic question, and the opening of No-Man's-Land was a victory of poetics, not just Reaganomics. Along with most idealists, one could be excused for imagining that such a site holds the potential of that which is not yet written. One could

be excused for being disappointed with predictable urban developments which threaten to fill up the void of No-Man's-Land as the West convinces itself of its natural rights to the end of history.

No-Man's–Land is not just another piece of real estate, but, in similarly prosaic terms, it is a massive open space system, a greenbelt, the potential of which is long gone in most large cities. The apprehension of No-Man's-Land as a continuous ribbon of public open space could become as important to the future of Berlin as Olmsted's Central Park became for New York. With this potential in mind, we propose that this 102.5-mile ribbon of land should be secured from development as an open public site.

In contemplating a designed future for No-Man's-Land, one has a desire to preserve much of the site's existing rugged authenticity, but this can easily become melancholic or a touristic fetishization of aberration. Alternatively, simply to develop the land or smear it with the predictable veneer of tasteful landscaping or typical parkland

is effectively to erase it. To preserve that which is not designed, by design, is of course a primary aesthetic conundrum of sites such as this, sites the Spanish theorist Ignasi de sola Morales theorizes as "terrain vagues."

An answer to No-Man's-Land seems to be first to secure its entire terrain as open space and encourage a thickening of its defining edges. Then, without a master plan, simply encourage a pluralism of projects intermittently along its entire length. Since the whole world was caught up in its creation, No-Man's-Land should now be deemed a world heritage site, but as opposed to heritage that freezes things in time, No-Man's-Land should accommodate diversity and pluralism. Just as is done for national parks, No-Man's-Land should be designated as an urban wilderness and valued for its ecology of information. The only caveat over the whole thread of land is that it remains open public space.

In between intermittent nodes of intense design and experimentation, the anti-aesthetic of No-Man's-Land's existing crust should simply prevail, devoid of maintenance or other sanitary ameliorations. As has been amply demonstrated by the ways in which individuals and community groups have used the land since its opening, No-Man's-Land should be reserved as a rugged base for the ephemeral, the impromptu, and the self-organized. Architectural development should be encouraged only at No-Man's-Land's edges as if to demarcate and dramatize its openness.

There are two projects in this volume that conceive themselves as nodes of design experimentation along the larger ribbon of No-Man's-Land; the Bestiary and the Herbal and the Park on Potsdamer Platz. The former is explained briefly on page 116 in Chapter 4. The latter is explained below.

The Potsdamer Platz
Berlin 1991-1992

Of all the fascinating sites along the length of No-Man's-Land, the Potsdamer Platz is the most hallowed. Here, amidst mounting conservative pressures to rebuild Berlin's nineteenth-century city center, we believed that an urban park would be a preferable typology. However, given that the urban design and redevelopment of the area was imminent, we agreed, upon invitation, to support and contribute landscape designs to Daniel Libeskind's submission to the 1991 urban design competition.

Libeskind's scheme is a labyrinthine and provocative rumination upon a new urbanity. Unlike almost every other plan submitted to the competition, which timidly elected to end the twentieth century by clinging to the palimpsest of the past, Libeskind's proposition has little use for simplistic tracings of nineteenth-century grids. Rather, he casts and interweaves nine main lines of force, one for each muse and each deriving from his own radically subjective reading of the city's identities, events, and images. Significantly, a general and objective history is replaced with the author's own poetic selections, which in turn transmogrifies into urban form. Paradoxically, in this sense an entirely new urbanity arises from intimate interconnection with the past. Hermeneutics replaces ideology at its ground zero, as the architect asks that we remember exactly where we are by forgetting its old form.

The muse lines of Libeskind's master plan reach out in all directions and transgress any boundary they encounter. They could constitute large linear buildings, partially underground, on ground, and hovering above ground. These enormous beams stir up a maelstrom in which fragments of other cities, people's signatures writ large, and the cubes of the periodic table all jostle for a place. The plan is intentionally ambiguous as to what is open space and what is built space, what is street and what is building, what is figure and ground. As a representation the plan hovers between the real and the impossible, between a catalytic mindscape and a cityscape. Overloaded with information and brought about by relative indeterminancy, the drawing asks that we consider building a new, more complex city, one that might require new developmental processes. The architecture for this new city is in fact not a plan, but rather a map. The map figures a labyrinth which offers a way out of the twentieth century, beckoning us into a city that is foreign to everyone and hence a place anyone might make home.

In support of Libeskind's city we proposed, first, a vast forest of linden trees planted on a template of glass shards which we used as a base plan. Second, we proposed a path out of the labyrinth, from the Potsdamer Platz to Paris in the West and Moscow in the east (see the Trans-European Songline, p. 36). Third, we attempted to earth Libeskind's labyrinth literally in new ground.

That is, the main landscape design proposal is not a design so much as an international event. It is proposed that earth samples be collected from the world's political borders and delivered to the Potsdamer Platz. The existing barren ground of the Potsdamer Platz is to be excavated and permanently stockpiled as an earthwork on site and replaced by the new earth from the world's nations. Within this extraterritorial zone, some of the existing bunkers under the Potsdamer Platz are excavated and left exposed.[1] With these landscape contributions to add to its impossibility, Libeskind's scheme was unsuccessful so let us, for argument's sake, return to our stated preference for a park.

---

1   As it turned out, it seems Libeskind's drawings suggested that the new earth from the world's political boundaries would be kept inside an enormous winglike blade which he proposed to hover over the redevelopment of the Potsdamer Platz. See Daniel Libeskind, *The Space of Encounter* (New York: Universe, 2000), pp. 142–144. Discussing this project, Alan Balfour noted that this would have been the "ultimate symbolic landscape," although, through no fault of his own he has not referenced the design to Room 4.1.3 and Müller Knippschild Wehberg. See Alan Balfour, "Octogon," in James Corner, ed., *Recovering Landscape: Essays in Contemporary Landscape Architecture* (New York: Princeton Architectural Press, 1999), p. 96.
The proposition to remove and replace earth is reused in two other projects, first for the 1996 design competition for the new government quarter of Berlin (Spreebogen), and second for Reconciliation Place in Canberra, Australia.

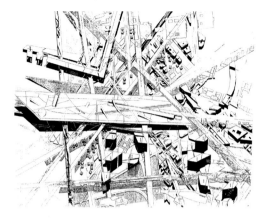

MASTER PLAN FOR THE REDEVELOPMENT OF THE POTSDAMER PLATZ BY STUDIO DANIEL LIBESKIND, 1991. COURTESY STUDIO DANIEL LIBESKIND.

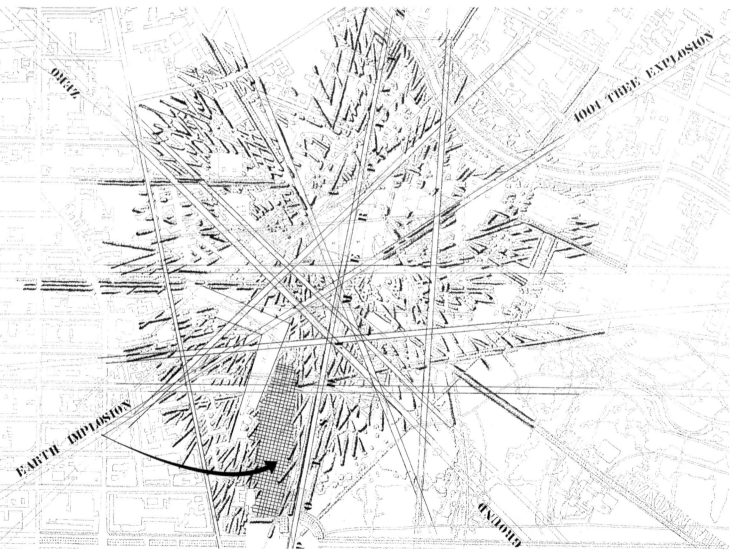

LANDSCAPE PLAN FOR THE POTSDAMER PLATZ. ORIGINAL COMPETITION DRAWING BY RICHARD WELLER WITH CORNELIA MÜLLER AND JAN WEHBERG IN MKW SUBMITTED IN ASSOCIATION WITH THE MASTER PLAN (ABOVE) BY STUDIO DANIEL LIBESKIND FOR THE REDEVELOPMENT OF THE POTSDAMER PLATZ. COURTESY MKW.

The Park

Berlin 1991–1992

In spite of its spectacularly banal redevelopment, we believed that the vicinity of the Potsdamer Platz would be best designated and designed as an urban park, a contemporary public space abutting Peter Josef Lenne's nineteenth-century Teirgarten. Regardless of the corporate resurrection of the Potsdamer Platz as a nineteenth-century ghost town, and the impossibility of a landscape of ideas ever arising there again, the following material remains of academic interest as our answer to the implicit question: What, then, is an urban park at the close of the twentieth century?

The Park on Potsdamer Platz comprises the following layers:
1. The Earth Work
2. The Day Theatre
3. The Night Theatre
4. The Machine Elysium
5. The Living Machines

The five layers of infrastructure are organized upon two templates: the former plans of the site and a network diagram derived from interconnecting the main cities in Europe's post–cold war geography, a landscape stretching from London to the Urals.

EARTHWORK

DAY THEATRE

NIGHT THEATRE

MACHINE ELYSIUM

LIVING MACHINES

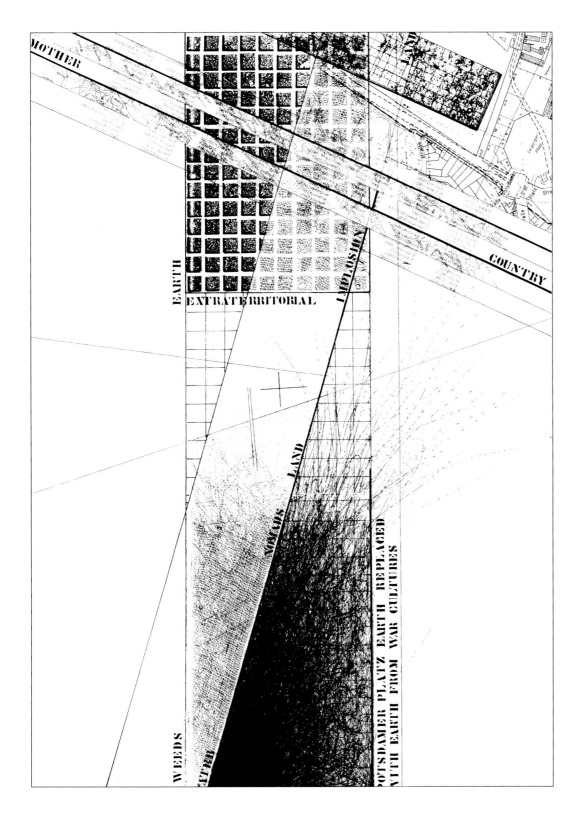

THE EARTH WORK (HEIDEGGER'S GARDEN)
LAYER ONE

Centered on the former Potsdamer Platz, abutting Lenne's Tiergarten and spreading north toward Pariser Platz, the first layer of the park involves a ritualistic preparation of the ground, as originally proposed in association with Libeskind's urban design (see page 20).

The existing earth of the site is excavated so as to partially reveal the World War II bunkers underneath. In the main, however, the excavation is replaced by donations of new earth delivered from all nations willing to participate. Ideally, participating nations take several tons of earth from the boundaries they share with other nations and ship it to Germany. The new earth donations are ceremoniously placed in situ and mixed with other earth samples. The old earth is simply stockpiled and left on site.

This proposal is not so much a landscape design as a rite of passage for the resurrection of the twentieth-century's ground zero. It amounts to an implosion of Berlin's history of global territorial influence and complicates any singular notions of *blud, boden, und gemeinschaft* (blood, ground, and community) which bedevil German reunification. The ritual replacement of the earth also recalls Etruscan rites of city founding whereby, as Joseph Rykwert explains, earth from a mother city was mixed into the ground of the new city site.[2]

This fundamental initiation of a new site prepares the ground for the following layers of infrastructure.

2   Joseph Rykwert, *The Idea of a Town: The Anthropology of Urban Form in Rome, Italy, and the Ancient World* (Cambridge, Mass.: MIT Press, 1988).

The Day Theatre
The Picturesque
Layer Two

The Berlin Wall, which from 1961 to 1989 forbade this space, has dematerialized. Now societies are more subtly segregated and manipulated by the postmodern currency of images. The proposal here is that thirty-six screens, each the size of large billboards, are set on tracks so as to move constantly and randomly across the space of the park. There is one screen for each of the thirty-six main cities within the larger European cold war "theater."

A diagram of a network that interconnects all of the thirty-six main European cities to each other is transposed onto the site as a template with which to locate the tracks along which the screens move. As well as local projections of any sort, each screen has the potential for receiving and projecting imagery to and from the distant European city with which it is associated. The screens could be virtually coordinated in themed events of varying sophistication in the manner of an open-air gallery. The screens mainly utilize conventional data projectors for virtual imagery, but could also in part use LED and LCD images as well as orthodox advertising, posters, graffiti and art.

The Day Theatre is a cubist field of moving images as if the cinematic strip of Bernard Tschumi's Parc de la Villette has been unedited, fragmented into thirty-six frames, and set off on a network of different trajectories.

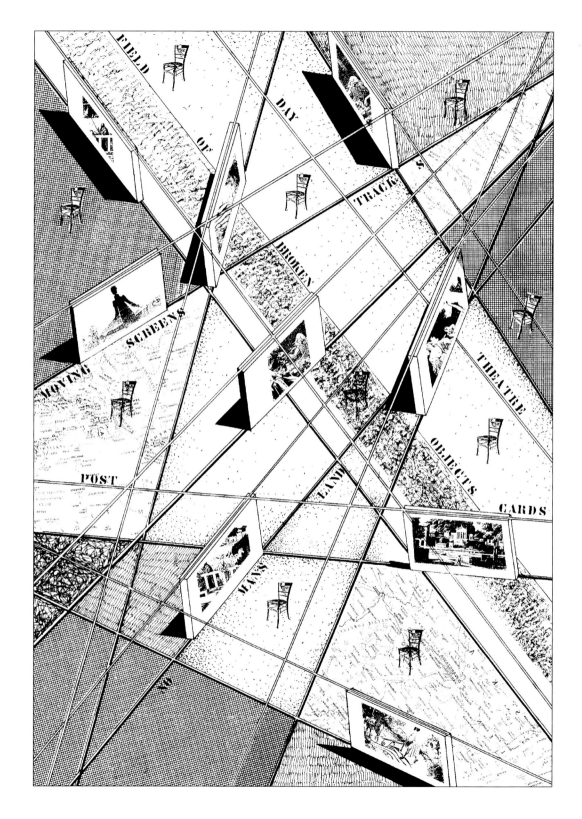

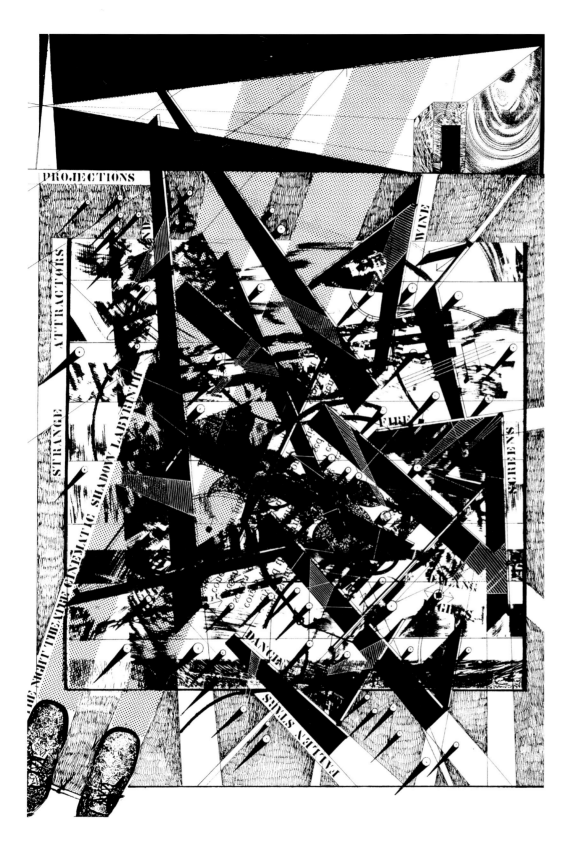

THE NIGHT THEATRE
THE SUBLIME
LAYER THREE

Across the ground surface of the park, the nineteenth-century urban plan of this area of Berlin is registered in areas of dark paving. The paving demarcates the shadows of the former buildings, not their footprints.

The paved shadows could trace the course of the sun through a day over the former city so that the paving patterns stretch across the ground plane of the park. Alternatively a particular moment in time can be selected to project the shadows. Lines of lighting then pick up the edges of the former buildings and cast sheet lighting across the shadow paving at night. People can then stand between the edge of the old city and the present so that their own shadows dance across the park, reaching across space and time. Fireplaces animate further shadows and entice aspects of Berlin's bacchanalia outside.

This night theater is Plato's cave, a landscape of the negative, dramatically acknowledging the palimpsest of the past.

The Machine Elysium
The Industrial
Layer Four

The Machine Elysium is a collection of spent military, industrial, and agricultural machines, equipment that commonly litters eastern European landscapes. Unlike objects in a museum, tanks, tractors, and turbines are scattered across the area of the proposed park and left to corrode—a monument to the bloodbaths of war, the engine rooms of utopia, and the mechanistic hell of the industrial revolution from which they arose. This godless Elysium harkens to landscapes beyond the park and the city, European landscapes that, as the painter Anselm Kiefer remarked, cannot be painted as such, because tanks have passed through them.

This field of dead machines is a carbon counterpart to the final layer of infrastructure of the park, the Village of Living Machines, which operates on silicon.

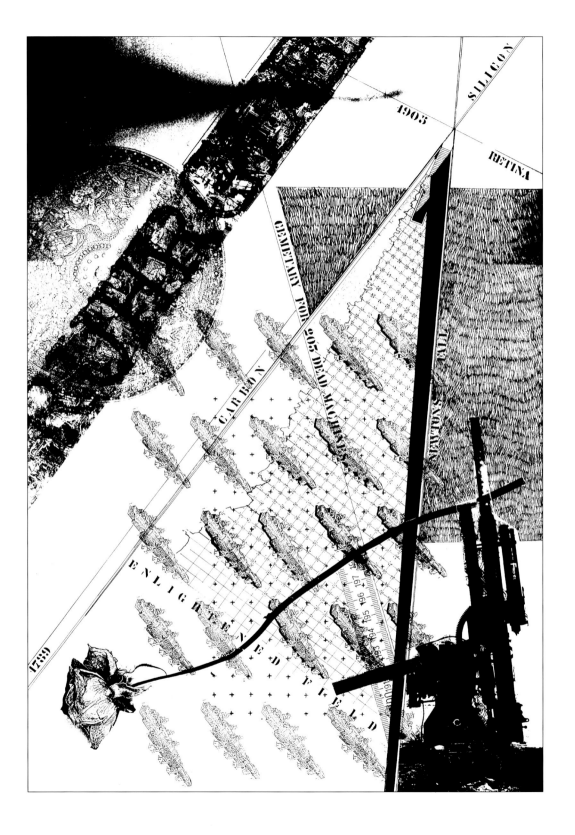

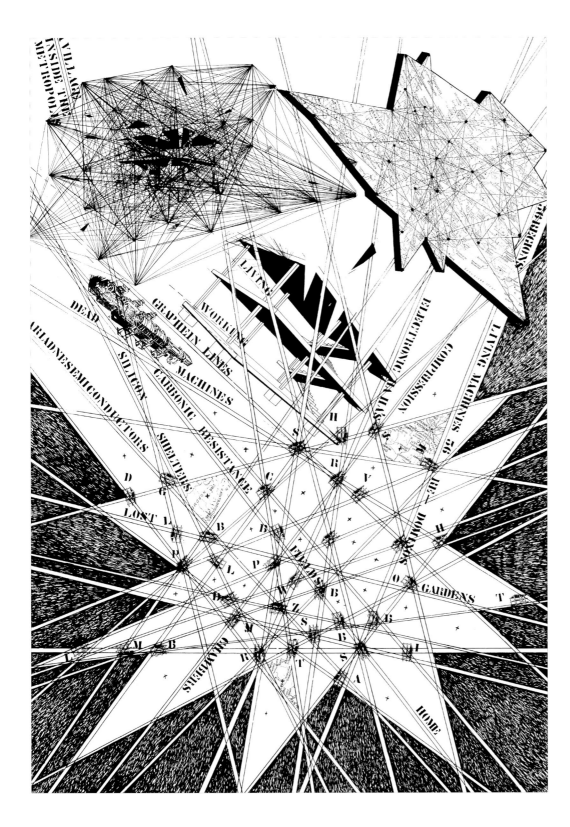

THE LIVING MACHINES
THE POSTINDUSTRIAL
LAYER FIVE

The Living Machines are habitable, working copies of Le Corbusier's Dom-Ino house, the quintessential modernist cell he designed in 1915. There are thirty-six dominos, one for each of the main European cities. Each Domino is sited accurately on a map of Europe scaled to the site, the same template used to lay out the Day Theatre. The network interconnecting all of Europe's cities across the old cold war frontier is boldly emblazoned over the ground surface of the park as a series of paths. Every Domino is thus connected to every other.

Each European city is responsible for sending a delegate or small teams of representatives to live and work in the Dominos in the park. One of the initial and ongoing tasks for these park inhabitants is to de-form and remake the Dominos in any manner seen fit. In this sense the provision of the bare Domino structure offers the park an initial architectural program. Not unlike artists in residence, the representatives living in the Dominos are also responsible for intervening in the outdoor landscape of the park, potentially generating public interaction on a range of self-determined projects, so that within its basic structure the park accrues complexity and detail over time. Indeed, projects would be encouraged to spread out along the whole length of No-Man's-Land to which the park is central.

The Village of Living Machines is not a field of follies or an art park, not a trade show or an expo, not a diplomatic quarter or a think tank. Rather it is potentially something in between all these things.

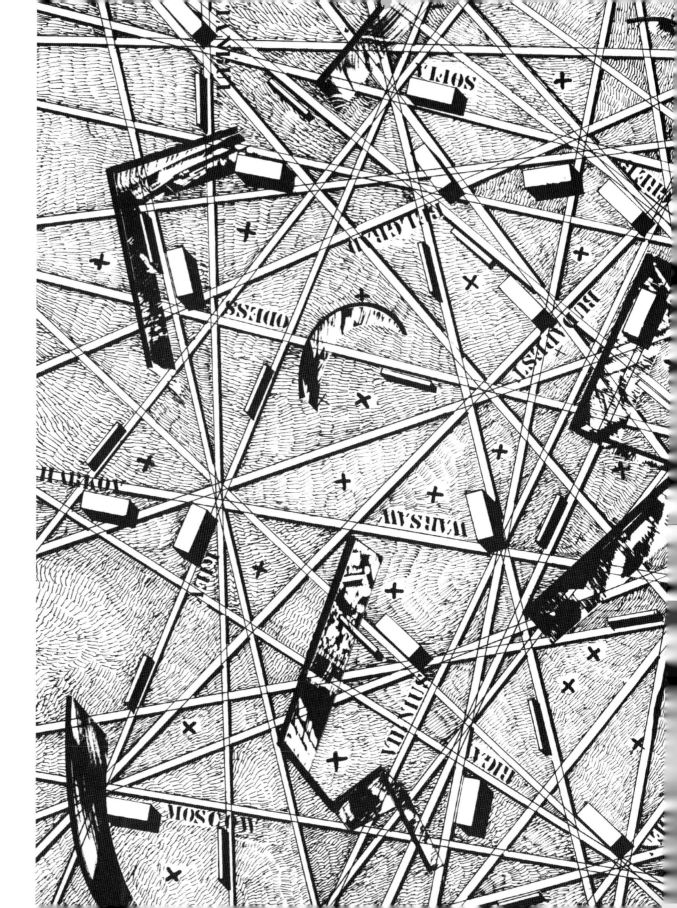

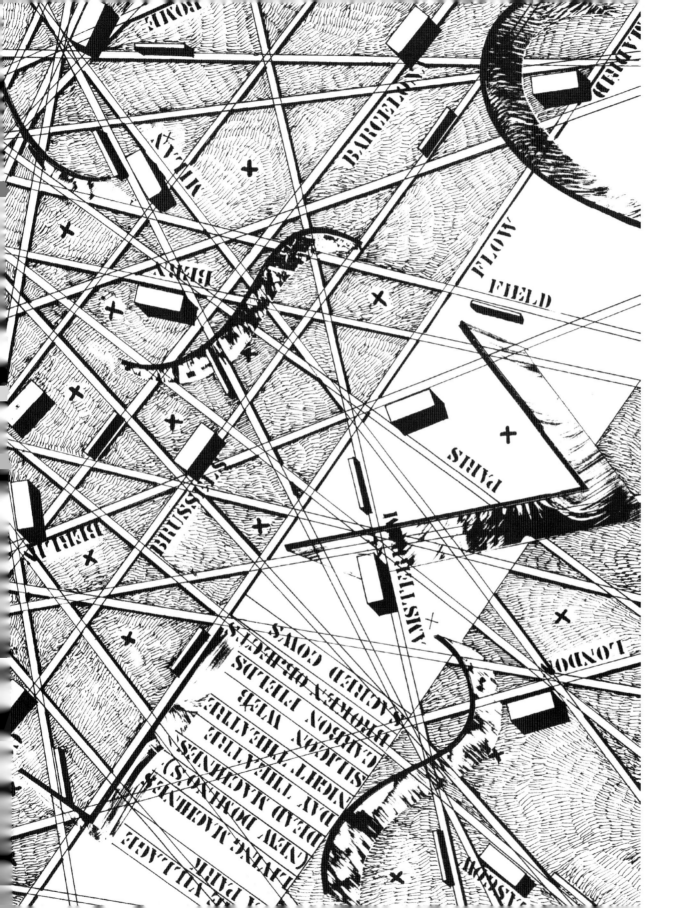

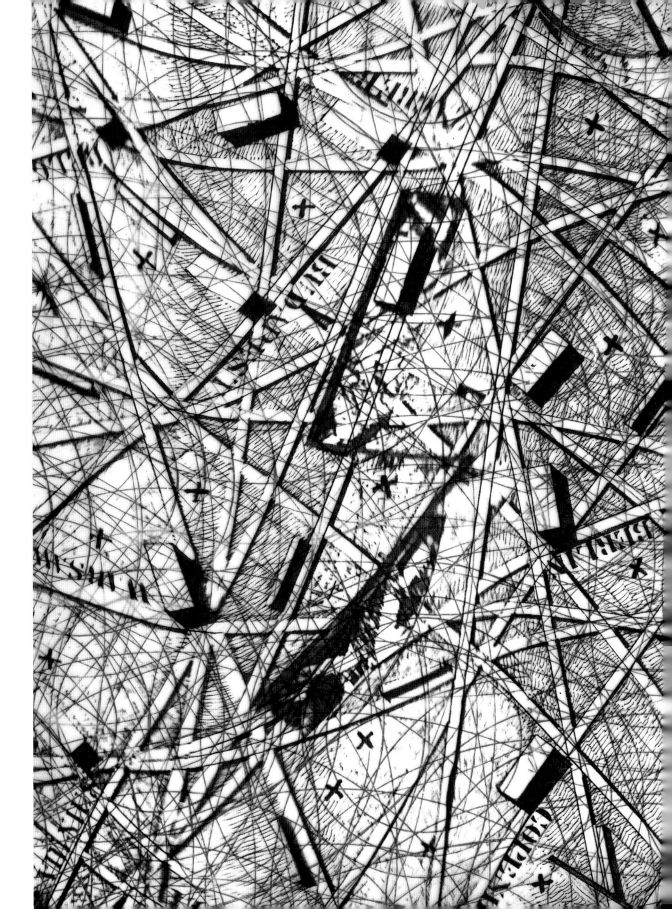

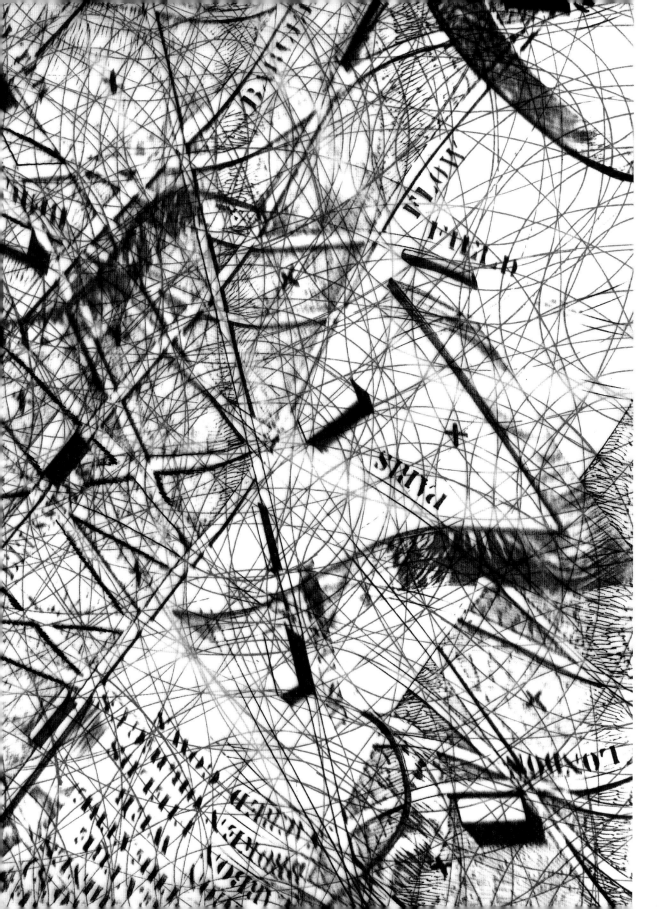

Postindustrial Park

Gelsenkirchen, Ruhrgebiet 1992

The main infrastructural components of the park on Potsdamer Platz
are here transposed to a postindustrial site for the competition to
design the 1997 Bundesgartenshau (German National Garden Show)
at Gelsenkirchen, in the Ruhrgebiet.

The Bundesgartenshau is a major event on the German design calendar and also a significant development opportunity for regions that
compete to host it. The horticultural and exhibition requirements
of the garden show were simply written into the Dominos and
the spaces between the paths of the network of an interconnected
Europe as used to set out the original park on Potsdamer Platz.

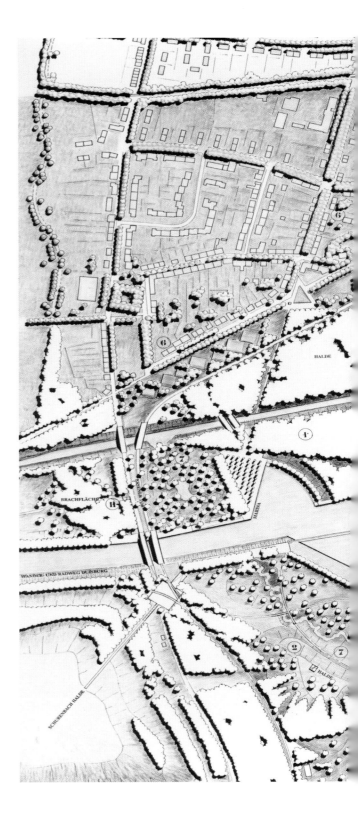

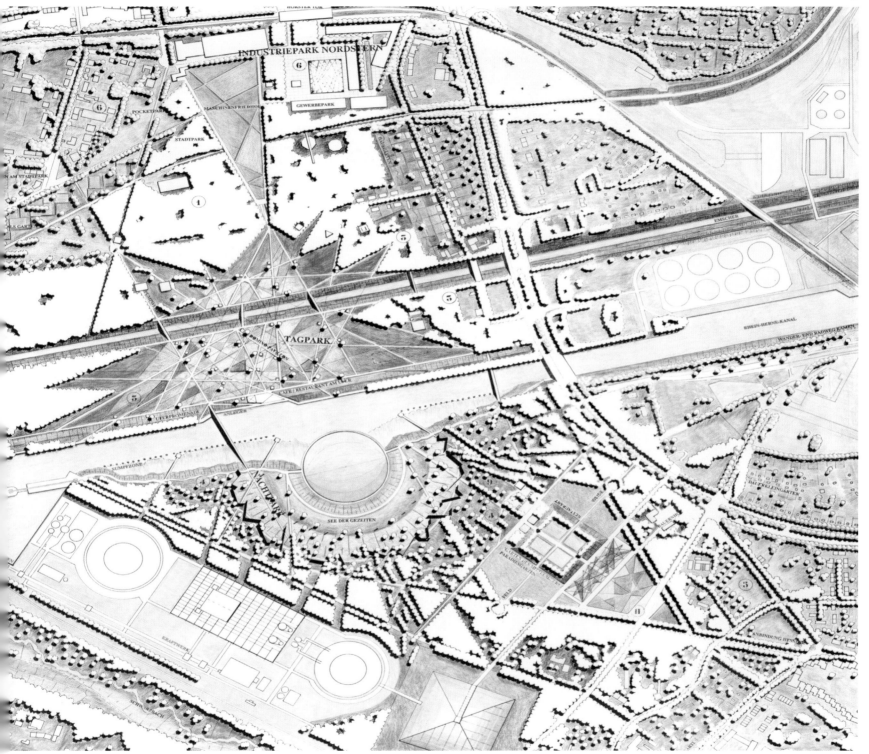

MASTER PLAN FOR THE BUNDESGARTENSHAU (NATIONAL GARDEN SHOW), GELSENKIRCHEN, GERMANY. ORIGINAL COMPETITION DRAWING BY RICHARD WELLER WITH CORNELIA MÜLLER AND JAN WEHBERG IN MKW. COURTESY MKW.

THE TRANS-EUROPEAN SONGLINE
BERLIN 1991

Having dominated the history of modernity, Paris, Berlin, and Moscow lie on a notorious cultural axis. As a landmark for a reunified Europe it seems appropriate to link the metropolises by building a humble path across the landscape.

The Trans-European Songline is a yellow path 2,489 kilometers long lined by an avenue of 248,900 trees. The path, for pedestrians and cyclists, follows insofar as possible, a straight line through the Potsdamer Platz in the heart of Berlin. One hundred and ttwenty-four buildings formed from copies of Ludwig Hartwig's Bauhaus chess pieces punctuate the path to offer shelter to travelers. Like small hostels, the shelters also include libraries facilitating the documentation of regional histories.

The Songline is a thread along which sharing of stories and places in between the cities are the main modes of exchange.

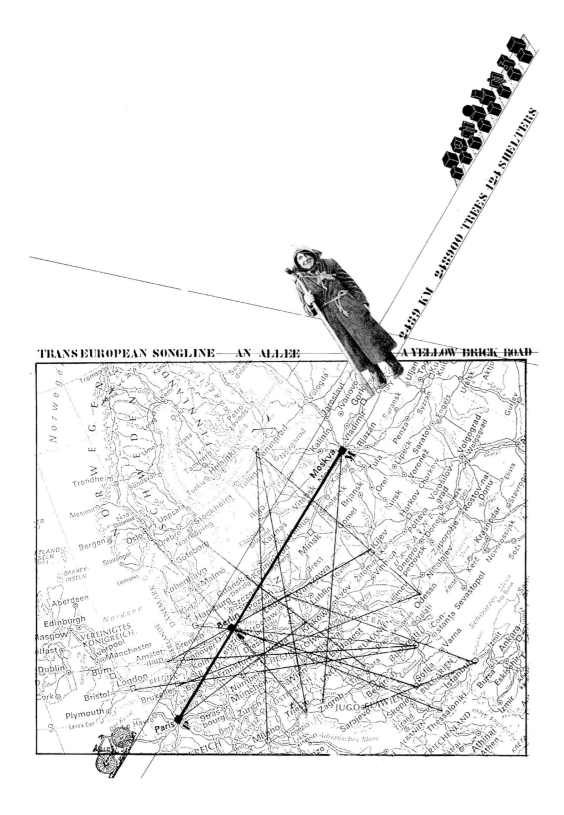

2469 KM 248900 TREES 124 SHELTERS

TRANS EUROPEAN SONGLINE — AN ALLEE — A YELLOW BRICK ROAD

Das Berliner Zimmer (The Berlin Room)

Berlin 1995

Most nineteenth-century bourgeois residential buildings in Berlin have a Berliner Zimmer. A Berlin Room is a type of drawing room in an apartment where the family would come together and receive visitors. Such a room housed memorabilia and functioned as a space for reflective activities somewhat apart from domestic life, a place for reading, writing, and the contemplation of winter's depth.

The idea of such a room is extended to the design for a public space in the midst of the redevelopment of the Potsdamer Platz, a triangular splinter of land with a hypotenuse of 75 meters. Fitting into the triangular void, the proposed Berlin Room becomes a public water garden enclosed by a massive wall. Apart from an internal, peripheral path, the entire surface area of the garden is dark water, within which is a forest of birch trees planted in steel barrels flush with the water's surface. Parts of the inside surface of the garden's perimeter wall is lined with mirrors which, as one approaches the corners of the room, multiply the birches into forests of infinity. In the water are some floating postcard-size images and snippets of text related to the lives and deaths of the Potsdamer Platz—frozen moments in an island of water.

The cue for this small act comes directly from Wim Wenders' film *Faraway, So Close*, in which Cassiel, the fallen angel, reaches down into the black water of the River Spree in East Berlin to see a floating newspaper page on which the death of Willy Brandt is announced. Birches are used because they rampantly colonize postindustrial and military wasteland throughout eastern Europe and also because, as Herbert Bayer has illustrated, their trunks appear to have eyes.

This heavily walled garden turns away from Sony Corporation's new development across the road, a dazzling, white noise cathedral of the new Berlin, replete with Peter Walker's paving patterns. This garden is unashamedly nostalgic, a reservoir of memory containing a loss of innocence and a pathos peculiar to the old Berlin.

PLAN OF THE BERLIN ROOM. ORIGINAL COMPETITION DRAWING BY RICHARD WELLER WITH CORNELIA MÜLLER AND JAN WEHBERG IN MKW. COURTESY MKW.

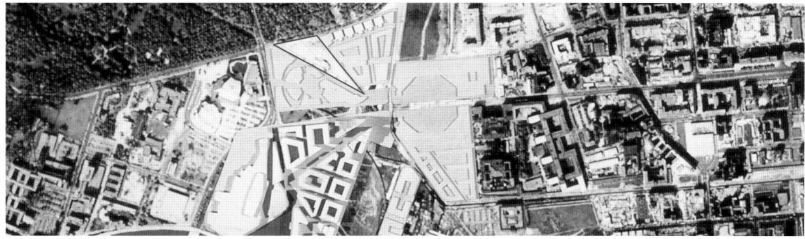

THE BERLIN ROOM: A WALLED WATER GARDEN SITUATED AS A SHARD IN THE MIDST OF THE REDEVELOPMENT OF THE POTSDAMER PLATZ IN BERLIN. COURTESY MKW.

 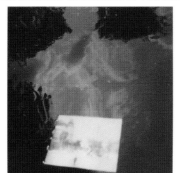  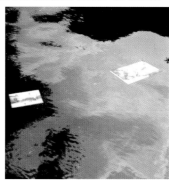

INSIDE THE BERLIN ROOM, HISTORICAL IMAGES OF BERLIN FLOAT ON THE WATER IN BETWEEN BIRCH TREES.

MONTAGE EXPRESSING THE INTERIOR QUALITY OF THE BERLIN ROOM. ORIGINAL IMAGE: HERBERT BAYER, *IN SEARCH OF TIMES PAST*, DENVER ART MUSEUM.

Eyelands
Diomede Islands 1988

The two Diomede Islands in the Bering Sea, one Russian and the other American, were politically separated during the cold war even though they are within view of each other. The islands also lie on different sides of the international dateline.

The proposal is to link the two islands by cutting a staircase into the steep granite faces of each. The staircases lead to chambers. The chambers contain large camera obscuras so that each island holds the image of the other inside itself. Both staircases are set on the arc of one logarithmic spiral invisibly bisecting the invisible date line.

In this way, the islands are literally given eyes, which would suggest that the landmasses are the substance of memory. Not only can the islands "see" each other, but also, via the invisible structure of the logarithmic spiral they share in the curvature of their staircases, the islands are interconnected on the same arc of a time and space other than that set out by the Mercator grid.

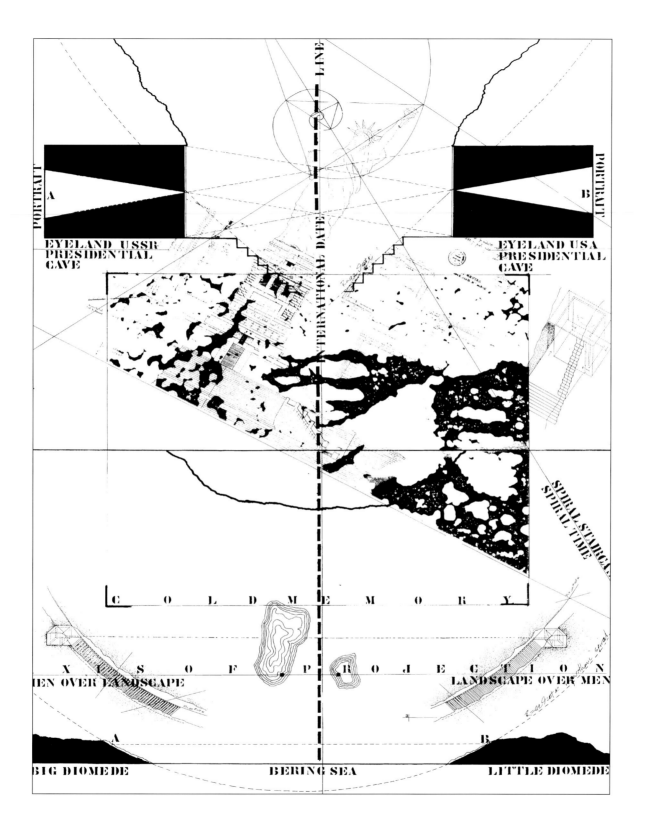

PORTRAIT A

PORTRAIT B

EYELAND USSR
PRESIDENTIAL
CAVE

EYELAND USA
PRESIDENTIAL
CAVE

INTERNATIONAL DATE LINE

SPIRAL STAIRCASE
SPIRAL TIME

C O L D   M E M O R Y

X I S   O F   P R O J E C T I O N

IEN OVER LANDSCAPE

LANDSCAPE OVER MEN

A

B

BIG DIOMEDE

BERING SEA

LITTLE DIOMEDE

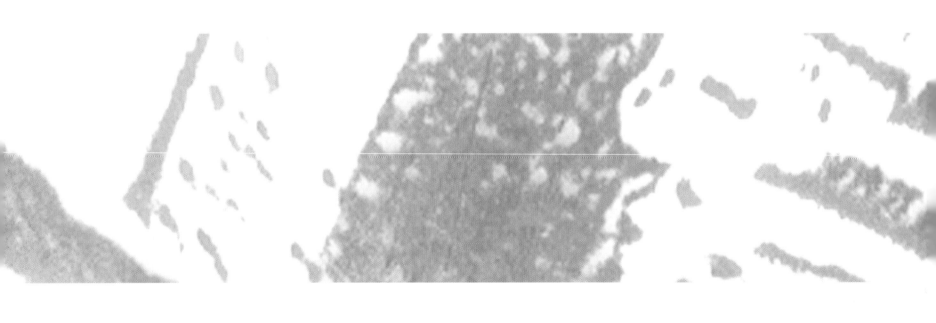

II. INFRASTRUCTURES

The Farm

Fossoli, Italy 1987

The site for this project in northern Italy is an abandoned World War II internment camp in a degraded agricultural landscape outside the town of Fossoli, near Carpi. The question posed by the competition was how to appropriately memorialize the camp and simultaneously create a large public park.

Our master plan proposes to develop a park from forms, materials, and land management practices common to the surrounding agricultural landscape and community. Simply, the park is conceived to celebrate seasonal change and accommodate the local calendar of social occasions.

Allées, bosquets, fields, and wild areas establish clear landscape rooms and structure the design. These rooms are scaled to facilitate a range of different outdoor events, and each includes some kind of attraction such as water features, fireplaces, picnic shelters, playgrounds, sporting equipment, and follies. All the main surfaces of the park are made of ephemeral crops into which ever-changing paths can be slashed. Nearly all plant species are chosen for their seasonal aesthetic merits but also for their productive agricultural potential. Functions and programs are often doubled. For example, the car park doubles as a vineyard, orchards define social areas, and farm animals roam through much of the park. Larger bosquets and small forests are left to their own devices so as to support local flora and fauna minimalized by regional agricultural practices. Drainage patterns allow the creation of a small lake, over which is constructed a central Banquet Hall, where food from the farm is prepared.

The existing, derelict internment camp is a grid of barracks. Rather than preserve these macabre fascist remains, we propose to enhance their ruination. The roof and floor of each barrack is removed and the domain of the building filled with saplings. There is one sapling for each bed in the barracks. As the trees grow up out of the barracks, the barracks decompose, ultimately forming an architecture of landscape, a ghost landscape, whereby the living copses of trees commemorate those who struggled to survive in these buildings.

Additionally, Time, landscape architecture's primary asset in a project such as this, was celebrated in a 100-meter-by-100-meter forest of columns, one of which is replaced by a sapling each year, for a century.

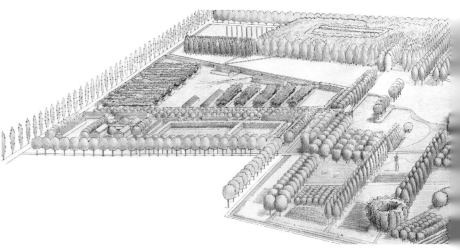

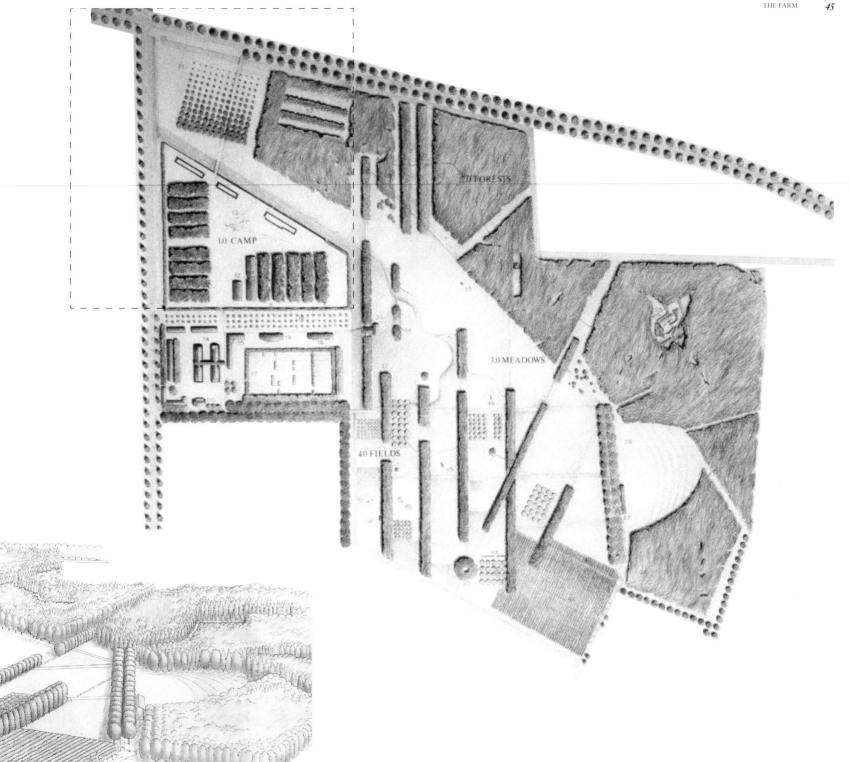

1.0 CAMP

2.0 FORESTS

3.0 MEADOWS

4.0 FIELDS

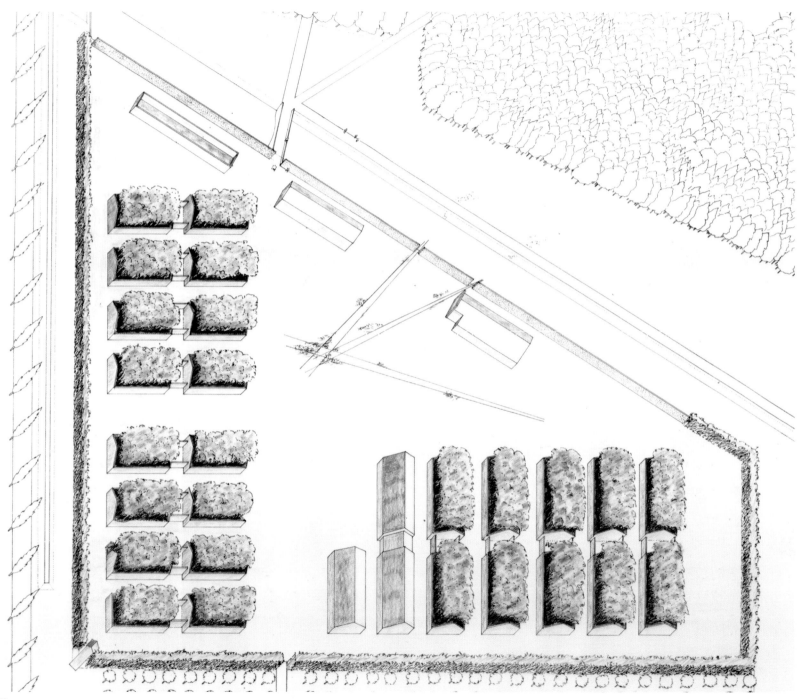

The roofs and floors of the former internment camp barracks have been removed and the interior spaces planted out with saplings.

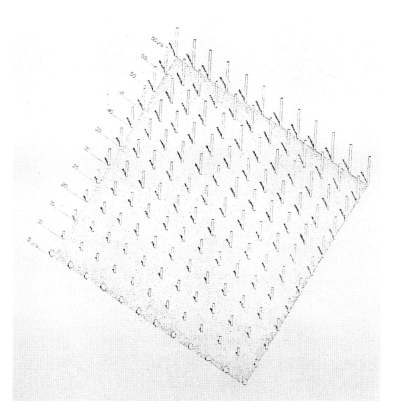

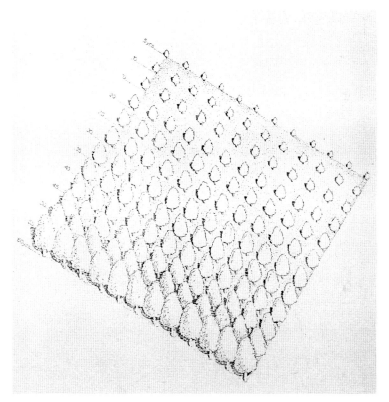

THE TIME GARDEN INVOLVES THE ANNUAL REPLACEMENT OF A POLE WITH A TREE.

THE TIME GARDEN AFTER ONE HUNDRED YEARS.

Blood Lines
Master Plan for Gallipoli Peninsula
Turkey 1998

As strategic ground between the Mediterranean and Black seas, between Europe and Asia, Gallipoli Peninsula, now part of Turkey, has been controlled by many different cultures. In the early twentieth century, it was the Allied forces (comprising many Australian and New Zealand soldiers) who had the peninsula in their sights. It is with this history in mind, coupled with contemporary environmental concerns, that the brief for this international design competition premised the establishment of a park on the peninsula. "Peace" was to become the grand theme or supra-identity, unifying a strip of land 80 kilometers long, with countless archaeological and cultural sites, extensive agricultural lands, nature reserves, and three major towns with a collective population of more than ten thousand people.

The brief called for master plans that
- undo past environmental mistakes,
- give more prominence to the archaeological heritage and the battlefields,
- demonstrate how to curtail and deflect undesired construction,
- provide alternative sources of income for resident,
- reorganize activities and stage new scenarios, and
- reevaluate the identity of the park and create a new identity, vis-à-vis peace.

Typically, the brief overwhelmed entrants with information and scope of work. This and a general lack of faith in master plans in any case led us to submit a tentative map, a tangle of lines that demarcate various critical edges. These lines could be superimposed upon more traditional planning and zoning schemes which should ensue from finer-grained analysis.

Lines have several guises: on the one hand, they procure division and separation, marking and fixing the edge between opposing entities and forces; and, on the other hand, lines render palpable connections between seemingly disparate entities, leapfrogging hostilities or indifference to link one point to another. Also, a line is pure folly, dancing in an errant choreography that neither divides nor connects, but traverses a wandering route of continual renegotiation.

Our project represents an exploration into the line, and into the neutral space of "potentiality" that the line constitutes. It is this neutral space, the no-man's-land found within the infinite thinness of a line, that is a metaphor for our interpretation of a "peace park." "Peace" becomes located in the exchange, interconnection, and negotiation of the middle ground, rather than in the frozen edge between absolutes. The scheme thus embraces notions of blurred, negotiated and confused lines. The lines we have unraveled have no ideal geometry or precisely predetermined trajectory. But if these lines confess to inaccuracy now, it is because later they would find their way on the ground.

Strategies and Maneuvers / Degrees of Error
1. The Wild Garden

In 1915 the ANZAC (Australian and New Zealander Army Corps)
soldiers landed two kilometers north of where they intended, and
the consequent loss of life under Turkish attack was the Australian
nation's formative sacrifice. We have built this fundamental degree
of error into our mapping. That is, our first move was to trace the
existing coastline and move it inland by a similar degree of error.
This new coastline is superimposed upon the existing accurate ridge
line of the eastern coast, against which so much blood was spilled.
The two lines, the existing ridge line of the eastern coast and our
shadow coastline–then interweave across each other so as to form a
zone, a space in between the lines, as it were. This in-between zone
or blurred zone is proposed to become a wilderness, an ecological
no-man's-land running the eastern length of the peninsula.

To the west of this wilderness across to the coast is a zone entitled
the Refuge Garden and to the east, the Cultivated Garden. The
Refuge Garden comprises the main battlegrounds and tourist areas
of the peninsula, and the Cultivated Garden comprises quotidian
working agricultural landscapes.

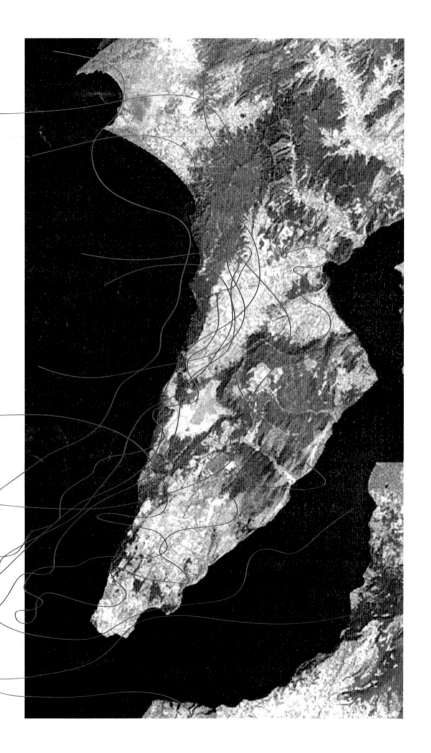

This simple tripartite banding of the peninsula into zones of refuge, wilderness, and cultivation is then further delineated and structured according to the following overlays of poetic and programmatic guidelines.

2. THE REFUGE GARDEN

The Refuge Garden is the western precinct of the park comprising the main battlefields and tourist circuits. As a zoned area of land in our plan it is further articulated by the Battle Lines, the Blood Lines, and the Song Line.

2.1 BATTLE LINES

Maps of the military campaigns across the peninsula typically utilise a simplistic range of colors and graphics to illustrate the military machinations that have taken place. With a range of brightly colored materials, lighting, sounds, and bold directional markers, we propose, insofar as possible, to build these graphic map conventions in situ so that the actual landscape corresponds to the tourist's military map.

2.2 BLOOD LINES

Within the Refuge Garden the drainage lines of the landscape are planted out with red flowering trees. The red tree lines become the "trademark" image of the Peace Park, identifying the landscape as a body while also serving to secure eroding catchments.

2.3 SONG LINE

The Song Line is represented as a path linking four major new amphitheaters proposed for four dramatic coastal sites. The amphitheaters facilitate an annual week-long festival of operatic performances whereby patrons are encouraged to walk to the next venue

on a circuit. It is proposed that four major operas be specially commissioned, each devoted to describing a millennium of history so as to plumb the depths of the cultural history of this landscape beyond its twentieth-century prominence. Supporting the performances is a flotilla of period ships celebrating the maritime history of the Dardanelles and the Aegean.

3. THE CULTIVATED GARDEN

The bulk of the peninsula is dedicated to the Cultivated Garden, where essentially the same activities of peasant agriculture are conducted. Little is changed or modified in this area, with the exception of the Life Lines, the Ghost Line, and the Section Line. These guidelines all concern the peninsula's working landscapes and are aimed at maintaining and improving the quality of fertile land while providing economic incentives and advantages.

3.1 LIFE LINES

The Life Lines are simply mass plantings of indigenous vegetation along drainage lines of the entire area of the Cultivated Garden. The implementation of the Life Lines occurs gradually, ultimately reconfiguring agricultural allotments so as to respect and accord with the "natural" systems of the peninsula.

3.2 SECTION LINE

The Section Line is a programmatically complex insertion of new infrastructures along an axis cutting across and interconnecting the Refuge Garden with the Cultivated Garden. It is a major new transport corridor across the peninsula and a service route containing nurseries, shops, information kiosks, and accommodation and transport hubs. The Section Line begins on the west coast with the battlefields and crosses the peninsula so as to join with the shipyards;

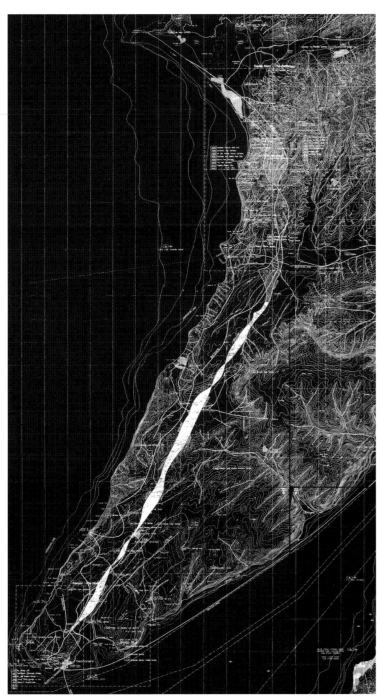

MASTER PLAN OF THE GALLIPOLI PENINSULA, INCLUDING THE GHOST LINE, THE HORIZON LINE, THE LIFE LINES, BATTLE LINES, AND SONG LINE.

it is proposed so as to build and maintain the proposed Dardanelles Flotilla.

3.3 GHOST LINE

The Ghost Line wanders the coast of the entire peninsula so as to demarcate a zone of no development. It also traces out the edges of the major towns, a mapped line of jurisdiction preventing certain land uses from sprawling into others.

3.4 HORIZON LINE

The Horizon Line consists of beacons of light floating in the water equidistant off the coast visible from the no-man's-land of outer space, where satellites play "join the dots."

New Singapore City
Singapore 1987

In 1987 "Marina South" was the name of 372 hectares of landfill fronting the Singapore Central Business District. Completely empty, it provided the rare opportunity for tabula rasa speculations regarding a new urban development. Our proposal, a bio-superstructure, developed on behalf of the design group Creative Design and Technology (CDT) for consideration by the Singaporean government presents a modernist ecology. The proposal sought to maximize urban density and functional green space.

As opposed to land ordinance grids and street patterns determining development on the ground, here an enormous five-story super-structure provides a skeletal structure for the city to grow into. Constructed as stage one of the new city, the bio-superstructure is 30 meters wide and 25 meters high forming 70-meter by 70-meter open courtyards.

Initially the bio-superstructure becomes the structural frame for mixed-use buildings which "grow" into it over time. The entire structure is conceived also to support vines and hydroponic food crops, with the top level devoted to recreational public space, pleasure gardens, and market gardens. On its various levels the super-structure also contains major urban services and transport systems.

Piecemeal architectural developments can begin in the framework of the superstructure but are expected to quickly extend out into the voids (courtyards) of the grid. As illustrated in the model the scheme actively anticipates, supports, and encourages a tension between the ideal order of the grid and its traditional nemesis, the labyrinth.

The bio-superstructure is an enormous pergola or trellis covered in vegetation that cools and filters the air and creates shade for the dense city below. The bio-superstructure forms the skeleton of a new hybridized and mechanized confluence of market gardens, parkland, and inner-city landscapes. In New Singapore City the city becomes a wilderness and wilderness becomes a grid.

MODEL OF THE PROPOSED NEW SINGAPORE CITY BY RICHARD WELLER AND VLADIMIR SITTA IN ASSOCIATION WITH CDT (CREATIVE DESIGN AND TECHNOLOGY PTY LTD.), 1987.

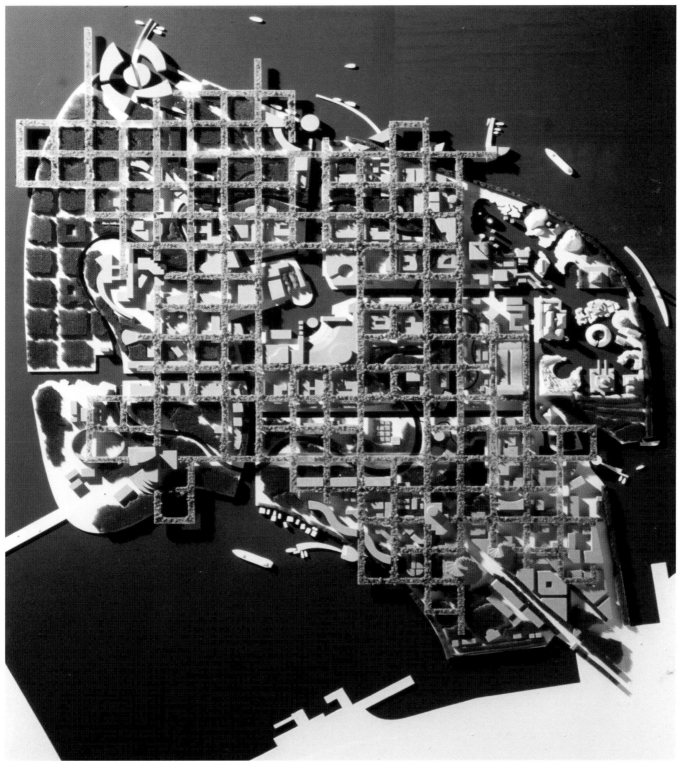

PLAN VIEW OF THE PROPOSED NEW SINGAPORE CITY. RICHARD WELLER AND VLADIMIR SITTA IN ASSOCIATION WITH CDT (CREATIVE DESIGN AND TECHNOLOGY PTY LTD.), 1987.

Sun City
Perth 1995

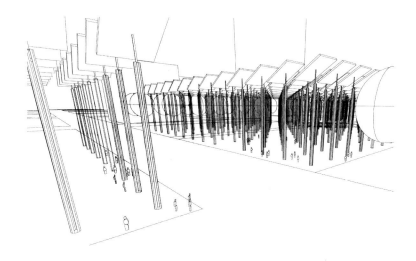

In front of the central business district of Perth toward the river is a flat strip of land approximately 2 kilometers long and 150 meters wide. In 1991 a design competition was held for this site, and as a result fights broke out and nothing happened.

Ironically, in its undesigned state the site works well to facilitate a range of ephemeral events. Its vast emptiness is also strangely appropriate to this isolated, underpopulated, and overengineered city on the edge of a desert.

Generally the site is hot and empty, leading one to think the city should grow out into it. There is money to be made. Attractive as that might seem now, in a century it might well be regretted. We propose to secure and maintain the site's emptiness while simultaneously extracting higher social and economic value. The entire site is to be covered in solar panels set high on a forest of columns. This solar temple could provide up to one-third of the energy requirements for the adjacent central business district, offer shade to increase activity, and simultaneously celebrate the culture of big, beautiful engineering solutions Western Australia is proud of.

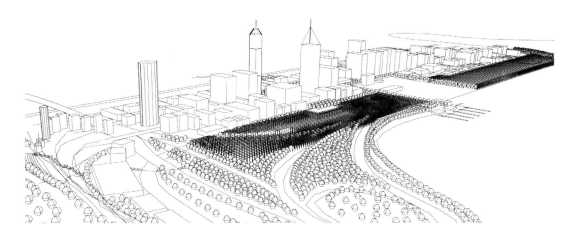

FUTURE GENERATIONS UNIVERSITY
WYONG, AUSTRALIA 1996

I consider sustainable development to be a contradiction. What we need is sustainable life. In the 20th century the glory of the human has become the desolation of the earth. The desolation of the earth is becoming the destiny of the human. All human institutions, activities and programs must be judged primarily by the extent to which they inhibit, ignore or foster a mutually enhancing human - earth relationship. There are enormous creative possibilities if only we would take them.
– Thomas Berry in discussion with Paul Collins, "Encounters" (Australian Broadcasting Corporation, 1995)

An international design competition for a "Future Generations University" (FGU) was commissioned by private investors in association with the Future Generations Alliance Foundation in 1996. The Future Generations Alliance Foundation is an international organization, begun in 1992 by Katsuhiko Yazaki in Kyoto, devoted to the ideals of a sustainable future. The Alliance believes such a future is predicated upon cultural (r)evolution to which new modes of education are considered essential.

The idea of forming a new, private university for postgraduate studies, dedicated to the theory and praxis of sustainability, came about after the Rio de Janeiro Earth Summit in 1992. Australia, and ultimately Wyong, north of Sydney, was chosen as an appropriate Australasian intersection for such a project.

The Eco-Design Foundation in Sydney, known locally for its scholarly critique of orthodox design practices was commissioned to draft the brief and manage the competition. Introducing the project, the Eco-Design Foundation's director, Dr. Tony Fry, explained that the competition was "to encourage a different kind of design process, one that moves beyond a limited conceptualisation of design as 'problem solving'." For the Eco-Design Foundation the Future Generations University was explicitly premised upon a critique of current academic culture. Fry began a conversation which entrants were expected to extend by provocatively stating that:

The modern university has been founded on and as the institution of reason. Its current problems are not merely its growing irrelevance, ineffectiveness or compliant anachronism, but more destructively, its inability to overcome liberal pluralism and focus on reversing the degradation of the world that has been caused by instrumental reason. The failure of all current universities to generate responsibility for what is known, how it becomes known and what happens to that knowledge calls for the reinvention of the idea of the university. The idea that the university preserves society's freedoms through pluralism has been revealed to be illusory—the inability to preserve the future for future generations is the most active removal of freedom.[1]

In order to engage with this project the brief stressed that specialist design teams should be formed and that they would best be international, multicultural, and interdisciplinary. Following this advice Room 4.1.3 established a group of twenty-three people from eight cultures, speaking ten different languages, representing fourteen different professions and ranging from twenty-one to seventy-two years of age.[2] This group came together for a week to discuss the project.

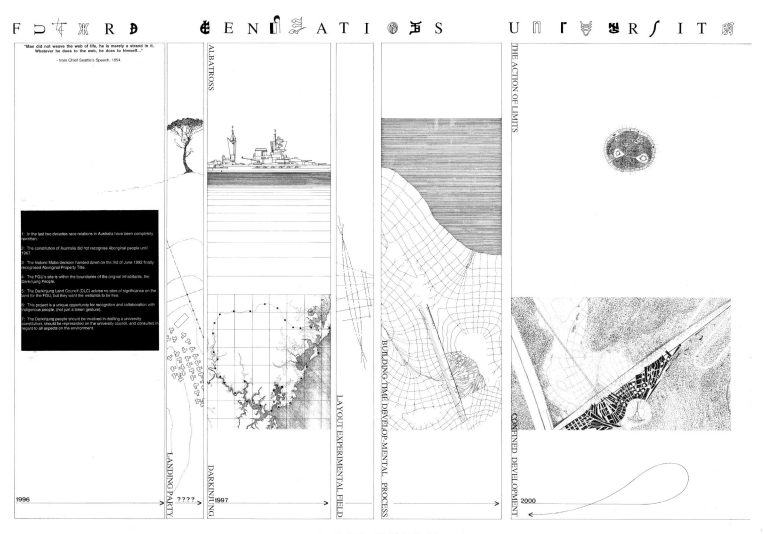

FUTURE GENERATIONS UNIVERSITY

"Man did not weave the web of life, he is merely a strand in it.
Whatever he does to the web, he does to himself..."

- from Chief Seattle's Speech, 1854.

1: In the last two decades race relations in Australia have been completely rewritten.

2: The constitution of Australia did not recognise Aboriginal people until 1967.

3: The historic Mabo decision handed down on the 3rd of June 1992 finally recognised Aboriginal Property Title.

4: The FGU's site is within the boundaries of the original inhabitants, the Darkinjung People.

5: The Darkinjung Land Council (DLC) advise no sites of significance on the land for the FGU, but they want the wetlands to be free.

6: This project is a unique opportunity for recognition and collaboration with indigenous people, (not just a token gesture).

7: The Darkinjung people should be involved in drafting a university constitution, should be represented on the university council, and consulted in regard to all aspects on the environment.

ALBATROSS

THE ACTION OF LIMITS

LANDING PARTY

DARKINJUNG

LAYOUT EXPERIMENTAL FIELD

BUILDING TIME DEVELOP-MENTAL PROCESS

CONFINED DEVELOPMENT

1996   ????   1997   2000

EVOLUTION

DIAGRAM OF THE TIME DEVELOPMENTAL CONCEPT AND INFRASTRUCTURE FOR THE PROPOSED FUTURE GENERATIONS UNIVERSITY.

The brief stipulated that the university:

- Will be a private institution.
- Will function both locally and globally.
- Will be an institution with an ability to change and re-create itself.
- Will foster the creation of new communities of learning.
- Will focus on new ways of learning.
- Will seek to produce students who can transform existing professions and create new ones.
- Will develop practices of co-creation as opposed to egocentric production.
- Will form and promote an intercultural ethos that does not destroy cultural difference.
- Will ensure that educating processes and modes of organization are innovative, critically reflexive, and modifiable while nonetheless being coherent and directive.
- Will be of an architecture that is educational, not architecture for education, and that entrants in the competition must conceptualize built forms, uses, and informational means through which the whole site's ecological sustainability instructs and is instructed by all its uses.
- Entrants are expected to challenge the idea of the university as it is currently being formulated and develop their own interpretations of what a new university devoted to sustainability ought to be.
- Entrants are also expected to notionally design the university's curriculum.
- The university will accommodate up to four thousand international postgraduate students.
- The site has been designated as a piece of land adjacent to a wetland, outside the town of Wyong, just north of Sydney, Australia.

In order to be chosen as a finalist and move to a design phase teams were required to submit a polemic that responded to the idea of the new university and the rubric of sustainability in general. The following points summarize our written response and underpin our penultimate design propositions for the new university.

Regarding the University

- We are unqualified to offer instrumental solutions; our work is gestural.
- We agree with Charles Jencks when he says "form follows worldview."[3]
- The project is already somewhat flawed since local Aboriginal groups were not consulted about the project.[4]
- We might expand upon or contradict the chosen site and are uncomfortable with it's a priori selection.
- The site is both local and global, theoretical and material.
- We reserve the right and tradition of the university as a critical institution. It is essential that the notions of sustainability as part of a popular culture of environmentalism be academically retrieved, just as it is necessary to academic operations that a popular culture surrounds its more indulgent ramblings and end games.
- We believe international cooperation and scholarships can expand the student representation beyond that of a privatized exclusive institution.
- We understand the university as a center for excellence, and on-campus students ought to be selected internationally for their outstanding abilities. However, through virtual systems the university should be open.
- The Bauhaus reminds us of an integrated educational model that responded to conditions of crisis and also redesigned not only a range of objects but also reappraised design processes and techniques.
- We understand this university as an extension and reinterpretation of the idea of the Bauhaus. That is, central to the new university is the aim of designing products. However, unlike the Bauhaus, the sciences, landscape architecture, and broader humanities components would be part of the program.

- The FGU is not a tabula rasa project in competition with existing educational facilities; rather, it is understood as a conduit between institutions.
- Its difference to existing institutions is that it can focus on the philosophy and practice of sustainability relatively free of the contingencies affecting the development of new programs in existing institutions.
- In principle the FGU is understood as something akin to a United Nations which focuses a sense of global community even when a global community can be said to already exist. For example, the Bauhaus could never have achieved what it did if it had been dispersed throughout the existing design programs of Europe. In this way we are for the project, despite its utopian undertones.
- The university is understood as generally part of the region's existing infrastructure, yet case-by-case analysis might determine whether autonomous, site-specific systems of energy and waste can be deployed. The obvious contradictions at this level are part and parcel of the new institution's concerns and realities.
- For example, students do not produce their own food, but the university would address issues of alternative agriculture and global agribusiness. A local farm might be established later as a community project if the university perceived itself as a model project and saw the need to hinge its integrity on a withdrawal from the status quo.
- Over time the university can design, prototype, test, and market sustainable technologies.

Regarding Ecology and Sustainability

- Both virtual and "real" spaces are understood as environments.
- The land should be understood as an existing living architecture.
- An aesthetic of sustainability does not exist as a generic type; it must be created site-specifically by critical inquiry.

- We are not convinced that structures that appear to "touch the earth lightly" have any more ecological merit than those that do not.
- A more eco-logical way of understanding objects is that of relationality, whereby anything must be perceived as only the final manifestation in networks of prior exchanges and transformations which have socioecological effects far above and beyond the final appearance of a thing.
- We are not interested in environmentalism that finds humanity repugnant, although we are fascinated by the challenges to humanism which the ecological crisis entails.
- Sustainability calls the teleogies and theologies of civilization into question: this is the theoretical power of this new university.
- Biocentrism is best understood as an enrichment of humanism not its antithesis.
- We do not agree with an institution or movement that posits environmentalism as truth according to which culture must be simply corrected.
- We are interested in the contradictions and impossibility of sustainability as a point of departure for this project.
- Sustainability is both a poetic and economic problem.
- Sustainability, for us, is not a new global narrative imposed by the first world, but rather it is something specific to sites and cultures.
- Sustainability is not about harmony; rather, life systems need to be placed within the dynamic and unstable processes of evolution which push away from equilibrium and stasis.
- We suffer no illusion that culture is to be redeemed by a pure nature or vice versa. We work within the intellectual frame of the denatured, an entanglement of human and nonhuman systems.
- Rather than a separation of culture and nature in physical and conceptual terms the future is cyborgian.

- We accept postmodern readings of nature as a cultural construct while recognizing that nonhuman life systems have autonomous, intrinsic value beyond cultural construction.
- The earth does not need to be saved, nor is it feminine. Rather, culture needs to be technologically refined, and values need to be contested.

THE CURRICULUM

We propose that students attending the Future Generations University would enter a three-semester study period. Each semester is four months. Each semester is themed according to local, regional and global scales of reference.

1. The first (local) semester is spent in situ at the main campus, a village comprising Re-city and The Edge. Re-city can accommodate three thousand people, and the Edge is the main teaching space.
2. The second (regional) semester is spent in the Darkinjung Cycle, an educational experience whereby up to six hundred students walk the boundary of the local Darkinjung people's tribal lands, stopping for three- to four-day workshops with scholars in thirty residences set at six-kilometer intervals along the circuit.
3. The third semester is spent in the global educational program aboard an ex-military vessel, the *Albatross*.

THE MAIN CAMPUS: RE-CITY AND THE EDGE

RE-CITY

Re-city, the main residential area of the campus, is largely created from waste and scrap products. The FGU should set an example by researching and implementing a system of recycling which will provide compound materials for construction. Resident designers administer the necessarily highly detailed and contingent construction, utilizing unorthodox salvaged and recycled building materials and components.

Re-city contains facilities common to a vibrant urban neighborhood. The FGU is neither a monastery nor an ashram. Re-city, as sketched, claims to be the densest urban development in Australia (disregarding high-rise apartments), yet it will accommodate only three thousand people. In our view this is the sustainable limit for this site. The university's aim of four thousand students is, however, satisfied since at any given time up to one thousand additional students are engaged off site in the regional concept of the Darkinjung Cycle and the global concept of the *Albatross*.

Moving west along the site's ridge, Re-city breaks down according to the logic of the way in which water moves over the contours and the positions of existing trees. Where Re-city meets the Edge it is comprised of buildings more suited to educational activities.

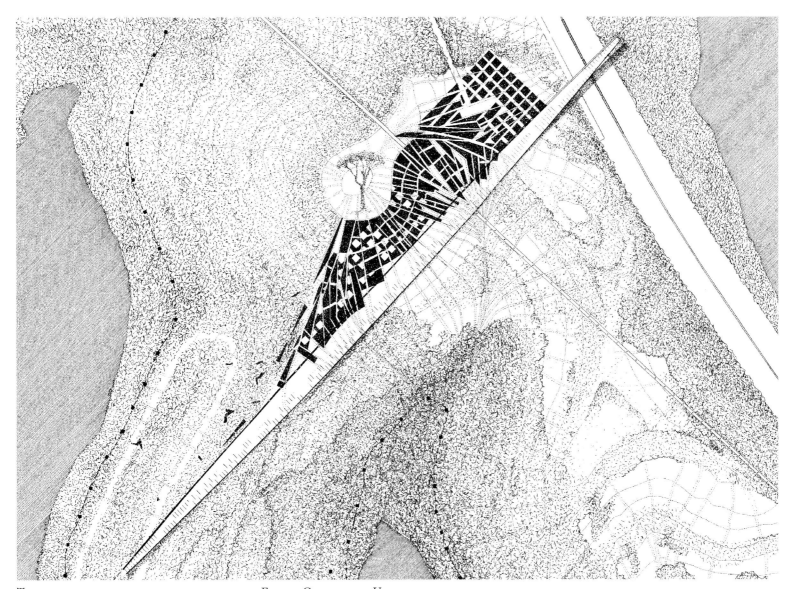

THE MAIN RESIDENTIAL CAMPUS OF THE PROPOSED FUTURE GENERATIONS UNIVERSITY.

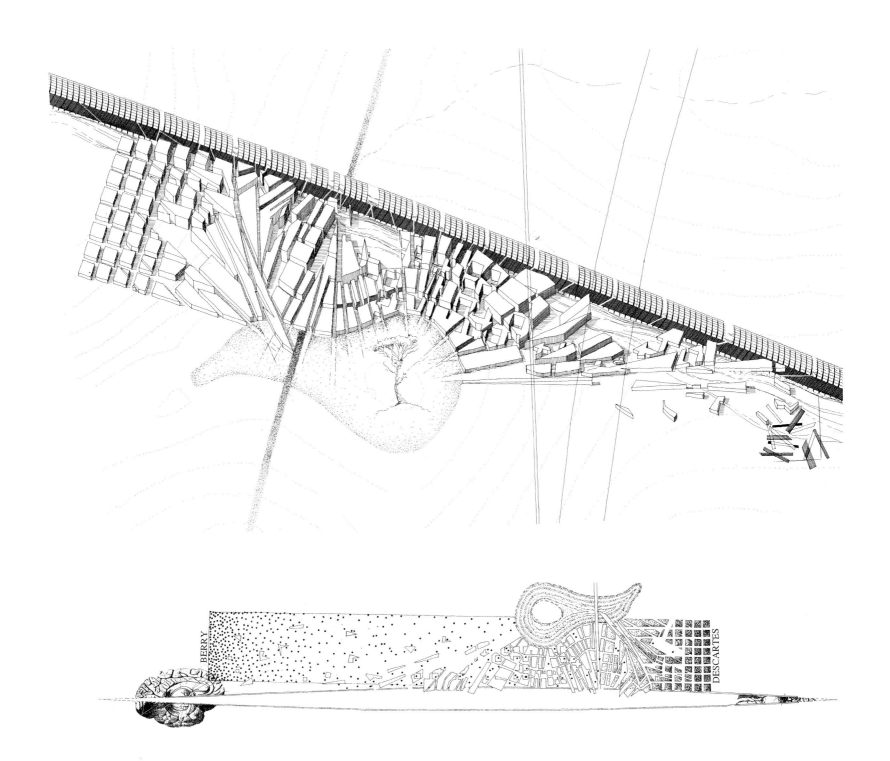

The Edge

The Edge runs for exactly one nautical mile (1,852 meters) in an east-west direction along the site's ridge and is 40 meters wide. It is a not a picturesque building that pretends to nestle in the landscape. It is made of two massive walls that form a long axial corridor and a framed view of the sky. The northern wall is solid so as to absorb and retain thermal energy, and the southern is glazed, offering views out over the site's wetland. The eastern extremity of the Edge becomes a bridge, which crosses over the existing railway line adjacent to the site and then cantilevers out toward the Pacific Ocean, in view some 12 kilometers away.

The Edge marks a boundary: southward the land is revegetated, whereas northward is the dense urbanity of Re-city. This use of architecture as a boundary condition stresses limits, not a naive dialectic of culture and nature. While externally asserting a limit to the use of the site, internally the Edge is flexible. The space inside the massive volume of the Edge is subdivided by large movable partitions. The partitions are taken from a time line of western history—a linear calendar of cultural change that the FGU now loops into a different reading. The flexible inner spaces made possible by the partitions provide relatively private tutorial spaces or larger spaces depending on the university's needs at any given time. The entire length of the Edge can be emptied of partitions, forming a grand, formal architectural enclosure.

While Re-city and the Edge offer intense interaction and crowding, the Darkinjung Cycle offers relative quietude.

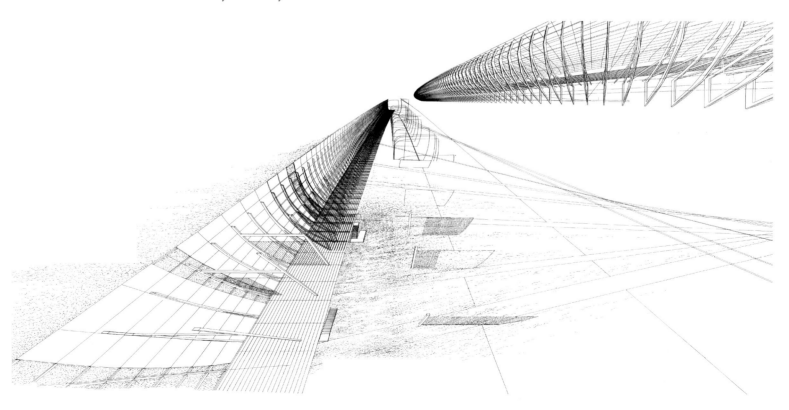

The Darkinjung Cycle

The Darkinjung are the indigenous Australians upon whose land this project is proposed. As a mark of respect and intercultural landscape appreciation, their tribal boundary sets the path for one semester of the university's educational program.

The boundary of the Darkinjung land is identified and marked by a (serviceable) 180 kilometer bicycle and walking trail. Punctuating this circuit are thirty houses and camps, one of which operates as a Darkinjung cultural center. The houses are approximately 6 kilometers apart from each other. Residing in each of the thirty houses for a specified period is a guest scholar of the FGU international program. The cycle has six hundred students in circulation at any given time.

The students meet with the resident scholar and are involved in a three-day program, then move on to the next residence, and so on. The entire journey takes approximately four months with one and a half days off between each workshop.

The thirty scholars in residence in the Darkinjung Cycle are in close communication with one another to determine the educational narrative that unfolds along the path for the duration of the semester. The Darkinjung Cycle extends Aristotle's peripatetic mode of education at the Lyceum and Plato's outdoor classroom, the sacred grove at Academos. In a Socratic sense, as opposed to the general tendency of education today to amount to the mere accumulation of instrumental information, it could be that the Darkinjung cycle is about unlearning.

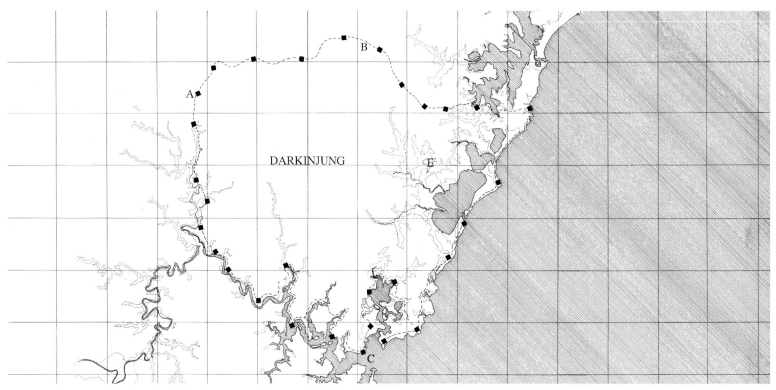

The boundary of the Darkinjung lands are marked by a bicycle and pedestrian path connecting thirty scholars' residences. The inlet in the south of the map (C) is Sydney Harbor. The site for the main residential campus of the Future Generations University is marked (E).

THE *ALBATROSS*

The *Albatross* is an ex-military vessel converted into a traveling class-room specifically engaged in cross-cultural programs at strategic international ports of call. The *Albatross* is also a mascot and traveling exhibition of projects undertaken by the FGU. The *Albatross* is not a self-appointed environmental police unit in the manner of the *Rainbow Warrior*, but it is understood as an extension of this successful concept and practice.

The vessel will have a rich turnover of students and scholars depending on the global paths it takes. In the manner of any large ship visiting a place, the ship will dock for some time and afford student and community interaction. Not only does a military vessel have to be secured, but also a flexible annual program of migrations must be developed which makes educational and symbolic sense.

The vessel could contain up to seven hundred students (probably half the number for which the vessel was designed). These students should as far as possible represent the world's bioregions and not an elite of wealthy first world students indulging in an intellectual cruise. This means governments and corporations must award *Albatross* scholarships for the concept to have any strength.

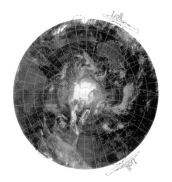

Subverting the Design Process

These ideas for the Future Generations University amount to a sketch of a place where the intellectual challenges of ecological awareness and the role of design could be focused upon with an intensity and concentration in proportion to the magnitude of the problematic.

Although we have set out a series of potential ideas for how this university might work and what form it might take, we also believe that the Future Generations University presents such a complex range of issues that a larger group of international consultants need to live and work together in situ to fulsomely design the university's programs and structures.

This larger in situ design team was, for the purposes of presentation, entitled the Landing Party and their accommodation was based on "Cells." The Cells are small transportable buildings based on a hybrid of the Japanese teahouse and the caravan. Once construction begins, the Cells can accommodate construction workers. Once the main campus (Re-city) is constructed, the Cells might be kept in situ and used to accommodate short-term students and visitors. Each Cell can be constructed for under US $20,000. The design and construction of the Cells is expected to be the first of the university's marketable sustainable products.

1   Tony Fry, Eco-Design Foundation unpublished design brief for the Design Competition of the Future Generations University, Sydney, 1996.
2   The team members and other finalists are listed on page 249 under Project Credits.
3   Charles Jencks, *The Architecture of the Jumping Universe: A Polemic. How Complexity Science Is Changing Architecture and Culture* (London: Academy Editions, 1997), pp. 10–14.
4   Room 4.1.3 included indigenous representation.

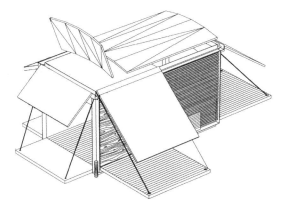

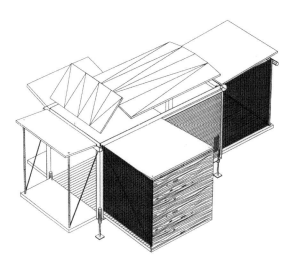

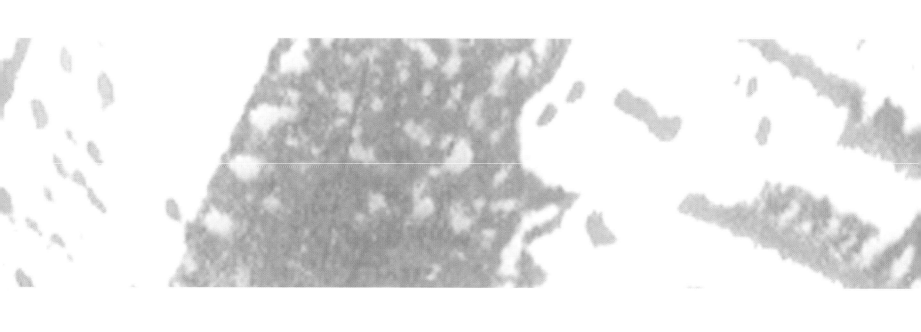

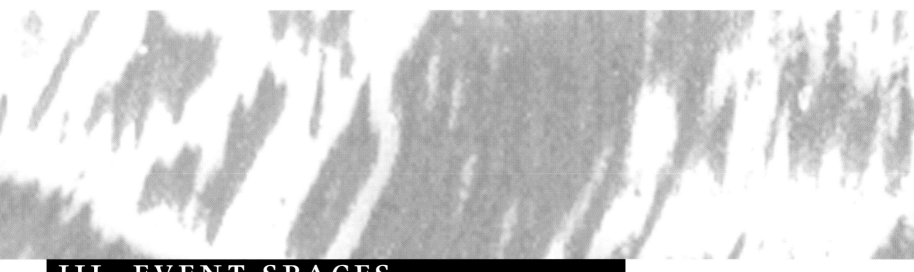

III. EVENT SPACES

A-Political Project(ions)
Berlin 1996

As information merchandise becomes indispensable to productive power it passes naturally into the global competition for power. Just as nation-states in the past have fought to acquire and master territories in order to dominate the means of production associated with those territories it is today imaginable that they will fight to dominate information. And yet the war for information will be a war without territory, without space, what Virilio has called "pure war." [1]

In 1990 when Germany was reunified, Berlin was ratified, once again, as the capital. This meant the infrastructure of West German government in Bonn had to be moved into a massive new development in central Berlin, an area of land defined by the arc of the River Spree entitled the Spreebogen.

The Tiergarten to the southwest, the Reichstag to the east, and the Spree River to the north bound the site. This land is directly adjacent to the ground upon which Albert Speer proposed to build the Great Hall of the German People, a mad temple at the head of the main axis of the proposed reconstruction of Berlin as Germania, the capital of the Third Reich (see the Twentieth Century Monument, page 128).

In March 1993 the Berlin architects Axel Schultes and Charlotte Frank won the international architectural competition to design the new government offices. Aspiring to the metaphor of a bridge between East and West, and apparently structured along the lines of an undeclared musical score, their master plan allowed for a large open space in the arc of the Spree River. Further to the architectural competition, in 1996 we submitted the following proposal to the

landscape design competition, which focused on the open spaces provided for in the Schultes-Frank plan.

In the large public space at the heart of the Parliamentary zone we propose a process based on the importation of donations of earth from all nations willing to contribute. This is an idea we developed in 1992 while preparing designs to assist Daniel Libeskind's entry in to the urban design competition for the Potsdamer Platz (see the Park and the Potsdamer Platz, page 20).

Donor nations send earth excavated from borders they share with other nations. Naturally some nations, which share no borders, cannot do this, and others might prefer to select their own specifically symbolic sites of extraction. Regardless, each donation of earth should fill a shipping container, and upon arrival in Berlin it is ceremoniously poured onto the site of the Spreebogen, as an individual cone of earth. The multitude of individual earth donations can be read off the plan as a grid of circles, each circle representing an individual conical pile of earth. It is estimated that approximately 273 containers of earth are needed to create a truly global microcosm.

Once poured onto the site the new earth deposits are mixed and somewhat smoothed out by people moving over the area. As the landform hardens, the site is topsoiled and turfed. Once the turf has taken root it is cut away from the western-facing side of the conical landforms and replaced with white concrete. This white side of the landforms then receives projections from projectors set on the peaks of adjacent landforms. Thus one side of the conical undulating topography is brilliantly illuminated with imagery, while the other remains dark, a literal illustration of the two-faced nature of politics. The field can contain a pluralism of images, or a single image can be programmed across all the projectors.

The passivity of receiving this spectacle is interrupted in two ways. First, when in this place at night one is projected upon, and yet one's shadow erases parts of the image. Second, it is proposed that anyone, anywhere, can orchestrate these images via the Internet. In this way politics is figured not so much as a war of words and ideas but a battleground of images cast around the world. Beyond politics, however, the project attempts to incorporate and conflate the categories of the real and the virtual, the netscape and the landscape. In trying to bring the depth of the earth to the surface of the image, the sublime extremes of postmodern culture are compounded.

To further animate and activate this site the topography is threaded with a soundscape. This too could be orchestrated (mixed) internationally over the Internet, bringing a world of ever-changing cacophony into the frames of Schultes' frozen orchestration. Finally, the topography is richly patterned with concentric wave patterns emanating from the four cardinal directions, recalling the Christian moral coding of Temperance, Fortitude, Justice, and Prudence, once symbolized in the four quarters of medieval gardens.

After having deposited their loads of earth the 273 empty shipping containers can then go back into circulation. Or, as we prefer, they can be randomly placed around the city to facilitate artful public dioramas. Some of the containers can also become "Direct Democracy Capsules" in which publicly accessible computers allow the disconnected to send messages directly to the ministers in the new government buildings. We would call this the "Ministry of the Disconnected."

As a representation of the world, this global earthwork creates an extraterritorial zone, a status churches once held. This project is then a new cathedral of the earth and a diplomatic, multicultural field. It is also saccharine political symbolism. But if this idea overindulges a millennial optimism, so too it is simply a sign of ecological, political, and corporate geography, a personification of what David Harvey has identified as global postmodern spatial and temporal compression.[2] More specifically, in the local symbolic order this

THE PROCESS NECESSARY TO THIS PROJECT BEGINS WITH THE EXCAVATION OF EARTH FROM A BORDER BETWEEN TWO COUNTRIES, THEN THE EARTH DONATIONS ARE SHIPPED TO BERLIN AND DEPOSITED ONTO THE OPEN PUBLIC SPACE AT THE HEART OF THE NEW PARLIAMENTARY QUARTER IN BERLIN.

proposal explicitly embodies core values of German democracy as opposed to simplistic nationalism and its specious notions of *blud, boden und gemeinschaft* (blood, ground, and community). In addition to the main proposal of an international earthwork, we offered a wooden platform to serve as a performance space and forum and in front of the Reichstag, three long tables to sit one thousand people.

1   Peter J. Burgess (1996), "European Borders: History of Space/Space of History," www.ctheory.net.
2   David Harvey, *The Condition of Postmodernity: An Enquiry into the Origins of Cultural Change* (Oxford: Basil Blackwell, 1989), pp. 284-307.

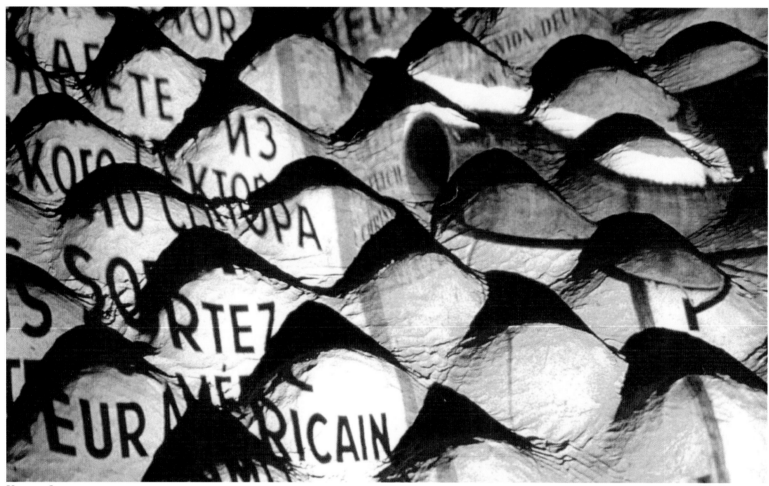

VIA THE INTERNET, MULTIMEDIA IMAGES ARE PROJECTED OVER THE FIELD OF EARTH DONATIONS.

1. Reichstag
2. Site for field of earth deposits and projections
3. Parliamentary offices
4. River Spree
5. Wooden stage (Forum)
6. Three long tables to seat 1000 people

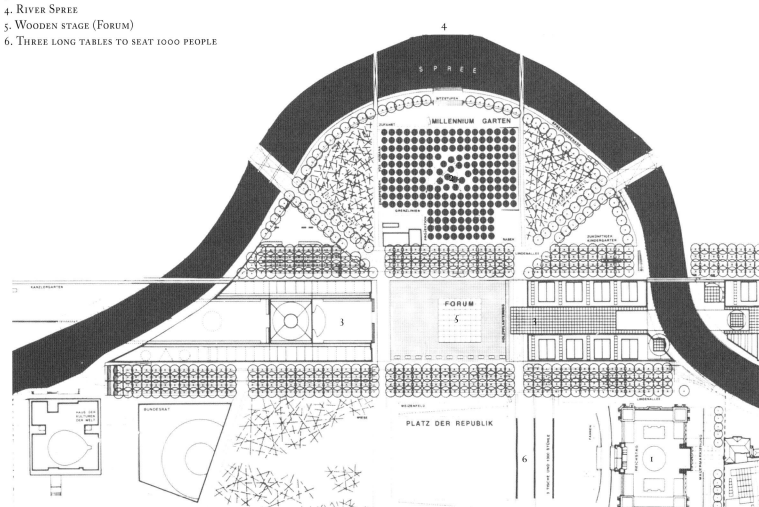

Master plan of the design for the Spreebogen.

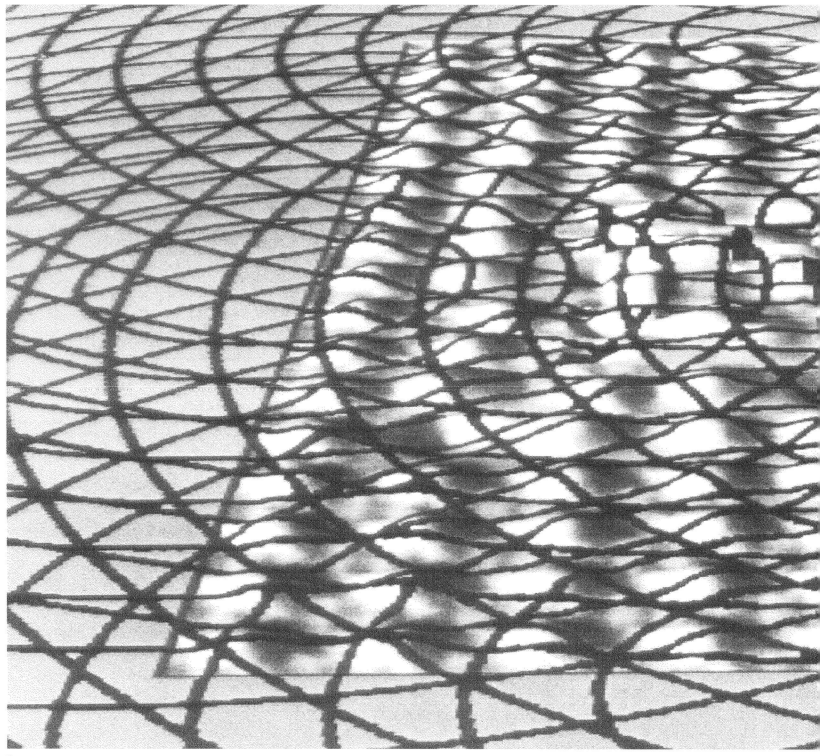

INSCRIBED OVER THE FIELD OF EARTH DONATIONS IS A PATTERN OF FOUR INTERSECTING CONCENTRIC CIRCLES

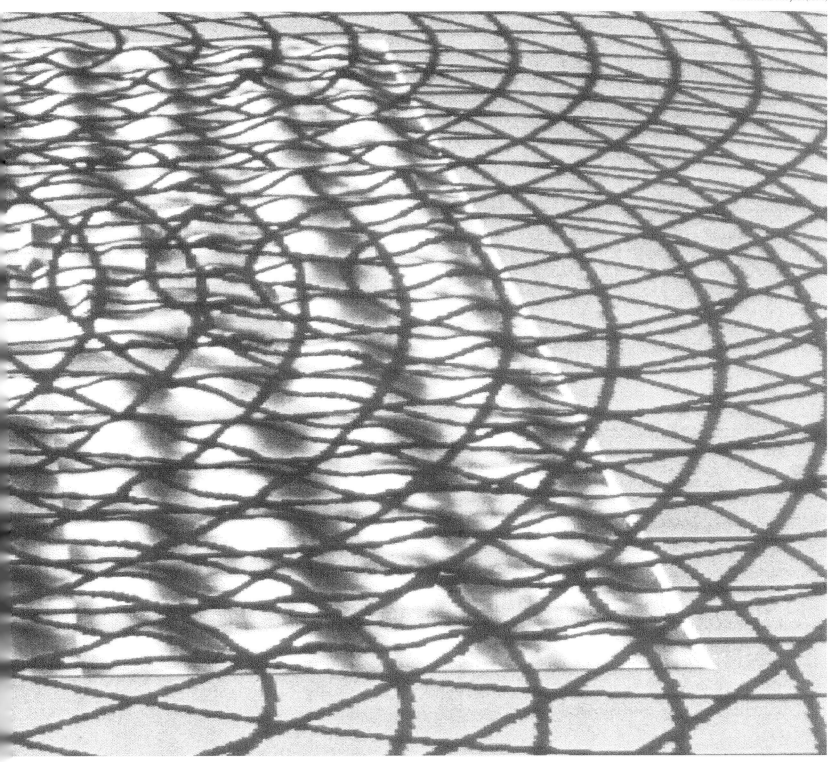

The Women's Rooms
Berlin 1992

Originally royal pleasure gardens, in 1992 Park Monbijou ("my little jewel") was a typically frayed and drab (ex)East German park. The park is located opposite Berlin's prestigious Museum Island in the midst of the former Jewish quarter on Oranienburgerstrasse. In a unified Berlin the area has rapidly become an edgy and fashionable arts district. Having traded their socialist youth uniforms for bunny costumes and suspenders, some women work the streets adjacent to the park.

This proposal argues that there is ample open public space provided by our master plan for the area, and that in this part of the city it is appropriate to propose that a portion of the existing non-descript parkland be devoted to a specifically themed program. Entitled the Women's Rooms, approximately one-third of the existing park is subdivided into a labyrinth of forty rooms and tight passages formed in hedges.

Each room in the labyrinth is clearly signed with the name of a particular woman, all of whom are significant figures in Berlin's social and intellectual history. Most of these women remain relatively unacknowledged in the official history and urban nomenclature of Berlin. Although the rooms could remain empty (but named), the proposal is best thought of as a gallery without a roof, a place where certain responses to changing themes could be curated as an ongoing public arts and entertainment program.

Some of the rooms are used for outdoor dining and are available for rental as private event spaces. An adjacent building services the arts and entertainment program of the site. It offers catering and a range of period costumes and fancy dress. When rented or containing artworks, installations or performance equipment, all or some of the Women's Rooms can be easily secured.

Figurative statues of Eros, Thanatos, Cupid, and Demeter overlook the labyrinth, and the Garden of Venus, as described by the fifteenth-century author Francesco Colonna (1433-1527) in his text *Hypnerotomachia Poliphili*, is superimposed as a circular pattern and water feature.[3]

The women to whom the rooms are dedicated were chosen from 1770 to the present and include Rahel Varnhagen von Ense, Amelie Beer, Henriette Herz, Dorothea Schlegel, Rebecca Friedländer, Marianne Schadow, Julie Heyse, Sar Levy, Marianne and Sara Meyer, Rebecca Ephraim, Friedchen Limann, Dorothea von Courland, Fanny Lewald, Eliza von der Recke, Helmina von Chezy, Caroline de la Motte Fouqué, Felicité de Gemlis, Miriam Itzig, Philippine Cohen, Jente Steiglitz, Rosa Luxemburg, Hannah Arendt, Lise Meitner, Berta Pappenheim, Anna Freud, Anna Seghers, Nelly Sachs, Else Laska-Schüler, Sarah Kirsch, Christa Wolff, Gabriele Wohmann, Tatjana Gsovsky, Rebecca Horn, Nina Hagen, Angelika Domröse, Gisela Breitling, Susanne Specht, Irmtraud Morgner, Katharina Thalbach, and Elvira Bach.

3 Francesco Colonna, *Hypnerotomachia Poliphili* (Padua: Editrice Antenore, 1980).

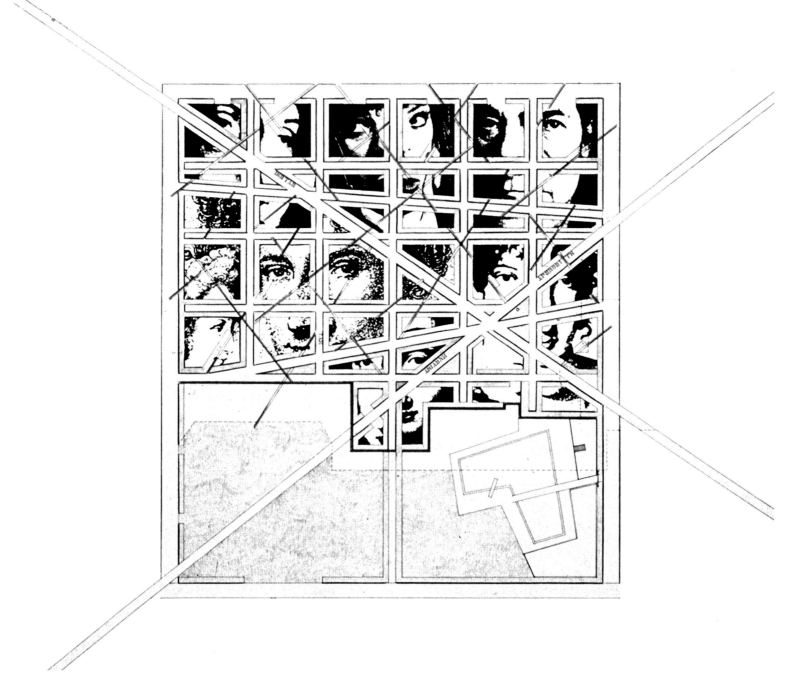

CONCEPT IMAGE OF THE WOMEN'S ROOMS. ORIGINAL COMPETITION MONTAGE BY RICHARD WELLER WITH CORNELIA MÜLLER AND JAN WEHBERG IN MKW. COURTESY MKW.

L O C U S   A M O E N U S

ΠΑΝΤΩΝ ΤΟΚΑΔΙ

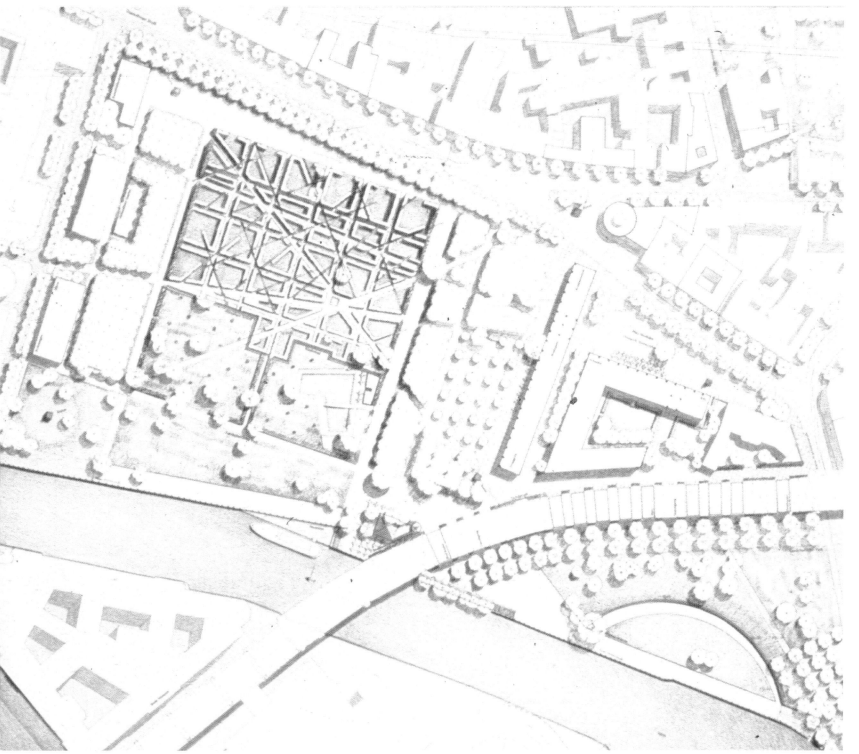

MASTER PLAN OF THE WOMEN'S ROOMS. ORIGINAL COMPETITION DRAWING BY RICHARD WELLER WITH CORNELIA MÜLLER AND JAN WEHBERG IN MKW. COURTESY MKW.

The Esplanade
Melbourne 1998

The Docklands, the former working port of Melbourne, is the site for Australia's largest urban redevelopment project. As we approached the competition calling for landscape designs to give the Docklands identity, cohesion, and useful public space, the developer, Grollo Pty. Ltd., had just announced its intention to build the world's highest tower at one end of the site.

At odds with this boyish intention is the fact that the primary characteristic of this site is its vast horizontality. Hence our first move is to take the tower and lay it on its side. With some stretching and bending, the original tower becomes a template to organize a landscape design. The bold supergraphic of a section through the fallen tower serves to mark out a coherent pattern for a 2.1-kilometer-long esplanade. The fallen tower effectively unifies the site as opposed to dominating it if it were to be built vertically, which, incidentally, is unlikely.

A section through the tower's 240 floor levels and its lift shafts is clearly marked across the ground plane of the proposed esplanade as a bold supergraphic. The floor levels form "bays," each clearly numbered so as to operate as an address system for the length of the site. The individual bays are also reinforced by lines of trees so as to convert the pattern into volume and form subspaces running perpendicular to the main flow of the esplanade. In this way, the singular, monumental urban gesture of the fallen tower unifies the site in the north-south direction, while the individual bays subdivide it in the east-west direction, linking the city to the water's edge.

Having set down this basic identity for the esplanade, other elements could be superimposed so as to animate and activate an urbane promenade. For example, food and information cafés occur every forty bays, and a shipping container is placed on every fifth. The containers can be used as outdoor studios and storage areas for a comprehensive public art and entertainment program.

One of the main ways to experience this site is also to drive through it. Therefore, we propose a linear sequence of large billboards receiving advertising revenue on one side and art on the other. Finally, the architects, Ashton Raggatt McDougall, with whom we have collaborated on this project, propose to bind the whole event space with a sculptural shade structure that loops and waves its way through the site.

Perspective view of the Esplanade. Grollo's proposed world's tallest building stands to the right. Original competition drawing by Ashton Raggatt McDougall in association with Room 4.1.3. Courtesy ARM.

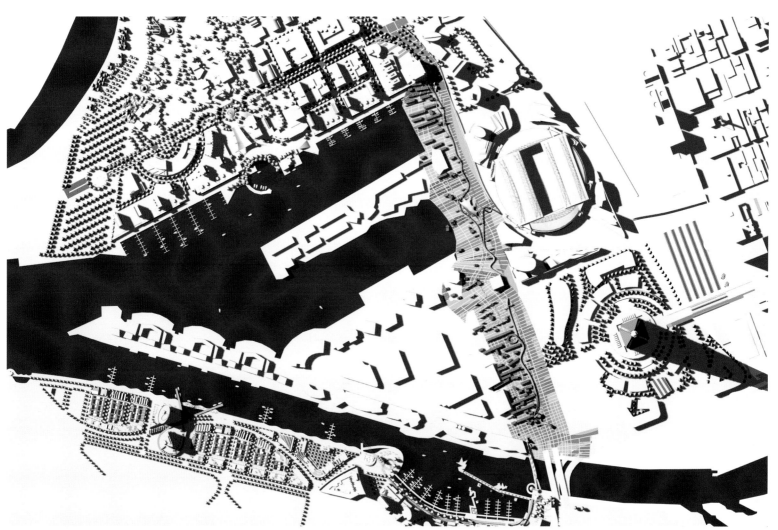

PLAN OF THE ESPLANADE IN THE CONTEXT OF THE MELBOURNE DOCKLANDS. ORIGINAL COMPETITION DRAWING BY ASHTON RAGGATT McDOUGALL IN ASSO-
CIATION WITH ROOM 4.1.3. COURTESY ARM.

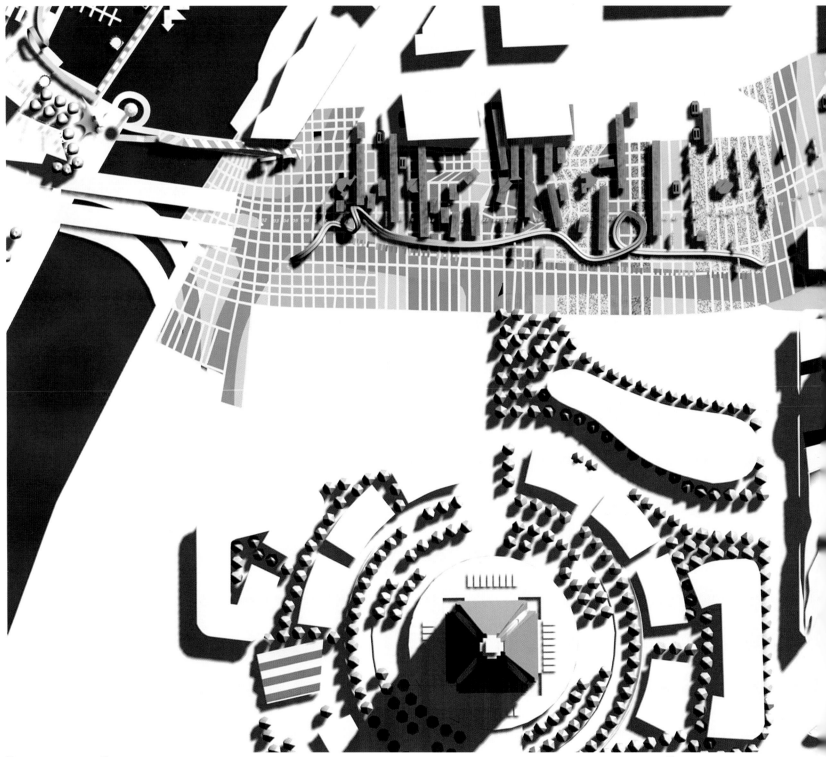

PLAN VIEW OF THE ESPLANADE SHOWING THE CURVILINEAR SHADE STRUCTURE, GROUND PLANE STRIATIONS, AND LINEAR GROVES OF TREES. ORIGINAL COMPETITION DRAWING BY ASHTON RAGGATT McDOUGALL IN ASSOCIATION WITH ROOM 4.1.3. COURTESY ARM.

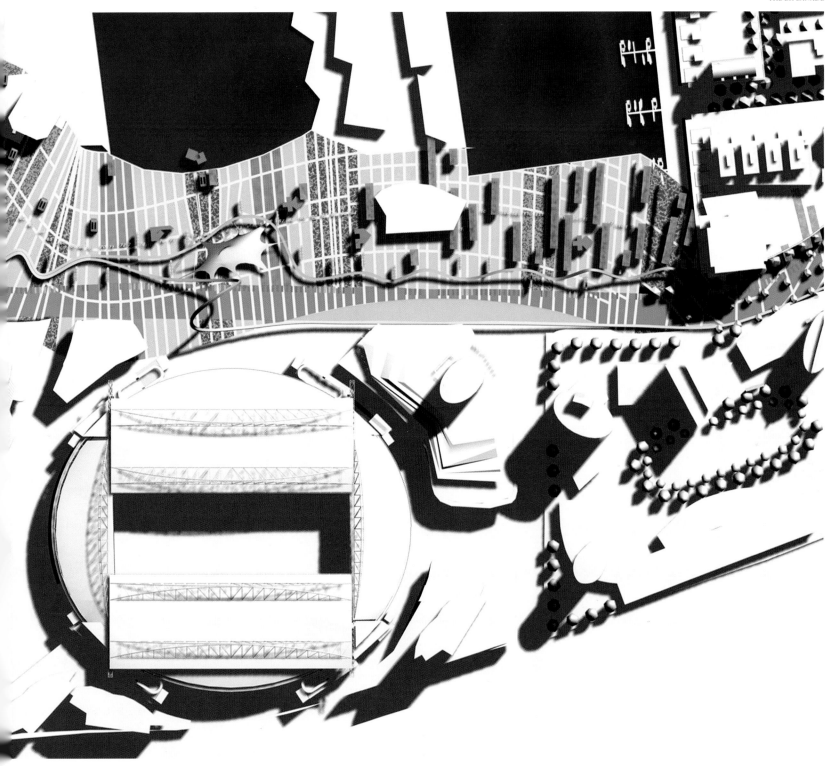

Namesti Miru
Prague 1995

Translated as the "Peace Square," this urban plaza near the center of Prague in the Czech Republic is a significant public space in the life of the city. The urban morphology of the square dates back to the nineteenth century and is structured along an axis that links the town hall and a prominent cathedral. While this connection between civic and divine power is still evident, years of meddling has dissolved the square's clarity. So, too, the public's faith in *res publica* as the stage set of civic institutions they could trust has been eroded.

As it is now, the square is a conduit, whereas it should be a container. Our approach was to significantly reorganize circulation patterns, erase the flotsam and jetsam that have confused the space, and then increase the gravity of the square's center. To this end, the basic strategy is to create a homogenous ground plane of decomposed granite and plant a bosquet of linden trees. The lindens are shaped (undercut) so as to decrease in height, thus creating a false perspective toward the square's center. The grid of lindens stos, so as to create a green room open to the sky at the heart of the plaza.

The centerpiece is a sculptural water feature based on the notion of equilibrium or, rather, its impossibility. Rather than making glib claims for peace, we propose water and fire as elemental opposing forces set on either end of a 10-meter long and 4-meter-wide swaying beam. The beam of steel and stone is mechanically manipulated in the manner of a seesaw, an enormous lever. One end of the beam is punctured by gas jets, which ignite only to be gradually extinguished as the beam lowers into a surrounding pool of water. Steaming, the beam reappears, and as it rises out of the water, it reignites—and so on. Inscribed into the beam are the names of battle fields past and present.

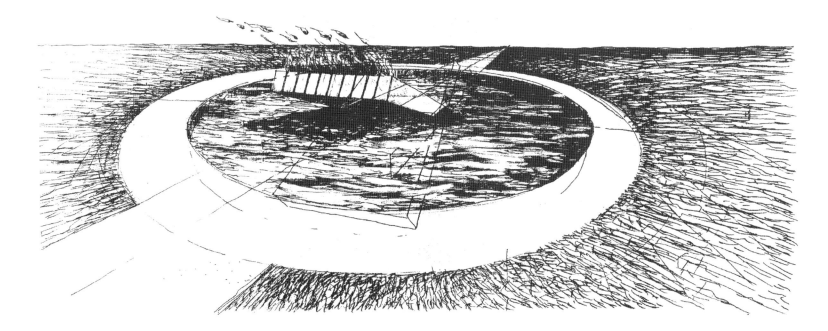

The Field

Wellington, New Zealand 2002

The brief called for a vibrant urban park while expressing a desire to retain the site's current role as a parking garage.

The Field is a grass-covered artificial topography draped over parking for three hundred cars. The form of the Field meets all surrounding levels and is framed by a proposed mixed-use building at its western flank and a proposed Asia-Pacific Market and Courtyard Garden on its eastern flank. Superimposed onto the basic superstructure of the Field are the myriad programs that would constitute a democratic and pluralist urban park. This messiness is held in place by the gravity of the Field's unifying form.

The undulating topography of the field is formed by initially placing prefabricated culverts in three rows to cover the basic parking garage layout of three rows of one hundred cars. Smaller pipes are then used to backfill in between the three main rows so as to form the porous skeleton of a second, finer-grained set of undulations. The culverts and pipes are simply covered with lightweight fill and finally sealed over with topsoil and grass.

The Field's topography enables both oceanic panoramas and protection from the site's prevailing winds. The spatial strategy of the Field offers a broad homogenous green surface as a public park on a civic scale while containing niches of difference within—an ambiguous response to the brief's emphasis on surveillance. Light wells are sliced into the smooth-flowing topography to reveal its mechanistic underbelly. Some of the slices and portholes into the parking garage underneath are covered in colored glass and backlit at night.

Legend

1. Te Papa (National Museum)
2. Mixed Use Development
3. Entrance/Exit to Underground Parking
4. Tidal Environmental Artwork
5. Soundscape
6. Hotel Drop Off
7. Main Event Space
8. Chaffer's Hotel
9. Chaffer's Beer Garden
10. The Field
    (Parking Under for 300 Cars)
11. Panoramic Ridges and Active and Passive Furnishings
12. Protected Valleys and Active and Passive Furnishings
13. "Geomorph" Skatepark
14. Geomorphic Section (Art Wall)
15. White Wall Backdrop to Chinese Garden
16. Chinese Garden
17. Pacific-Asia Neighborhood
18. Navigation Place: Time Tower and Lookout

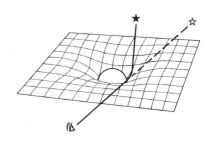

Black Nightshade Ink

Rod Barnett

Over the past fifteen years the work of Room 4.1.3 has engaged the complexities and ambiguities of the millennial world without itself falling prey to easy complexity and ambiguity. With clarity and a narcissistic self-belief Room 4.1.3 has charted its course through the heavy seas of alienation, memory, hybridity, and desire. Their graphic landscapes explode across our retinas scattering shards of nature, or burst like bags of black nightshade ink. Angry, moralistic, the work demands attention. That is bad, it says, this, this is good. There is good, and it is called landscape design. By means of a compulsive, but considered, investigation into the role of art in a society that has given up and rolled over–an investigation through design–Vladimir Sitta and Richard Weller have created a universe of images that form an indictment of collective sentimentality, lassitude, and venality. They invent landscapes that deny cozy liberalism and force reaction. This is what design is for, they seem to say. Not to cosset or reassure, nor to project history, or ideology, or aspiration onto the land or into comfortable little urban enclaves. Room 4.1.3's work is not an appearance medicine. In design after design they subvert expectation. That they can do this *and* win international competitions says no little about their skills in the witchcraft of signs.

An obsession with signification permeates the work of Room 4.1.3. It is, however, an interest in more than just signification; there is a need here for motivated, determined signification. In a universe otherwise deemed relativistic, any design work that calls itself "allegorical" demonstrates a touching faith in the possibility of communication. Allegory such as Room 4.1.3's requires a belief system of some sort not only to validate its ideological narratives, but to provide a baseline for the morally charged anger, derision, frustration, and desire that power these narratives. And so we find a paradoxical mix of motivated symbol (Richard Weller is always at pains to link his work with his meanings) and promiscuous sign (but we will have our wicked way with it anyhow).

The result is nothing less than an exploration of landscape architecture's potential to signify. This would seem to be the program behind their avowed interest in forging a landscape poetic out of environmental politics. What justifies Room 4.1.3's claim to a landscape "poetic" is, first, that this signification takes place on a number of different levels. It is a mixture of the correspondence theory of truth and semiotic chaos. Second, their ideas are sourced in the discipline's own unique thematic (it is landscape architecture and nothing but landscape architecture), and, third, the work is concerned with the concrete articulation of ideas rather than the ideas themselves. Despite their "allegorical" certitude, these designs are not simply vehicles for preordained theory.

If one is to pursue a landscape architecture of allegory, one must take a moral stance on the world. For allegory tells a story with a moral. One must believe in something. Landscape architecture has traditionally believed in the unassailable naturalness of nature. Room 4.1.3 cannot believe in this. For them nature is, if not constructed then at least part construction. Nature is in some way created. It too is a story. But that's all right because we have ecology—and we have technology. We have memory and desire. Out of these we can build an environment fit for human habitation. We have science and we have art. Contemporary landscape architecture, more than any other design discipline, has found it difficult to slough off the "eternal verities." Humanist ideas of truth and beauty tie it to a realist and physicalist interpretation of nature. A deep, enduring moralism is based on this idea of nature as a real physical entity, as an ultimate reality, as a life force that is under attack from humans themselves. Landscape architecture must believe in the primacy of nature. Even though three decades of poststructuralism have not left this particular verity in good shape, it remains the dominant paradigm in the discipline of landscape architecture. To be a landscape architect is to work within a paradigm framed by this understanding of nature.

But the postmodern confrontation of landscape architecture's nature-realism with relativism and constructivism has shaken the landscape architectural belief in nature. Nature now is discourse, nature is a construction, nature is culture. The question for landscape architecture now is: how to reconcile these beguiling (because egalitarian, ungendered, nonracially specific) theories with the foundational nature-realism so essential to a discipline that requires a metaphysic to validate its advocacy? It is the terrain marked out by this question that Room 4.1.3 has been exploring. If their work is allegorical at all, it is an allegory of the encounter of landscape architecture with relativism. There is a curious similarity between the work of Room 4.1.3 executed in the 1980s—caught in an incisive moment of transition—and the landscape architecture of the baroque. Both face an encounter with the new. Both articulate an allegory of change, of transition. Both have their sacred.

The seventeenth-century baroque discovered that the universe was infinite. Room 4.1.3's work discovers in ideas of the political a poetic that finds its infinitude in the endless Protean flux of information. The endless stories we tell ourselves about ourselves become woven by Room 4.1.3 into the landscape itself, not as a field of linear, fixed narratives but as a matrix of shifting songlines, culture-data that never settle into closure or meaning. This lore is just as likely to be uncomfortable or contested, or bloody and violent, as it is to be that kind of happy temporary tale of victory over adversity found in the six o'clock news. Similarly, Weller's early work in Berlin avoids solutions. He cut his critical teeth in that scarred, charismatic city. Only a commitment to a politicized poetics could serve landscape architecture in a city so "postindustrial," so "denatured" as to be beyond ecology, beyond sustainability, beyond the feeble legerdemain of plants, paving, and street furniture that normally passes for landscape design. The 1996 proposal for the German Government Center in Berlin entitled A-Political Project(ions) transposes 140 earth cones of soil from international borders. This project illustrates Room 4.1.3's commitment to political change through environmental transformation. Visitors to the installation are themselves "altered." Caught in a web of projected netscape images and short-wave white noise, they drift through an "allegorical topography" in an extended free-fall from national pride and political innocence which changes the landscape as it changes them.

And so this is a politicized design. It draws its sustenance from political issues, and links these with grand themes such as in the Trans-European Songline or Heidegger's Garden. Often the links are forged by means of linguistic or mathematical signs. Phonemes, phrases, quotations, place-names, neologisms, and grids of text trailing clouds of glorious memory lodge in the interactive webs of the poetic and the political. (And these are not poles. They are coexistent, even interpenetrating fields, and as such provide the shifting matrices through which a future for urban open space must be discerned, if at all.) The use of mathematics, and particularly the grid, provides an ordering system that can be upset, destabilized, "poeticized." The allegorical thrust of this simple principle underlies most of the work: contradiction and ambivalence–the tropes of a disturbed society. Is this not apparent in the deployment of the diagonal, especially in the early work? German literary historian Richard Aleyn has said of baroque space that "orientation, and, specifically, the possibility of crossing it on the diagonal" captured the imagination of the seventeenth century. It was "a device so elemental to the baroque that the space really only came into its own when there was movement."[1] In the early work of Room 4.1.3 the *contrario* itself is a function of the use of the diagonal. Diagonal lines cross and recross the grid of the city, establishing vectors for the movement of ideas and emotions away from and toward informational infinity. Of their design for No-Man's-Land in Berlin, Weller comments that the beauty of the space lies in its emptiness–but it is an emptiness crossed with meanings (conveniently provided for us by the accompanying text).

If *baroque* culture was characterized by a confrontation with contradictions, the universe itself was infinite, self-perpetuating, and determined by eternal laws. Both were still somehow overseen by God. Life at court was rich in ritual, ceremony, regulation, and manners, while life on the streets of the cities was unpredictable. The laws of nature were stable, but everything seemed to be in flux. In the late twentieth century, nature is chaotic and society unstable. Room 4.1.3's work demonstrates an attempt to navigate the contingencies of the postmodern world–a world we have now perhaps left behind us. This volume shows the development of an allegorical mode of landscape architecture in the service of a kind of romantic rationalist narrative of the world. A range of rhetorical devices are used to engage the viewer emotionally, to provoke and estrange us at the same time. Strategies such as negation (Nihilum), irony (Courtyard for the German Institute of Standards), naming (The Garden of Australian Dreams), and symbolism (the Federal Government Center in Berlin) are employed. Throughout the eighties work there is a heavily ironic representational vocabulary replete with stark black and white images, repeated found images, stenciled texts, panoptic geometries, a continual allusion to the mathexis of the baroque, its infinitude and certitude disrupted by moments of intimacy and delicacy.[2] All of it is drenched in a knowing/unknowing postindustrial *noir* which finds its potency in the virtuality of the denatured city.

It is here that we encounter the most interesting parallel: the investigation of a nature that is not reduced to or confined to exemplification by means of natural processes. Everything in the baroque garden is laid out according to rules, which, while they themselves are regarded as "natural," do not take account of the naturalness of the territory. The baroque rules of rhetoric determine the structure of the visual in very specific ways. The gardens of Room 4.1.3 invoke the moment when signs and conventions leap off the computer screen and onto the terrain to spread their codes across a horizontal field, engaging with the surface of a topographical ooze that awaits animation by an ordering principle (mere matter desperate for the input of mind). The baroque French garden reaches back through Descartes to Plato and beyond him to Euclid's ideal world where mathematics organizes chaotic nature. Room 4.1.3 is still using mathematics, but not to organize nature. There is no nature to organize. Here nature is occluded, rather than absent as in a piece of urban design. Nature is here, but placed under erasure, and a diversity of contested "natures" is allowed to flood through the garden (human nature is part of this flood). Instead of a set of passive objects to be used and worked on by people, nature becomes something people put together, using various elements from the chaotic field in which they find themselves immersed—willy-nilly, as they wish. And that is why at the heart of this unholy marriage of ecology and technology there is a darkness. That is why this searching for a future city of meaningful form in the spaces between architecture and art, the leftover, thrown-out bits of place, this relentless hopefulness, this grim millennial romanticism shares with certain kinds of contemporary music and anti-aesthetic art a project that finds its very optimism in the clarity of a luminous negation.

1   Quoted in Barbara Borngasser and Rolf Tolman, introduction, in Rolf Tolman, ed., *Baroque: Architecture, Sculpture, Painting* (Cologne: Konemann, 1998), pp. 7–13.
2   Mathexis refers to the mathematical ordering principle of the universe. During the seventeenth century (middle and high baroque), the notion that mathematics was the ordering principle of the universe (introduced earlier of course in Plato and Parmenides) found its modern champion in René Descartes. For Descartes the *mathexis universalis* is mathematical method, which he regards as the key to the universal science of nature. Descartes gives the new spatiality of the seventeenth century its coordinate system, which determines the position of a point in a plane by its distance from two fixed lines. He deploys the clarity and incontrovertibility of mathematical truth in the deduction of the universe and its laws. His geometry is set out at Vaux-le-Vicomte in France—a tableau of points, lines, and planes. For Leibniz, however, the *mathexis universalis* seems to be music.

The Satellite's Garden at Ground Zero

Denis Cosgrove

Richard Weller's preface to this volume makes an impassioned plea for design as a way of confronting the world and for the integrity of knowledge that comes through the processes of design. Design's autonomy is never absolute, and Weller fully appreciates the tensions between politics and poetics: the two poles that compel the compass of his work, and indeed shape the processes and form of all human landscape making. Recognizing design's inescapable engagement with these poles, he finds the twentieth century's term *field* preferable to the eighteenth century's *landscape*. The field, he claims, is "interdisciplinary and eco-logical, merging binary distinctions between landscape and object";[1] field design projects are relational, crystallizing within a web of connections. This is very much how places are conceptualized and interpreted today within the geographical sciences and planning. The most recurrent connection is that which the Room 4.1.3 projects also make: between the cultural and historical specifics of place (so often erased by the politics of colonial occupation or market utility) and the enduring spatialities of mobile human bodies subsisting within a limitless cosmos.

In this short essay, I reflect upon these claims and the ways they have been actualized through place specifics and cosmic spatiality in some of the projects illustrated in this book. The collection is rich; the scope of its creativity resists any purely textual capture. I have chosen, therefore, to concentrate on a limited set of projects: those that relate to Berlin, the Fossoli internment camp design, the Gallipoli Peninsula peace park plan, and the Memorial to Fallen Bodies in Los Angeles.[2] My choices are not random. They are governed by very immediate concerns at the time of my writing, above all by the inescapable recognition that the twentieth century closed, not with the banalities of millennium midnight firework displays over the world's great cities (Millennium Dome, Eiffel Tower, the Pyramid at Cheops), but on September 11, 2001, with the terrifyingly sudden, precise, and total extinction of a landscape. For thirty years, the twin towers of New York's World Trade Center had represented the heart of a globalizing world. There the politics *and* the poetics of the networked topography that constitutes the modern globe coexisted in the concrete and steel of two soaring geometrical forms. Their destruction was witnessed simultaneously and helplessly from every television set on earth, even by the satellite dwellers of the space shuttle passing 300 miles over Manhattan. Here was a very paradigm of place in the twenty-first century: a global center of financial, informational, and cultural connectivity, invisible flows and processes precipitated into the materiality of an intensely symbolic landscape form. Material destruction of buildings and the consequent loss of human life, powerful and shocking as they were, had relatively minor and transient impacts on the processes and flows realized at that locale, but they have activated other processes—military, economic, cultural—whose material consequences reverberate across a global field of activity.

One of the key cultural debates of the last decade—reflected in much of the work recorded in this volume—was how we should remember and inscribe into public landscapes, in ways that promoted understanding and learning, the violence of twentieth-century territorial nationalism, whose bloody stain soaked that century's history. Many of the sites that Room 4.1.3 has worked with are inescapably hued with the memory of violence: the institutional violence of war and the more casually individualized violence of urban crime. Treating them as sites or fields for landscape design must come to terms with many and conflicting features, including perhaps the poetics of violence itself. What can we learn from all this work? And do its lessons have anything to suggest for the wholly new context of that clotted, five-acre hole in the heart of New York City? My intention is not to enter the emerging debates over the future use of "Ground Zero," over the cultural politics of a monument to the firefighters who raised the Stars and Stripes over the smoldering steel in an aching echo of Iwo Jima, or even the possibility of memorializing an event that was at once so specific in location and so global in occurrence. Rather, it is to signal the ways that the events of that day have reshaped the questions faced by Richard Weller and his colleagues in 1990s Berlin, Gallipoli, and Los Angeles. Landscape architecture, like every other practice that concerns how humans organize their collective lives on earth, faces a new world in a new millennium. Design has to renegotiate its perennial challenge of speaking through place to both the eco-logics and the cosmo-logics of altered times.

At Gallipoli, the issues reflect very precisely the nature of the "Great" War that opened the past century—they are regional in scale and speak to clearly distinct, territorially based cultural and national differences: Christian and Muslim, Turk and Australian combatants: formal armies engaged in a conventional struggle over a landscape. To be sure, the mechanization of mass slaughter produced by the agents of industrial warfare brought to bear on the flesh of patriotic conscripts produced an especially horrific landscape of violence. It was the Great War that confirmed the idea of dignifying the deaths of individual soldiers by inscribing their names and deeds on the field of battle itself. The Peace Park plan for Gallipoli addresses this contradictory politics and poetics through the device of the line—metaphoric and material realization of both division and connection. Front lines, supply lines, dream lines, critical lines, peace lines, above all the planned "horizon line," visible only from the no-man's-land of space, the *line* simultaneously underscores and undermines the territorial sense of place and landscape that generated the violence. And the intention is to respect the complex dignity of place, seeking "to maintain the daily life of the peninsula's inhabitants while offering a viable economic world event, without further monumentalizing nationalistic sentiments or trivializing or defining notions of peace."

A different, horrifically characteristic place-feature of twentieth-century violence is confronted at Fossoli. This is the camp. Complex symbol of modernity's ambiguous relationship with mobility, nomadism, and transient habitation, the internment camp became–first in Boer South Africa and by mid-century in the jungles of Burma, the tundra wastes of Sweden, the deserts of California, and the chill estuaries of Baltic Poland–the paradigm place of the modern state's desire to discipline the body and systematically erase human identity and dignity. Regardless of the differences in the actual treatment of internees, the camp represents a different space of violence from the trenched field of battle or the exploitation spaces of mine, mill, or sweatshop. The camp's ecological relationships with landscape and territory are arbitrary; its impermanence is central to the project of dis-placement and consequent violence to the integrity of its subjects. Designing "clear landscape rooms, scaled to events and rituals that the people in this region follow," with saplings filling their ghostly outline, Room 4.1.3 seeks to recover at Fossoli some of the ecological integrity of the place, thereby restoring some dignity to those now-absent camp subjects, without obscuring the geometry of state violence that shaped the camp landscape.

Berlin, heart of darkness for mid-twentieth-century state violence, has become since 1990 a kind of laboratory for rethinking memory and place. Berlin's urban core was quite literally an ecology of horror–the "Wall" snaking over the bunkers and cellars of Gestapo headquarters and the open spaces choked with the ruined buildings from which the holocausts that ultimately visited all the peoples of Central Europe were planned and directed. Two of Room 4.1.3's plans seem to reach toward grasping the enormity of memory and place here. The Vertigorium, a great axis connecting the Hill of the Devil and the Hill of the Cross that shape the city's topography, through which, Icarus-like, we fall, from the all-seeing satellite eye to the dark void of the images composing pixels, is a powerful synthesis. Berlin's moral darkness, the possibility of salvation, and the final grounding of responsibility in the centered subject come together in an extended landscape vision. By contrast, No-Man's Land, postdialectical and postmodern, tracing along the line of the now-absent Wall the gash at the heart of the twentieth-century global space, begs, as Richard Weller says, an essentially poetic question: where are we now? And answers it in the "raw poetry of emptiness and antithesis," in "the pathos and fascination of ruination." Confronting Weller's question, Room 4.1.3 seizes the antithesis directly in two projects. Trans-European Songline and Heidegger's Garden address the poles of modernity's contradictory human geography: respectively, the frictionless surface of space and the deep-rooted ecology of place.

New York's Ground Zero is not like Berlin's Potsdamer Platz in 1990: a long-maturing absence, meaning evolving over decades out of the chaos of military destruction and totalitarian construction. The ugly wound at Manhattan's heart now sealing over with the scar tissue of memory was not incised by military or ideological weapons; it was not the sign of territorial or political ambition. It was the barbarism of sack and civilian mass slaughter. Terrorism is more than terror—it is calculated violence without prior warning or evidence of origin, with undeclared purpose, its victims wholly random. Visiting a place, it entails immediate and total change of meaning. Terrorism's incoherence cuts deep across those late twentieth-century debates about the cultural politics of commemoration; the sickening poetics of its violence acknowledge no identity in its victims.

Perhaps closer to the questions of place and memory confronting Manhattan today are those faced by Room 4.1.3 in responding to the Los Angeles brief for a Justice Park and Memorial to Victims of Violent Crime. Ironically, this competition referred to a quest for the "Heart of America." Fallen Bodies draws upon the lunar cycle and the movement of waters to signal a loss and to remember the deaths of victims. The kind of violence commemorated here—symbolized in the O.J. Simpson murder trial—is familial, or at least person to person. And the proxemics of attacker and victim "place" even the most apparently random crimes in an ecology of the local. This was a design for Los Angeles, for the heart of America.

While placed close to residential districts of New York, Ground Zero is neither territorial nor local in the conventional senses that apply to most of the sites discussed in this volume. The World Trade Center site truly is a founding site of the twenty-first century. Anticipated, to be sure, in terrorist acts of earlier years (just as the fields of Flanders and Gallipoli were foreshadowed at Appomattox and Sebastopol), the destruction of place and people on September 11, 2001, has nonetheless recast many of the questions about monument and memory that Room 4.1.3 faces in this collection. In the weeks immediately following the attacks, American newspapers such as the *New York Times* and the *Los Angeles Times* carried obituaries of individual victims. This was an unprecedented personalization of the casualties—an ephemeral fixing of mobile human bodies, halted forever within the limitless cosmos of opportunities and actions. Their deaths and the erasure of place that accompanied them were acts of "war," so framed by both those who condemned and those who justified them. But this was not war in the way it was known in the twentieth century; it was the indelible signature of a placeless, globalized terrorist geography into the equally global, hypermodern landscape of downtown Manhattan. If a new politics is emerging around the processes that sustain such global nodes, 9/11 was its most pathological expression. A new poetics, or maybe better, new languages of place poetics, will be necessary to respond to such a deterritorialized place-politics. To understand the landscapes and images collected in this volume is to appreciate that design will remain the surest way of grasping the knowledge that embraces these two enduring imperatives.

1   Richard Weller, "Re: Design," *www.Room413.com.au,* 2000.
2   At the time this essay was written Room 4.1.3's design for the World Trade Center Memorial was not available.

Diving into Stars

Gavin Keeney

The trade route of truth no longer passes through thought: strange to say, it now seems to pass through things.
—Jacques Lacan, "The Freudian Thing" (1955)

The work of Room 4.1.3 recalls Peter Greenaway's curatorial project at the Louvre, "Le Bruit des Nuages–Flying out of this World," especially his remarks regarding Atlas: "Atlas, the man who carries the world, becomes the book of the maps of the world. An example of man, or God, into book. Few have that honour."[1]

Room 4.1.3 recognizes the "broken premises" of classical metaphysics–that the world is not composed of a celestial and a sublunary realm. The semitragic view of the world portrayed in the representational exuberance of Room 4.1.3's projects (and notably those projects typically "withdrawn" or "unbuilt") comprises the synoptic view that the world is a plurality of forces held in suspension by unknown or inscrutable factors. This is also the inescapable state of things.

The installation in the Museum of Contemporary Art in Sydney entitled $Z^2 + C$ condenses this argument through the appropriation of the idea of entropy (so dear to Robert Smithson) and focuses the re-representation of nature as a provisional system of contrasting phenomena in a water wall that metamorphoses as time passes. Far from fetishizing the ritual excesses of the nature-culture dialectic, the dialectic is instead imploded to produce a map of the world or a petri dish for a new world based on conflicting claims of instrumentality and language. These latter two constructs are the body and soul of landscape architectural discourse.

The post-Arcadian games played today in landscape architecture–the materialist and utilitarian operations–are a conventional appropriation of antihumanist rhetoric, an earnest appeal to the latent desire of the architectural object/body for things heterogenous but, in fact, strictly nominal (abstract and arbitrary). This nominalism excludes the sublime and only ever represents the ideal as an image, or sign, without real content. The sign never refers back to anything other than itself. This is particularly so with the current fascination (vogue) for messing with postindustrial landscapes, and the oftentimes fetishizing of these ruined landscapes, that passes for avant-garde design. These games are a residue of a metaphysics that continues to tragically subdivide the world, while pretending otherwise. Content, after modernism, is the deferred, denatured, depleted surface of things or antimilieu (the thing without its most radical other–the sublime). The Sublime, a complex of psychophysical artifacts in itself, resides within things, but remains at a maximum distance in such denatured mechanistic landscapes, as mechanisms only appear sublime when they fail or inexplicably turn upon themselves and yield unforeseen expressions of the catastrophic and the tragic. Postindustrial landscapes are not sublime in themselves. As in the late paintings of Turner, or in the neoclassical landscapes of Poussin, landscape carries the imprint of the Sublime, but it is racing at light speed away from the subject. With modernity, the Sublime has become a vortex into which disappears milieu. The modern technological Sublime is, in fact, the complete absence of milieu. In a word, the machine ate the garden.

Room 4.1.3's landscape design for Daniel Libeskind's the Tenth Muse in Wiesbaden circumnavigates this deferential pose vis-à-vis the Sublime by invoking a region that is set up only to decompose and turn the anarchic nature of the city on its head. The worn-out logic of the grid is utilized to destabilize the very notion of territoriality and electronic "landscape"–hypertextuality–is superimposed within the fallen, discredited skeletal remains of rational orders.

Linking high and low in structuralist-inspired operations may perchance reveal the underlying or even metatactical secret effulgence that underwrites discursive, horizontal systems. This is the sublime potential of intertextuality as defined by Julia Kristeva.[2] Nonetheless, the openings to a "beyond" or a "below" are sufficiently irrepressible to guarantee that most stringent nominalist (abstract and formalist) projects will burst, in time, with their own inherent surplus–that is, the sublime or infinite vistas contained/buried in the amalgam will crash through the artificial limits of highly structured systems (including high-formalist landscapes). Room 4.1.3 negotiates this dynamic by building the latent anxieties of systems into the system itself. The Garden of Australian Dreams at the National Museum of Australia (Canberra) is the landscape-architectural equivalent of Artaud's infamous Sorbonne adventure, the Theater and the Plague. The garden is both a dream and a nightmare. It begs, like Artaud mimicking death by plague, for life in an expanded field. Its references are so dense that it induces vertigo in the hyperconscious adult subject. Children, on the other hand, will simply laugh and explore the built delirium.

Let us celebrate (with Room 4.1.3) reversing trends, negating fashions, and nixing compromises with utilitarianism and pragmatism. It is not enough to privilege minimalism and its autistic codes; the necessary conflict of fighting fire with fire requires more strenuous measures. Minimalism is merely a cool, numbing, sublinguistic territory that instills quietude–quiescence–versus resistance and renovation. It is the mute territory of unintelligible phonemes. It also passes passively into the annals of fashion and style with ease and considerable élan.

I propose, instead, the excess of loveliness–an excess of the minimal–through an excavation, stripping away, of the vulgar (ordinary) to reveal a commonality that is uncommon, uncanny even, and an interface for the immense complications–noise–"on the other side" of the object and the figure. This favors the slippery and the phantasmatic–the serious and grave, stringent, and suave–markings in time of vast other places and things. Such measures might reengage the cultural complex that produces works of art (and landscape architecture).

These markings in time are "footnotes" of the Sublime, of the material that does not fit into the prose or journalistic rapport of design idioms, and that simply cannot be accommodated whatsoever. Such things will remain forever outside the object, but through stripping and sifting, return in the extreme ambient matrix of voluble signifiers. They are presented simply by the act of not obscuring them. They represent the various milieus in which things swim. Here is the trade route of truth, running through things like an electrical current.

Such measures imply exemplary intertextual outings and/or grandiloquent appropriations of apparently unrelated and extraneous genres and disciplines. This is the territory of intertextuality. The fearlessness of this quest for protean fire must outstrip the conventional and cautionary tales of the guilty and colluding ravens of the hour, or those who would complain that such things are too obscure, dense, and elliptical. To strip away the layers of deceit and structural anomie will also reveal the beneficiaries of not doing so. Neither cause nor effect will go quietly. The reversible, the recondite, and the real are buried in the didactic, diurnal machinations of magpies. Landscape architecture has been too long at pasture. It is so, and it has always been so. It need not be so, and therefore the sojourn elsewhere begins here in the absolutely quotidian, ordinary confines of the "just so." This just so is the irrepressible milieu.

Stringent measures are required, very large erasers (erasures), and number nil graphite pencils ground to a stub. Whole lines, run-on paragraphs and propositions, treasured locutions and clever clauses, excuses of craft, haughty self-congratulatory treatises, and endless bylaws and wherefores are to be scraped away and sent packing into oblivion–a field day for vultures, if you will.

Mise-en-scène, a cousin of milieu, is central to landscape, given its relationship to primal artistic *jouissance* (to the free plays of drives beyond all authorized codes of conduct). This free play is the elastic boundary/ frontier of intertextuality–the interplay of multiple sets of references. Properly understood, mise-en-scène is the supporting apparatus for the linguistic games of the stage. It is what makes Room 4.1.3's Fire Garden so "otherworldly" and "elemental." It is also what makes the films of Peter Greenaway both so annoying and fascinating. Contemporary landscape architecture, and Room 4.1.3 in particular, has finally come round to acknowledging that mise-en-scène is more than just pretty scenery—it can also be portentous. Many of Room 4.1.3's projects play with entourage and context by inverting and renouncing the normative presentation of "scenic" resources. The Peace Square in Prague, for example, demotes the dialectic of church and state (town hall) to vestigial, bankrupt forms rising as apparitions from a bosquet of lindens. The "green" room within mirrors a well-known Czech bias for unmediated environments—or a default neopaganism—and the sculptural centerpiece negotiates the image of the void (the pool) as it seesaws between eternity (the flame) and noth-ingness (the extinguished flame).

Landscape architecture needs to destroy the formal languages that hold it in thrall, that have destroyed the immediate and immanent nature of landscape itself—im-materiality, im-modesty, and imagination all miracu-lously merge in the synchronic plenitude of immanence. Acknowledging immanence is acknowledging the immense interior life of things. The one-time blessing in disguise (the blessed curse) of modernist abstrac-tion—and its quest for the transcendent, the Absolute—is overturned (inverted) through the reemergence of immanence. Abstraction relies on repression. What is omitted is as important as what is admitted. Paradoxi-cally, the reduction of architectonic mediation to its essence, as detailing the immanent nature of things, or as a form of linguistic dust, is the return of the Sublime from exile, from the distant lands of abstraction and positivism, and from the wasteland of dialectical operations (metaphysics).

Room 4.1.3's Federation Garden set on an island summarizes the battlefield of contemporary aesthetics. The project revolves around an act of demolition regarding Western traditions associated with the idea of axis mundi, a holdover from post-edenic design speak. This almost primordial figure was, perhaps, the beginning of the end for undifferentiated unity. It is the ur-vector of all forms of colonization. Situated on an island, Federation Garden, the center of attention, contains all the design moves one could ever want in one small, highly integrated parcel. The central attraction of the Federation Garden is, in turn, the Fireplace. Here is the all-consuming image of fire, Bachelard's idea of "fire," locked in an eternal struggle with pretense and "offering a redefinition of 'paradise.'" It stands in opposition to the Waterbody, a "cross-cultural icon," and a "reminder of life's universal ecological rhythms." One detects here a nostalgia, but not a pathetic landscape fallacy. Redemption is an always-deferred analog to a fugitive condition that inheres in the primacy of things.

Mise-en-scène, in landscape terms, equals topology (not typology or topography), hence architecture's current fascination with systems theory and manipulated ground plane (MGP). MGP is not quite the same radical force as topology. Topology is the intellectual articulation of form—the secret meaning of "architec-tonic"—and the secret mathesis universalis behind all cultural systems (including those deemed "natural"). Built form carries both inherent, albeit unstable ideological content and pure, unadulterated content—poststructuralism's denials of transcendence notwithstanding. The latter resides in the interstices of semantic structures.

The key—alas—is language. And, as with Artaud's critique of theater, the problem is the overreliance on speech (semantics) itself. In landscape architecture the problem is, ironically, the derelict state of design syntax—form without semantic value. The empty formalism of much contemporary landscape architecture is the late reification of the modernist curse (and a bizarre, ready-made excuse for knowing nothing). The cause of this latter-day version of the curse is the empty vessel of landscape architectural practice. Once smashed, this vessel—which is not unlike a barren tree—will liberate vast repressed potential. By reengaging milieu (both symbolical and very real milieu), landscape architecture stands a chance of doing what architecture has repeatedly failed to do—that is, bring out into the open the hidden structures that condition life. Landscape architecture cannot do this if it remains stuck between the oscillating poles of contemporary practice, formalism and naturalism. In fact, the solution—vividly rendered in Room 4.1.3's projects—is a new type of landscape formalism! This new type of landscape formalism strenuously engages rhetoric and milieu, mise en scene and language. Those afraid of intertextuality will run, screaming, in the opposite direction. It is, however, not altogether impossible that that is exactly what is required.

1   Peter Greenaway, *Le Bruit des nuages* (Paris: Editions de la Réunion des Musées Nationaux, 1992), p. 21.
2   Julia Kristeva, "Word, Dialogue, and Novel," in *Desire and Language*, ed. Leon S. Roudiez, trans. Thomas Gora et al. (New York: Columbia University Press, 1980), pp. 64–91. See also Graham Allen, *Intertextuality* (London: Routledge, 1999).

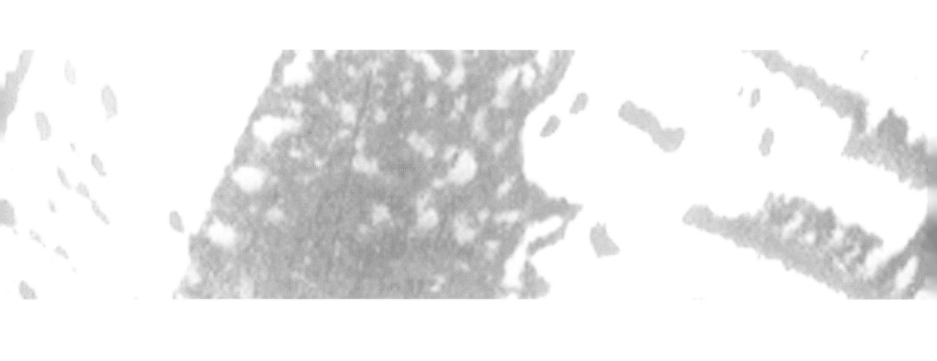

IV. DENATURED ECOLOGIES

$Z^2 + C$

MUSEUM OF CONTEMPORARY ART, SYDNEY 1998

From throughout Australia and New Zealand, Room 4.1.3 was selected as one of three finalists to exhibit their recent work in the Museum of Contemporary Art in Sydney. The installation is in three parts: computer renderings of the landscape designs for the National Museum of Australia on the side wall (see pages 212–213), thirty black-and-white drawings converted into conical shapes and set in black rutile on a titled plane across the floor, and a five-meter-high sculpture entitled $Z^2 + C$ propped against the back wall. Only $Z^2 + C$ concerns us here.

A golden frame hovers out from a canvas surface upon which is a grid of pockets holding living plants. Printed on the canvas is a definition of "Nature" from the *Shorter Oxford Dictionary*, and to the soft whir of an electric pump a thin film of water runs over the entire surface to be collected in a deep red trough at the bottom. The title $Z^2 + C$, the formula for the Mandelbrot set, is the latest in a long line of distinguished formulas which claim nature's quintessence. Mathematics, we are told, is the true language of nature, and so $Z^2 + C$ replaces the word "Nature," which is removed as the heading of the text constituting its various definitions.

Aesthetically, $Z^2 + C$ is in part a painting, a text, a machine, a plan, and an experiment. As a painting it offers no landscape scene or perspective; rather, it is a painting that paints itself as the plants grow and the surface develops ever-changing stains and flourishes of fungi.

Following the logic of the piece, we find manifold codependencies between viewer, machine, and organism. The viewing subject breathes the oxygen of the plants to then speak of "Nature" and make

I. 1. The essential qualities of a thing ; the inherent and inseparable combination of properties essentially pertaining to anything and giving it its fundamental character. **2.** The inherent and innate disposition or character of a person (or animal) ME. **b.** The general inherent character or disposition of mankind. More fully *human n.* 1526. **3.** With *a* and *pl.* An individual character, disposition, etc., considered as a kind of entity in itself ; hence, a person or thing of a particular quality or character. late ME. **b.** *Artillery.* A class or size of guns or shot 1813.
1. The Passion of Love in its N. has been thought to resemble Fire ADDISON. You have twice had warning of the fleeting n. of riches 1832. **2.** Men may change their Climate, but they cannot their N. STEELE. GOOD NATURE, ILL NATURE, SECOND NATURE : see those phrases. **b.** A just and lively image of human n. DRYDEN. Men have a physical as well as spiritual n. 1878. *Mod.* It's only human n. to do that. **3.** There are some Natures in the World who never can proceed sincerely in Business TEMPLE.
Phr. *Of* (a certain) *n.* : A plan of this n. 1765. *Of or in the n. of* ; A Peace is of the n. of a Conquest SHAKS. *In the n. of things, of the case* ; It is, in the n. of the case, probable that [etc.] PALEY. *By n.*, in virtue of the very character or essence of the thing or person ; He..ordained thy will By n. free, not over-rul'd by Fate MILT.
II. 1. The vital or physical powers *of* man ; the strength or substance *of* a thing ME. **2. a.** Semen. **b.** The menses. –1607. **3.** The female pudendum, esp. that of a mare –1750.
III. 1. The inherent dominating power or impulse (in men or animals) by which action or character is determined, directed, or controlled. (Sometimes personified.) late ME. **b.** Natural feeling or affection. Now *dial.* 1605. **2.** The inherent power or force by which the physical and mental activities of man are sustained. (Sometimes personified.) late ME. **b.** The vital functions as requiring to be supported by nourishment, etc. 1460.
1. 'Twas N., sir, whose strong behest Impelled me to the deed COWPER. *Law of N.* : see Law *sb.* 1. 9 c. *Light of N.* see LIGHT *sb.* 6 b. *Against n.*, contrary to what n. prompts, unnatural, immoral, vicious. **b.** Stop vp th' accesse, and passage to Remorse, That no compunctious visitings of N. Shake my fell purpose SHAKS. **2.** Tir'd nature's sweet restorer, balmy sleep! YOUNG. b. When with meats & drinks they had suffic'd Not burd'nd N. MILT.
IV. 1. The creative and regulative physical power which is conceived of as operating in the physical world and as the immediate cause of all its phenomena. late ME. **b.** Personified as a female being. (Usu. with capital.) late ME. **c.** Contrasted with medical skill or treatment in the cure of wounds or diseases 1597. **d.** Contrasted with art (see ART *sb.* 1. 2.). Also, naturalness. 1704. **2.** The material world, or its collective objects or phenomena, the features and products of the earth itself, as contrasted with those of human civilization 1662.
1. That common saying, that God and N. the minister of God doe nothing without cause 1594. **b.** Flowres which only Dame N. trauels with SIR T. HERBERT. **c.** N., in desperate diseases, frequently does most when she is left entirely to herself BURKE. *Against*, or *contrary to*, *n.* see DEBT *sb. Course of n.*: see COURSE *sb.* 13. *Law(s) of n* : see LAW *sb.* **III. 1.** In *n.*, in the actual system of things, in real fact. **2.** To enjoy cool n. in a country seat COWPER. *In n.*, anywhere ; at all. *The or a state of n.* : (*a*) the moral state natural to man, as opp. to a state of grace; (*b*) the condition of man before the organization of society; (*c*) the uncultivated or undomesticated condition; (*d*) physical nakedness.
attrib. and *Comb.*, a *n.-cure, -study, -worship*; **n.-god**, one of the powers or phenomena of n. personified as a god ; so **-being, deity** ; **-people**, people in a primitive state of culture ; **-spirit**, a spirit supposed to reside in some natural element or object.
v. late ME. [ad. med.L. *naturare*, f. *natura* NATURE *sb.*] *intr.* in pres. pple. or ppl. a. *naturing* [after med. L. *natura naturans*] : Creative, and giving to each thing its specific nature – 1694.

A DEFINITION OF "NATURE," FROM *THE SHORTER OXFORD ENGLISH DICTIONARY*, THIRD EDITION, 1964, THE TEXT USED FOR THE INSTALLATION $Z^2 + C$.

View of the three components of Room 4.1.3's installation in Sydney's Museum of Contemporary Art for the Seppelt Contemporary Art Awards, November 27, 1988-February 28, 1999. Z² + C, a framed text that supports plants and a flow of water, is on the left. In the foreground is a set of drawings of Room 4.1.3 projects folded into cones set in a tilted plane. On the far wall are the presentation drawings for the design of the National Museum of Australia (see pages 212–213). Courtesy Museum of Contemporary Art, Sydney.

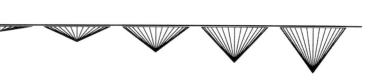

the world over into representation. Over time the text blurs into the fungoid surface of the canvas, suggesting a messy coevolution and synthesis of language and matter. So, too, the light by which we see in the gallery is the light by which the plants grow in the processes of creating and storing energy. We eventually tap this energy to fuel our technologies, and it is our technologies that serve to remake the world according to our conceptions of Nature and our relation to it.

Initially soothing and domestic like an innocuous indoor plant, or a waterfall in a hotel lobby, something in this decaying "word-fall" is disturbing and grotesque. In gently revealing its denatured construction and interdependencies $Z^2 + C$ compounds some of landscape architecture's anxieties, raising the specter that, as Jeffrey Deitch says in his remarkable visual essay "Artificial Nature," "genuine nature may now be more artificial than real."[1]

A signature of the loss of God is the garden. "Nature," modernity's supplement for God, is now a denatured ecology, a global, technologically manipulated and maintained garden. The earth and its human systems are a cyborg, but, as Donna Haraway points out, the cyborg was not born in a garden, so it contains no memory of paradise.[2] If $Z^2 + C$ cannot remember paradise, then nor can it imagine the future; rather, $Z^2 + C$ is an account of the limits of our representations. $Z^2 + C$ is a summation our failed utopias before it is a map leading to another.

DETAIL OF Z^2 + C. COURTESY MUSEUM OF CONTEMPORARY ART, SYDNEY.

---

1   J. Deitch and D. Friedman, eds., "Artificial Nature," introductory essay, D'este Foundation for Contemporary Art, exhibition catalogue, 1990.
2   Donna J. Haraway, "Manifesto for Cyborgs: Science, Technology and Socialist Feminism in the 1980s," *Socialist Review* 80 (1985), pp. 65–108.

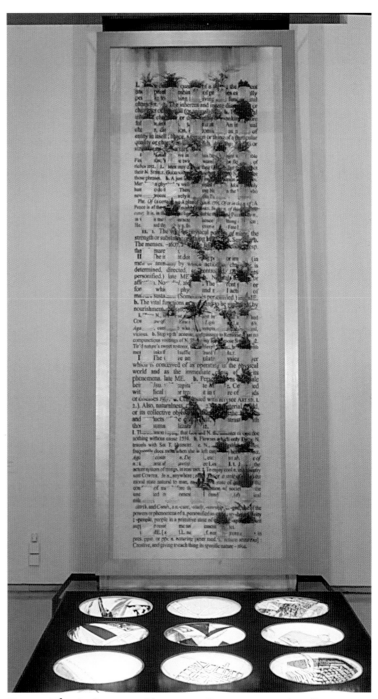

DETAIL OF Z^2 + C. COURTESY MUSEUM OF CONTEMPORARY ART, SYDNEY.

VIEW OF Z^2 + C. COURTESY MUSEUM OF CONTEMPORARY ART, SYDNEY.

Decomposition
Wiesbaden, Germany 1992

The entire landscape surrounding a new set of office buildings by Daniel Libeskind in Wiesbaden is covered in a wooden grid structure. The structure, an explicit manifestation of Cartesian abstraction, is a series of three-meter-wide, empty wooden rooms. The rooms comprising the grid are abutted to one another so that a one meter gap is created between each room. Into this gap is poured soil and seeds of the indigenous vegetation of this region. The grid is superimposed on the existing topography of the site in the manner of pixelated computer models of landform, so that the spot height of the site in the middle of each room is literally projected up by 1.5 meters.

Full of soil and seeds, the grid structure is then simply left to decompose and self-organize without any human intervention. Borne of processes of ecological succession, the plants will colonise the rotting grid and after approximately fifty years will form a young forest. This forest might retain some memory of the grid's original organization in its form.

This process challenges expressions of landscape design as manicured corporate image or amenity exclusively for humans. It also takes the static structure three-dimensional of Euclidean space and hands it over to the fourth. In this case humans are compensated for the loss of ground by highly patterned roof gardens, islands in a field of entropic (dis)order from which they can overlook the chaos. In that the coordinates of the grid opened up perspective and mapped the Euclidean world, its collapse here into a web of random growth can be seen as a landmark for the end of an era.

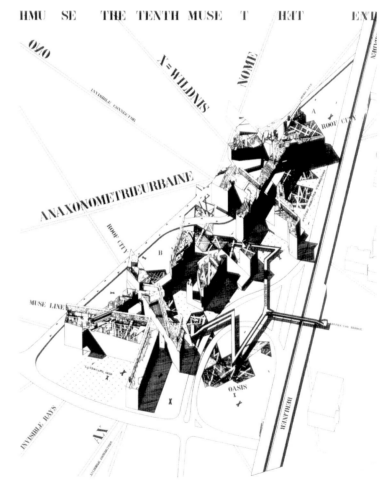

AXONOMETRIC OF THE PROPOSED OFFICE COMPLEX IN WIESBADEN ENTITLED THE TENTH MUSE BY STUDIO DANIEL LIBESKIND. AN INACCESSIBLE, DECOMPOSING GRID STRUCTURE COVERS THE ENTIRE EXTERIOR LANDSCAPE SPACES WHILE MANICURED ROOF GARDENS PROVIDE USABLE OUTDOOR SPACES.

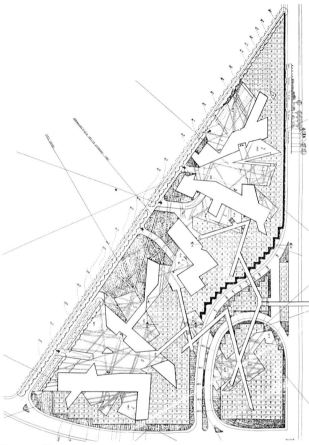

PLAN OF DECOMPOSITION. ORIGINAL COMPETITION DRAWING BY
RICHARD WELLER WITH CORNELIA MÜLLER AND JAN WEHBERG
IN MKW. THE LANDSCAPE BEGINS AS AN INACCESSIBLE WOODEN
GRID FULL OF SEEDS AND SOIL AND IS LEFT TO DECOMPOSE AND
GROW INTO A FOREST. COURTESY MKW.

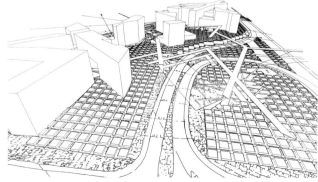

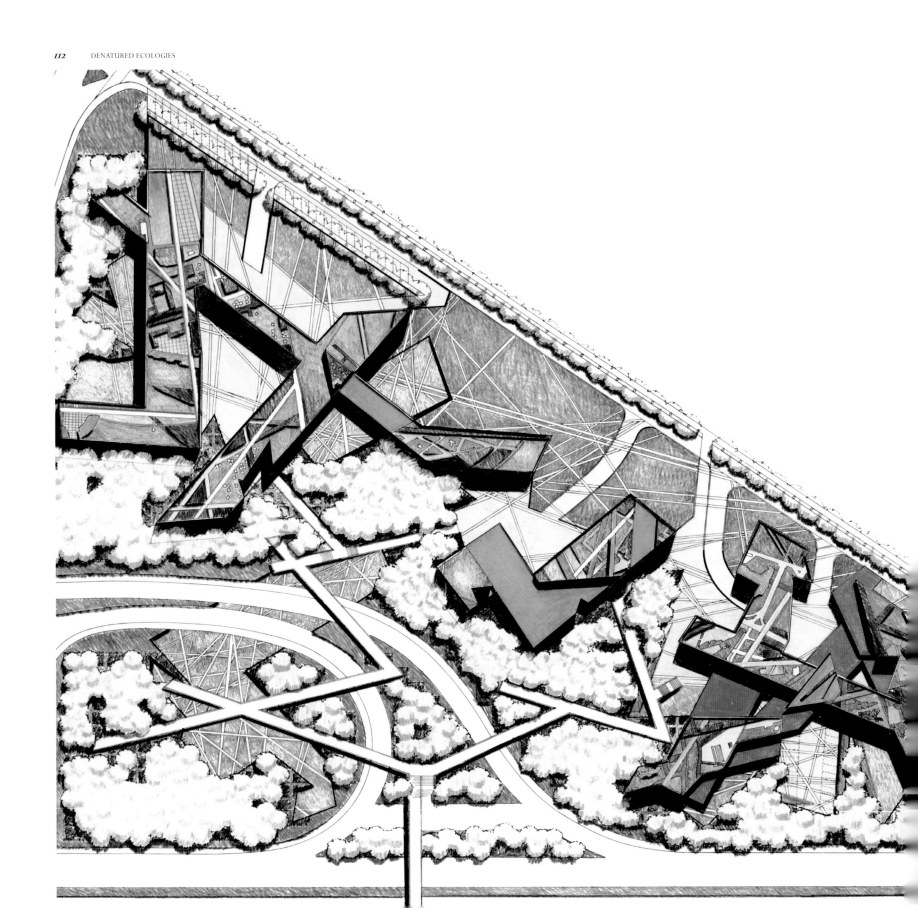

Year 1995

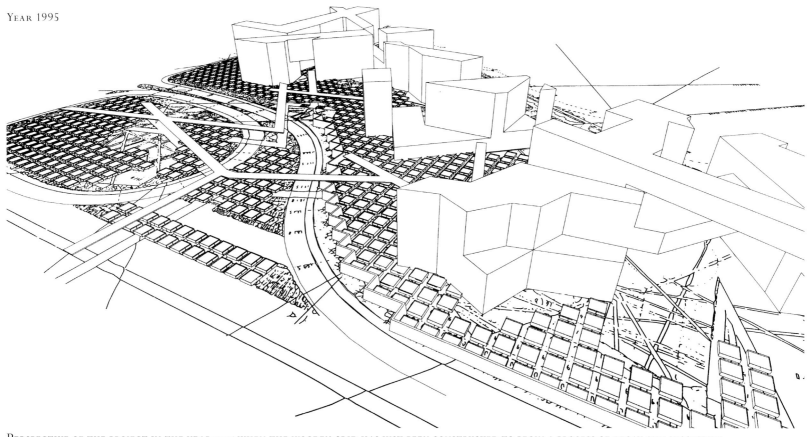

Perspective of the project in the year 1995 when the wooden grid has just been constructed to begin a process of decay and succession.

Year 2045

Plan showing the site in 2045 by when the landscape has become a self-organized semi-mature forest. Original competition drawing by Richard Weller with Cornelia Müller and Jan Wehberg in MKW. Courtesy MKW.

The Amber Room
Dessau 1993

In addition to the Bauhaus, the town of Dessau in former East Germany is also notable for its massive, derelict open-cut coal mines. The mines, like another planet sunken 30 meters below the level of the earth, stretch as far as the eye can see. This excavated landscape is littered with the heavy machinery that did the work of extracting brown coal. Specks of amber lie everywhere in the dust. The mines are naturally filling with groundwater and therefore destined to become lakes. Not far from the mines is the famous landscape park of Worlitz, in which there is a copy of the Isle des Peupliers upon which Rousseau was buried at Ermenonville in France.

This proposal is for a copy (of the Worlitz copy) of the Rousseau island to be constructed in the center of the mined landscapes at Dessau in anticipation of the incoming groundwater. With its stand of poplars the island will enhance the future picturesque scenery of a lake. Behind this veil, however, is a large sunken chamber—an engine room in which the old machine parts and much amber is gathered as a monument to work done. Within the chamber is also a new pumping system to assist in aerating the rising groundwater, thus increasing water quality.

DIAGRAMMATIC SECTION OF THE AMBER ROOM INCLUDING AN IMAGE OF THE EXISTING LANDSCAPE INSIDE THE OPEN-CUT COAL MINES. THE TOP OF THE IMAGE CAN BE UNDERSTOOD AS THE FUTURE WATER LINE DEMARCATING AN ISLAND INSIDE OF WHICH IS THE AMBER ROOM.

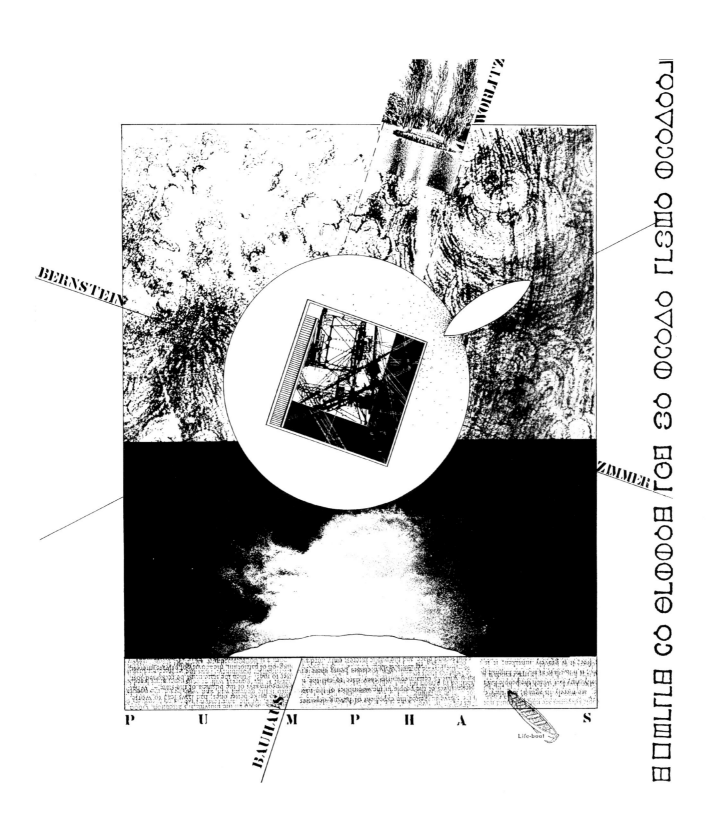

The Bestiary and the Herbal
No-Man's-Land, Berlin 1992

Sited notionally in a part of former No-Man's-Land on the periphery of the city not far from the great parks of Potsdam, the Bestiary and the Herbal is concerned with the thematic of ecology. The project is part of an argument to keep the entire stretch of No-Man's-Land as relatively nondesigned, public open space while intermittently punctuating its length with small designed projects.

The essential proposition of the project is that a budget is set in trust for one hundred years enabling a small, interdisciplinary council to manage the 15-hectare site. Although free from the antics of themed entertainment parks, the project is nonetheless distinctively thematic insofar as it is devoted to exploring contemporary notions of Ecology and Nature. It need not make a profit, but it should raise an eyebrow and draw a crowd.

For argument's sake, the council consists of a local philosopher, a farmer, a scientist, a politician, an entrepreneur, an artist, and a theologian. The council can decide to expand its membership as it sees fit. Council members serve a period of up to five years and act in the manner of a company board responsible for the management of the site and its intellectual property.

The council meets regularly in an old villa on the site entitled the Bestiary. The Bestiary not only is a meeting place but also operates as a gallery or small museum soliciting exhibitions exploring contemporaneous representations of "Nature." The Bestiary could also offer a "thinker in residence" program.

The council's responsibility is to determine the ongoing program for the whole project. It is charged with inventing and manifesting a program of events, installations, exhibits and experiments to take place not only in the Bestiary but also in the surrounding 15-hectare landscape entitled the Herbal.

The Herbal, a stretch of the former No-Man's-Land abutting degraded agricultural land, is initially marked out by surveyor's poles, instruments of measurement set on the intersections of a 30-meter graticule. In the zone of the former No-Man's-Land, these poles also mark the location of explosives. To mark the opening of the project, the explosives are detonated, resulting in a cathartic landform. If left unaltered, the detonated landscape is suited to water retention and a range of self-organizing random plant growth; alternatively it is also suited to being continually remodeled, according to whatever range of events and projects the council might later instigate.

To begin this project we would also suggest a small orchard be planted and propose that a gardener live on site. The gardener's responsibility is general site maintenance but also primarily to manage a series of wooden enclosures. The enclosures, randomly located across the site, are not unlike houses without roofs. They contain and protect a range of threatened botanic associations once endemic to northern Europe. The public can look into these locked gardens of precious botanic diversity through peepholes and telescopes fixed to the wooden walls.

Somewhat contrary to the dumbed-down demonstrations we have come to expect from ecologically themed landscape designs, the Bestiary and the Herbal hopes to set up the catalysts for a philosophical engagement with issues related to nature's continual reconceptualization. Paradoxically, in the first instance this project risks being overly contrived so as to set in train a relatively unpredictable, experimental field.

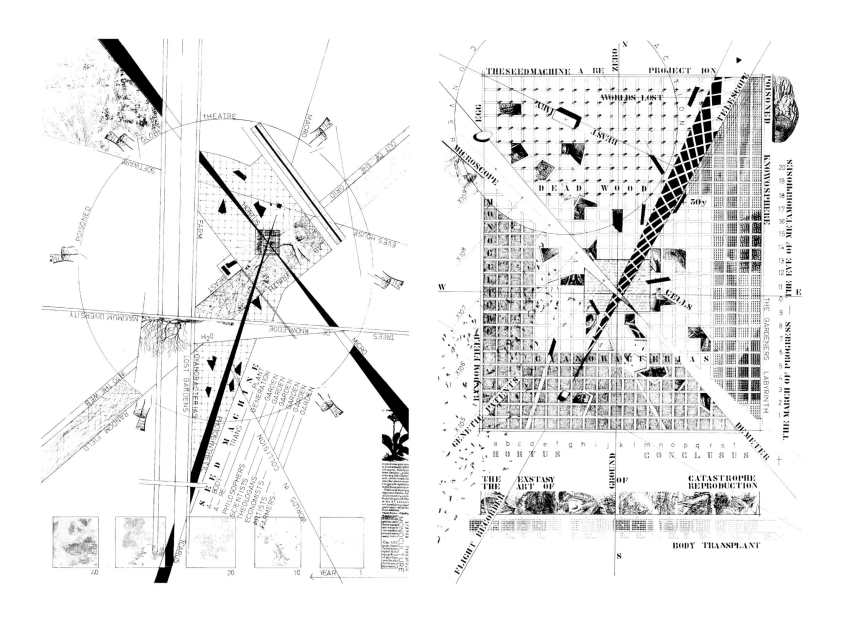

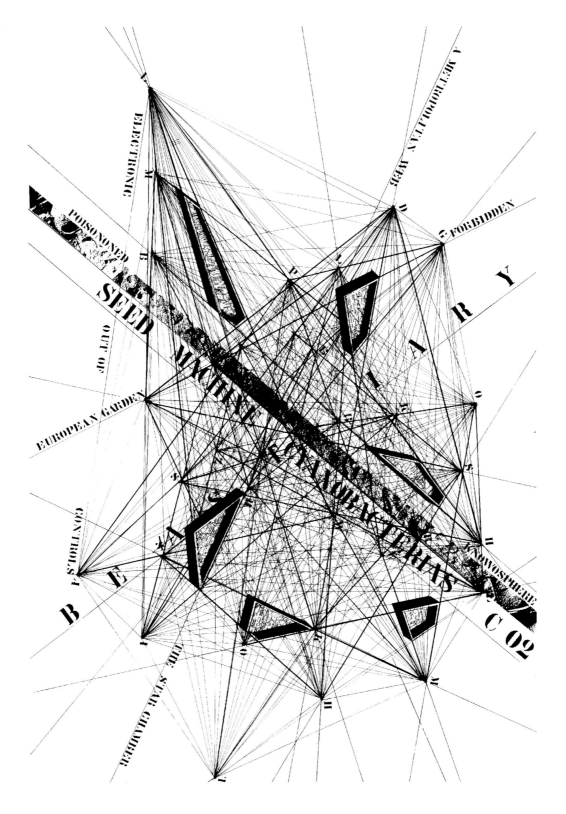

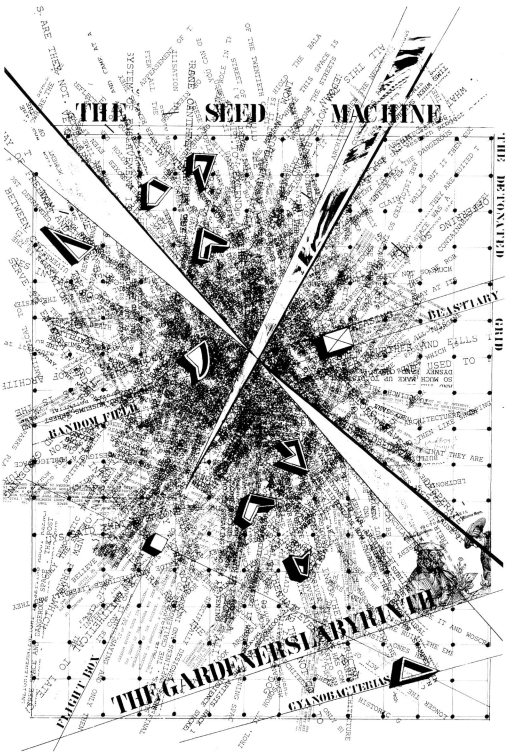

THE SEED MACHINE

THE DETONATED GRID

BEASTIARY

RANDOM FIELD

FLIGHT BOX

THE GARDENERSLABYRINTH

CYANOBACTERIAS

Animale Ignoble
Cockatoo Island, Sydney 1995

Now derelict, Cockatoo Island in Sydney harbor was dominated by naval shipyards and their associated industries. The island is consequently littered with exhausted naval machinery and toxic waste. It is a prohibited yet public place. Everything on the island is decaying except for some *ficus macrocarpa* (Moreton Bay figs), which grow voraciously in almost any circumstance. If the island were cleaned up a little, it would be a real estate gold mine in the midst of the world's most beautiful harbor.

This project responded to a competition for alternatives to the touted privatization of this public land and its typically incumbent culture of exclusive housing and pleasure craft marinas. Our polemical and eminently buildable response is as follows.

Historically, islands are often utopian sites, whereas contemporary literature deploys dystopian strategies often set in derelict, futuristic urban settings. Cockatoo Island would seem to contain the raw material for both utopia and dystopia. Islands are also sites of nostalgia, the exotic, and the paradisaical. Eden, however, is now a cliché, the stuff of three-star resorts and casino bars. Nonetheless, exotica are increasingly desirable in a world made barren by knowledge of everything. Hard science aside, ecosystems are our current mythopoeic sites, replete with narratives of sin.

With these themes in mind, the question we asked was how to create a dystopian, mythopoeic ecosystem on a derelict postindustrial island.

The answer is surprisingly simple. We propose that fig seeds be scattered randomly all over the island and that nobody enter the site for one hundred years. Thereafter it will function as a mysterious destination.

The fig trees often seed and sprout in a host tree (or a building), then grow roots down to reach the earth. In so doing they will strangle the host structure and grow into massive dark trees. The figs will colonize and gradually cleanse the toxic waste areas of the island, grow through and destroy the derelict buildings, and entwine and engulf the abandoned industrial equipment.

The figs will also attract fruit bats.

A mythopoeic creature par excellence, the fruit bats are a predictable feature of Sydney's nightscape. Every evening flocks of bats fly across the city to feed on the figs lining the streets and parks of Sydney's eastern suburbs. By dawn the bats return to caves outside the city.

The bats are appropriate heirs to the island. By eating fruit, these little devils will reenact Christian lore every night. But unlike man, bats do not fall. Rather, they hover and hang in a permanent purgatory. Moreover, by providence bats possess the radar technology the former military occupants of the site hope to master. Bats also read topography in contoured, virtual flight. There is nothing vague about their terrain. Their world is an echo chamber, whereas with humans eyes get in the way of everything. Bats do not have aesthetics, but they have sense(s). Bats do not make objects, they avoid them.

Not unlike the Zone in Tarkovsky's film *Stalker*, in a century from now, the island will have become part of Sydney's mythology. In the year 2095 an architect can be selected to design an appropriately wild restaurant and bar. The restaurant and bar are nocturnal and open to no more than two hundred people, who arrive at sunset and leave at sunrise by boat. Exclusive, expensive, but nonetheless public, the island is perfect for special occasions, romance, and bacchanalia.

In a culture dominated by economic rationalism this project is notably, a bargain. The main elements, fig seeds and time, are both free. With patience, by the year 2095 this proposition could create a mythopoeic zone in the midst of Sydney harbor, and myths, as Australia's Tourism Commission knows, are priceless. Indeed, it is not

unlikely that some tourists will extend their spendthrift itineraries in Sydney for one night specifically so as to dine on the mythic isle.

This proposal is also for an ecology emerging from injury, yet from across the waters of Sydney harbor no deformities will be visible. The island of figs will appear verdant and pristine. It will fit seamlessly into Sydney's picturesque frames, but it also reminds us that beauty is wicked.

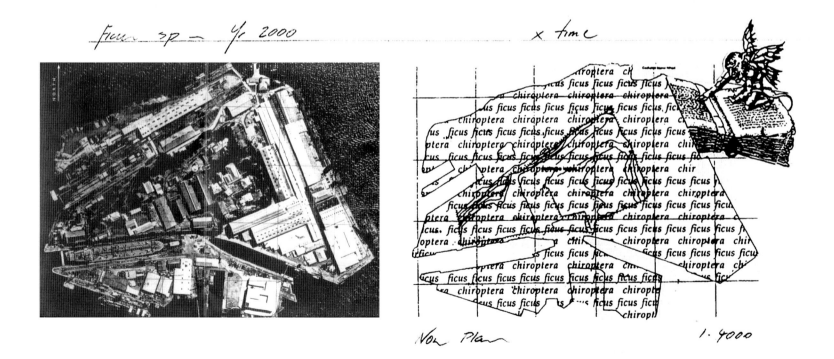

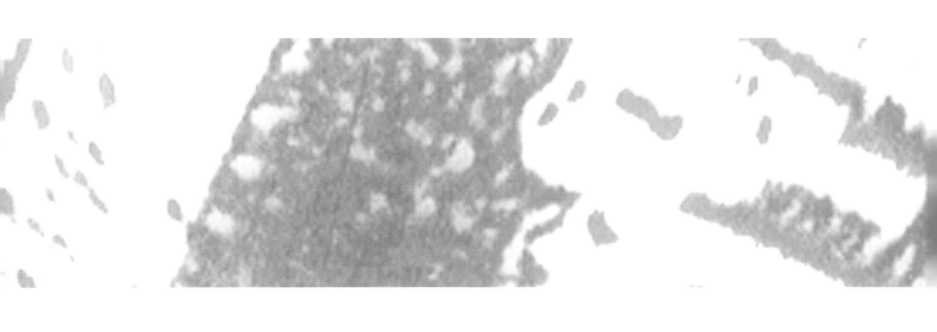

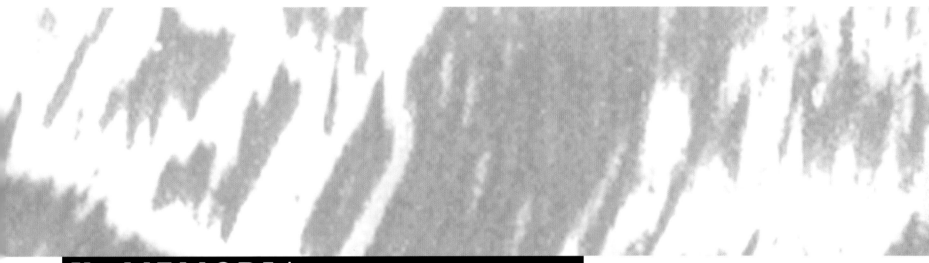

V. MEMORIA

The Memorial to Fallen Bodies and the Virtually Free Market

Los Angeles, 1995

This project departs from a call for designs for a "Justice Park" as a memorial to victims of violent crime in Los Angeles on the occasion of the trial of O. J. Simpson. The site is a city block outside the Criminal Courts adjacent to City Hall in the Los Angeles Civic Center.

The brief asked whether symbolic form and the design of public space could meaningfully commemorate the dead and also speak of social justice to a nation of the living. Identifying itself as a "romantic competition," competitors were also asked to try to create a place that would personify the emotional "heart and soul of America."

Our response to this curious brief is in two parts. The first, entitled the Memorial to Fallen Bodies, commemorates victims of violent crime, and the second, entitled the Virtually Free Market, seeks to activate a relevant, contemporary public place related to the overriding theme of social justice.

The Memorial to Fallen Bodies

The Memorial to Fallen Bodies is a large water feature based on the moon, our chosen icon of America's late twentieth-century heart and soul. Water fills and empties from this terraced pool in accord with the lunar cycle, mimicking the shapes of the lunar calendar. Victims of violent crime are signed in silver on the terrace of the lunar time at which they were killed. The actual moon, named with great figures of science and the arts, is here reflected and named with those sacrificed to the city, the anonymous, fallen. The moon—beacon of romanticism, home of the dead, and icon of insanity—is brought down to earth, as it was once thought only witches could do.

The Virtually Free Market

A scaled-up copy of a fragment of St. Augustine's description of the eviction from Paradise is used as a base plan for a large urban space adjacent to the Memorial to Fallen Bodies. Whereas the water body of the memorial is quiet, open, and reflective, the Virtually Free Market is crowded, noisy, and hi-tech.

The narrative of expulsion from the garden, reiterated by Augustine for the medieval mind, explains a split between this world and an ideal one. It also conflates sin with knowledge and punishes humanity's hubris in aspiring to become gods—themes that bear upon the America that put man on the moon. Christian morality, fearing the Dionysian moon, forms the substrata of justice and our law. Christianity is structured upon a dual conception of space and time, one heavenly and eternal and the other earthly and finite. Margaret Wertheim argues that postmodern culture is similarly dualistic, although instead of heaven it has cyberspace.

Each word in Augustine's text is literally extruded as a block and built as a habitable booth. Each booth is networked and cybernetically fitted out so that it can be rented out to computer nerds, cyber traders, and hackers, in exactly the manner in which an arts and crafts market is rented out to artisans. However, the Virtually Free

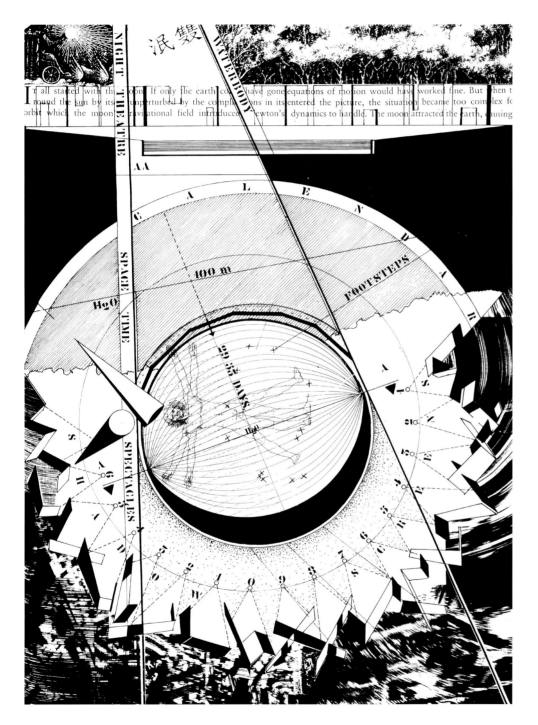

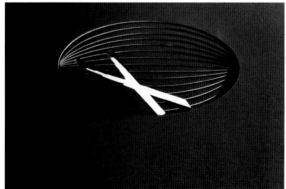

Market deals in information and cutting edge, virtual experiences, not talismans. The extruded text, now a labyrinth of cyber-booths, is constructed in metal as if it were a giant print template tilted to the sky or a microchip now enabling many different paths through the old linear structure of print.

The Virtually Free Market is put forward as an urban proposition for public space in an attempt to increase basic access to technology and information because, as Mike Davis points out, "the Ghetto is defined not only by its paucity of parks and public amenities but also by the fact that it is not wired into any of the key information circuits."[2] The project will also manifest the immaterial subculture of the Internet in urban form, enshrining and enhancing the creative competition of designing and selling cyberspatial experiences.

The Virtually Free Market is presented with a view to one of our contemporary cyber Medicis—those who typically boast that information society will offer all information to all people at all times—acting as patron.

1   Margaret Wertheim, *The Pearly Gates of Cyberspace: A History of Space from Dante to the Internet* (Sydney: Doubleday, 1999), pp. 44–75.
2   Mike Davis, in Michael Sorkin, ed., *Fortress Los Angeles: The Militarization of Public Space* (1990), p. 155.

The Twentieth Century Monument
Berlin 1993

In a small fenced-off and overgrown fruit garden in the middle of Berlin is an enormous block of concrete.

Approximately eight meters high and seven meters wide, the block was originally constructed as a test foundation to provide calculations for the final density and size of the footings intended to uphold Albert Speer's Great Hall of the German People, the unbuilt temple of the Third Reich, and its intended capital, Germania, a.k.a. Berlin. The Great Hall was conceived to be the largest dome construction in the history of architecture and was to sit on approximately two hundred of these monstrous individual footings.

One proposal is to slice the block in half, signifying a split atom of a consciousness that haunts progress. Inside the split, a small staircase would allow access onto the top of the block.

The preferred proposal is to carve up the block of concrete into large but manageable fragments and redeposit them unceremoniously in the midst of the open space at the center of the new parliamentary zone in central Berlin (see the Spreebogen). This land, now the heart of democratic, united Germany was intended as the site for the Great Hall for which this test foundation was made. Removing the massive concrete block would enable the small fruit garden to become an accessible public neighborhood park.

The fear with such highly symbolic moves is that they inadvertently establish shrines for those who gravitate toward Nazism's racial hallucinations. Indeed this grotesque pile of concrete is Germania's headstone, but surely it can only serve as a clear sign of megalomania's end point, the ideological *reductio ad absurdum* of the twentieth century.

Model of the Great Hall of the German People by Albert Speer.

The original concrete test foundation, Dudenstrasse, Berlin.

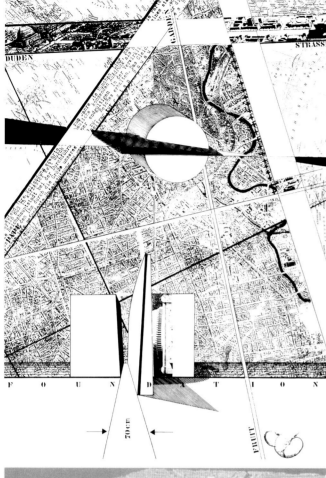

Detail view of the Berlin Plan (Germania) by Albert Speer focusing on the Great Hall of the German People sited at the arc of the River Spree, for which the original test foundation was built. (This site was later subject to an international design competition; see A-Political Project(ions), p. 70.)

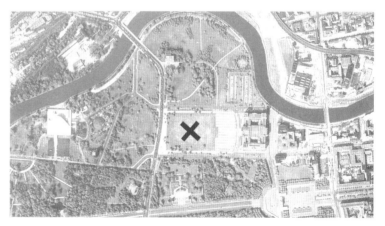

Proposed site for the location of the broken test foundation in front of the Reichstag, Berlin.

PLACE DE LA RÉVOLUTION

PARIS 1989

Both of the following propositions were conceived for "Inventer 89," an international ideas competition for monuments to commemorate the bicentenary of the French Revolution, 1789–1989.

The Garden of Emergence is simply an axis of trees that descend into or emerge from the earth. People can walk down along the axis to arrive at a final subterranean chamber in which Time itself is honored by a carefully regulated drip of water falling onto a hotplate.

A second proposal, the Place de la Révolution, is a sunken water garden inscribed with the cartography of the planet Venus, a planet where one finds several of the goddesses of antiquity. Upon this map, in the sunken garden, multiple decapitated copies of Rodin's *Thinker* are arranged in a grid. The volume of the sunken garden gradually fills and empties with water over a 243-day cycle–the time it takes for one revolution of Venus around the sun. When the water garden is full, the Thinkers' bodies are submerged, leaving only the disembodied heads suspended above water level in a web of wires.

The Pentagon Memorial Sky Garden
Washington, D.C. 2002

memory, *n. faculty of mentally retaining impressions of past experience, ability to remember; that which is remembered; commemoration; period during which something is remembered.*
Black Box Flight Recorder, *n. device in an aircraft which records the memory of a flight; chronicler of flight events.*

The Pentagon Memorial Sky Garden is a field of 184 hovering black cubes that contain water and reflect the sky.

The main metaphor for the proposal comes from the black box flight recorder, itself an Australian invention, and a crucial container of memory. In the proposal there is one flight recorder for each victim, but they are renamed Life Recorders and designed as 1-by-one-meter black cubes containing a deep conical well of water which reflects the sky.

At the base of the deep cone of water is a polished stainless steel disc creating a perspective to infinity. At the water level, in each of the 184 Life Recorders, bronze letters spell out the name of the deceased and their place of birth. By inscribing the place of an individual's birth at the place of that individual's death, the space and time of the individual's life is metaphorically held in the healing waters of the Life Recorder.

The 184 reflections captured in each Life Recorder create a cumulative crescendo of sky across the plaza, affording recognition of the immensity of the loss while also commemorating the individual. By creating a field of 184 individual memorials to make one collective monument, the design mediates between nationalism and individuality, the tension at the heart of American culture.

However, black box flight recorders are actually bright orange, and so, inserted into the larger black cubes are smaller, orange cubes. These are designed as precious chests, containers into which the relatives of victims are invited to place mementos of their loved ones. Once inserted into the larger shell of the black cube, the orange memento chests will be locked for perpetuity and the keys kept in the Pentagon. In this way, the design links both the public and private understandings of loss from September 11.

The Sky Garden of 184 Life Recorders derives its overall form and layout from the specific qualities of its context. The Pentagon's façade, immediately adjacent to the site, features ninety-two windows. This façade is reflected and doubled to provide the grid configuration for the Life Recorders. Thus the Sky Garden speaks directly to the building at the heart of the event. There is also a connection to the formality of nearby Arlington Cemetery.

The formality of the plaza, the configuration of the site, and the human scale of each individual Life Recorder lend the Sky Garden to a range of possible commemorative rituals. As a whole, the Sky Garden is a field of intense gravitas and permanence, yet its water surfaces change with every nuance in the wind and the sky.

I turned and looked back up at the sky,
Where we still look to ask the why
Of everything below.
—Robert Frost, "Afterflakes"

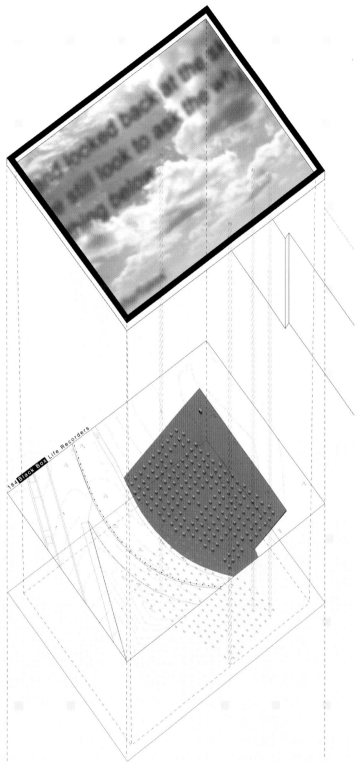

ROOM 4.1.3'S STAGE ONE COMPETITION ENTRY FOR THE MEMORIAL TO THE
VICTIMS OF THE 9/11 ATTACK ON THE PENTAGON.

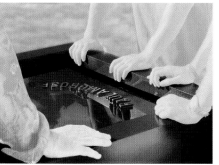

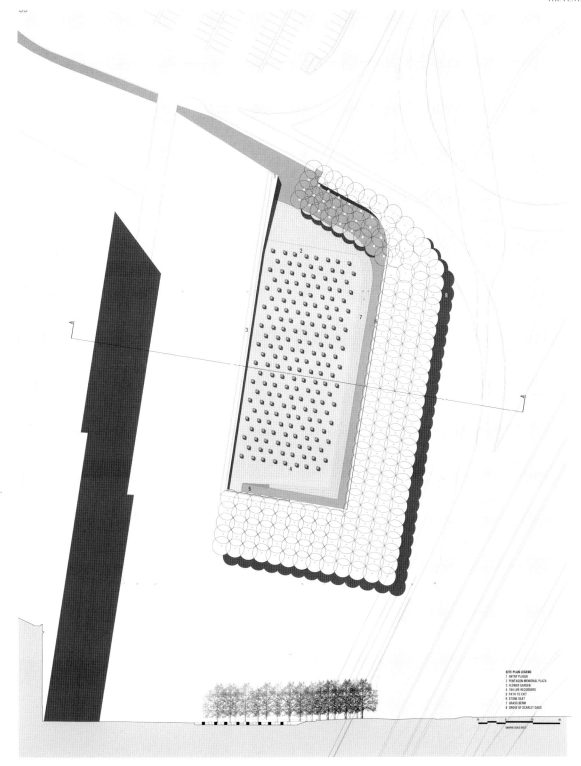

SITE PLAN LEGEND
1 ENTRY PLAQUE
2 PENTAGON MEMORIAL PLAZA
3 FLOWER GARDEN
4 184 LIFE RECORDERS
5 PATH TO EXIT
6 STONE SEAT
7 GRASS BERM
8 GROVE OF SCARLET OAKS

GRAPHIC SCALE (FEET)

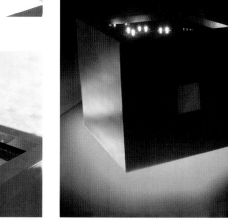

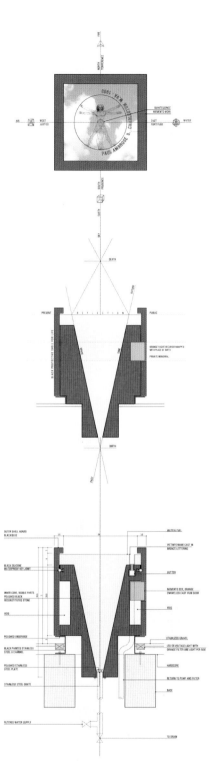

The World Trade Center Memorial
New York City 2003

This proposal for the World Trade Center Memorial includes the following components: the Book, the Grove, the Terrace, and the Ground.

The Book

In this situation, amidst Daniel Libeskind's phoenix, there is no need for heroics, spectacle, or glib signs of optimism. There is, however, a need for subtly joining the radically personal and radically global nature of post-September 11 culture in a manner that allows the community to regain the site for life and dignified reverence. The primary metaphor of this proposal is the Book: the book of the dead, the book of life, the book as the core of the enlightenment, and now the book as the ideological basis of fundamentalist misinterpretation cut from the tree of knowledge.

In the manner of sacred text this proposal writes the name of each victim into the palimpsest of the city. The two pages of the Book cover the footprints of the two World Trade Center towers. 3,016 names are spelled out as extruded letters, rising up from a fine gravel surface. Reminiscent of I beams in section, each letter is precisely made of indigo-colored reconstituted stone capped with a thick block of laminated, highly polished North American hardwood. Both the wooden letters and the stone shafts are precisely shaped to each letter. The wood is treated and can be simply maintained to last hundreds of years. By simple pin joints the tactile wooden letters appear to levitate slightly above the reconstituted stone shaft, and subtle lighting emanates from the gap between the stone shaft and the wooden letter, so that the whole field of text has a warm glow at night. The extruded letters making up the names of individuals

can be read close up or from a distance. The forms of the letters create nooks and crannies suited to a range of ritualized practices such as laying wreaths, lighting candles, or placing mementos. In addition, in between each victim's name is a plinth (grammatically a period) capped by a brass plaque upon which relatives and families are offered the opportunity to include personal obituaries and/or an etched image of the deceased. The simple, strong, and warm materials in this proposal can be exquisitely crafted but also lend themselves to mass production in regard to molding and laser cutting technologies. Overall the two fields of text bank up slightly from 1 foot to 5 feet, and tilt toward the sun. Gaps between the rows of names and between each name allow labyrinthine circulation, and the alphabetic listing of names creates logical locations.

At the center of each page of the book, enclosed by a small wall, is an inaccessible area necessary for the deposition of unidentified remains. Here, before the ground is sealed and covered in raked gravel, dignitaries and relatives may ceremoniously place small quantities of earth taken from the home countries of all citizens murdered on September 11. At the center of each enclosed plot is a small font of overflowing water reflecting the sky.

The Grove

In contrast to the public fields of the book is a small circular grove of trees. A place of respite, serenity, and togetherness, the grove is exclusively for families and relatives of the deceased. The circular grove is defined by a 12-foot-high stone wall upon which is inscribed a roll of honor including all the names of the living who were involved in rescue and reconstruction. This roll of honor effectively wraps and protects the interior seclusion of the grove. Mature trees planted into a grass berm form the grove. Each tree is angled toward the center, so that over time the branches intertwine to form a green chapel where relatives can meet and reflect. A gate at the entrance to the grove politely identifies the interior of the grove as a private place.

The Terrace

At the level of urban design, the terrace allows the broader context of the city to connect with the sunken space of the memorial gracefully and respectfully, without detracting from the architect's original intention for the site. The terraces allow easy access into and through the site and create generous levels of permanent and installed seating, accommodating daily life and crowds for formal occasions. Each terrace includes grass strips and garden beds which can be seasonally planted. At the top of the terrace, a bosquet of trees forms a shaded filter into the site. Via the terraces the quotidian public life of the cityscape can effectively join with the meanings of the site.

The Ground

The ground refers to all the flat paved space of the memorial site. The stone for this ground is delivered from all countries willing to participate. Each country sends a specified quantity of high-quality stone to New York, where the stone is cut so that each paving unit literally locks into those adjacent to it. Akin to a jigsaw puzzle, this paving pattern of multicolored stone symbolizes a global community united against terrorism, a renewed foundation.

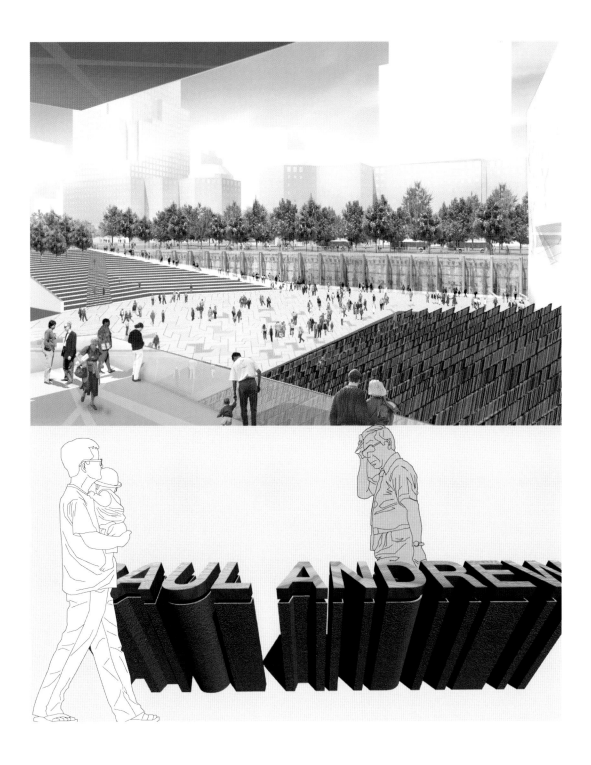

VI. GARDENS

DIN A4

Berlin 1991–1993

The courtyard garden for the German Institute of Standards in Berlin (Deutsche Institut Normen, or DIN) is not a public space, nor are the employees of the institute expected to enter it frequently. Instead, like a book, it is to be looked down upon, enjoyed in plan as one looks askance out the window. Unlike most projects where the plan is only a device of translation between ideas and three-dimensional reality, in this instance the plan is everything.

The scenario upon which the design is based is that an A4 piece of paper–itself a standardized DIN product used routinely by the employees in the building–has fallen out of the window and landed awkwardly in the courtyard. On the ground the A4 sheet is then scaled up to become a 16 x 7 meter black granite slab tilted from a height of 1.5 meters to grade so that a fine film of turbulent water flows over its surface. Some of the black granite stones forming the slab are cut askew in order to subtly buckle and warp the otherwise perfect graticule subdividing the A4 sheet. The enlarged A4 granite slab not only bears the institute's (DIN) letterhead, but also stainless steel letters and signs beginning with Babylonian script appear to tumble down the page.

Although adopting the lexicon of monumental stone inscriptions, this fallen monument announces no particular hero or deed; rather, it speaks of Babel and the entire effort of language as *the* standardized system to be meaningfully attached to the phenomenal world.

Just before the garden was formally opened, we were asked if the massive brooding stone tablet held a cryptic message. It does not. And yet surfaces become increasingly cryptographic, do they not?[1]

1   The main forms and ideas for this project were only sketch designed by Richard Weller. Müller Knippschild Wehberg modified the design, documented it, and ensured its high-quality construction.

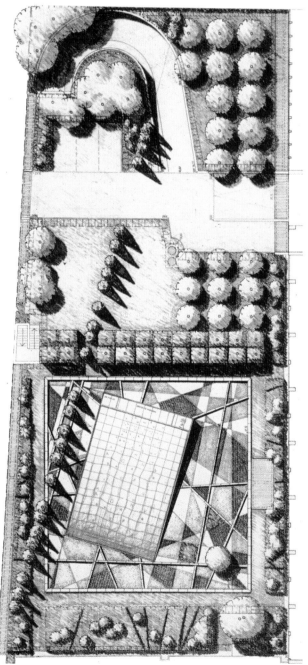

Plan of DIN A4, Courtyard of the German Institute of Standards. Original drawing by Richard Weller with Cornelia Müller and Jan Wehberg in MKW. Courtesy MKW.

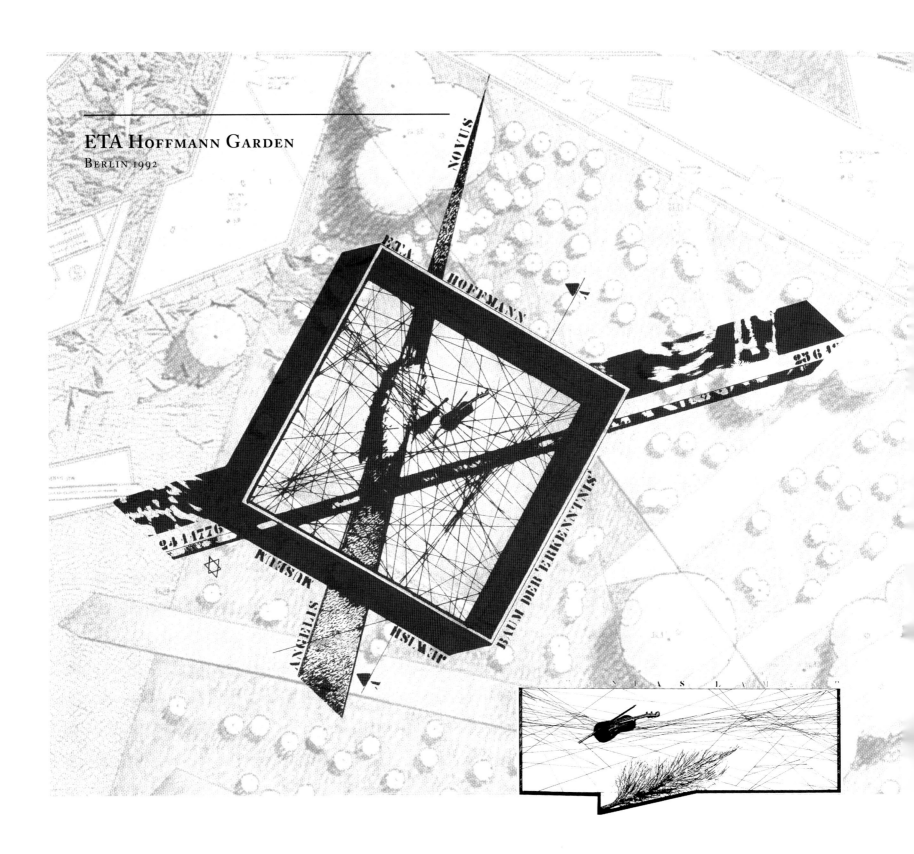

ETA Hoffmann Garden
Berlin 1992

Outside the recently completed extension to the Berlin Museum there is a tilted sunken room full of columns sprouting vegetation. Originally entitled the ETA Hoffmann Garden by the architect, Daniel Libeskind, for a long time it was a matter of speculation as to what exactly would happen in this space. This proposal, one of many, produced for Müller Knippschild Wehberg who designed and constructed the main landscape plan for the museum, comprises a fallen tree that grows toward a suspended fiddle. The axes marked across the ground plane align with a synagogue and a church in different parts of the city.[2]

2   As is now well known, the architect completed the garden himself.

PHOTOMONTAGE OF THE COMPLETED EXTENSION TO THE BERLIN MUSEUM (ARCHITECT, DANIEL LIBESKIND) WITH THE ETA HOFFMANN GARDEN IN THE FOREGROUND. BACKGROUND IMAGE: FRAGMENT OF THE LANDSCAPE PLAN FOR THE SITE OF THE EXTENSION TO THE BERLIN MUSEUM DESIGNED BY MÜLLER KNIPPSCHILD WEHBERG.

Vladimir's Folly

1970–

I long for the return of the dioramas whose enormous, crude magic subjects me to the spell of a useful illusion. I prefer looking at the backdrop paintings of the stage where I find my favorite dreams treated with such consummate skill and tragic concision. Those things, so completely false, are for that reason much closer to the truth, whereas the majority of our landscape painters are liars precisely because they fail to lie.
—Charles Baudelaire (1859)

Not many people imagine fantastic landscapes and record them in sketchbooks as a sustained practice. Vladimir Sitta has been doing so for more than thirty years. He conjures these little worlds while in meetings or on the bus going home from the office. They lie within the tradition of the grotto and the folly; yet since vegetation and topography are often incorporated, they can be understood as landscape gardens.

In the history of landscape architecture, the folly and the grotto have been receptacles for mythical nostalgia, desire, and all forms of alchemical tinkering. As Anthony Vidler explains, the old word "Folle" was used to refer to lewd, unchaste, and wanton behavior, and the grotto's generally subterranean situation makes it coterminous with the subconscious.

Vidler argues that the folly operated in bourgeois society as a controlled counterpart and container for specifically nonbourgeois qualities such as horror and decay. He explains that "the folly took its place beside the madhouse, the zoo and the botanic garden, the physiognomist's cabinet of shrunken heads and the phrenologist's

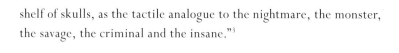

shelf of skulls, as the tactile analogue to the nightmare, the monster, the savage, the criminal and the insane."[3]

The sketches capture the capricious forces of creation and ruination, snapshots of troubled passages leading to seductive dead ends. Of course, along the way the sketches also indulge in carnival and mockery, which as Monique Mosser reminds us, is folly's twin sister.[4]

Sitta's sketches seem to operate similarly to that which Robert Harbison identifies at work in the Boboli gardens in Florence. There, Harbison explains that "far from a trivial decorative art, gardening of this sort provides calculated excitements and incitements to anarchic impulses. But this is not the whole story, for if the Boboli tempts us with the dream of release, it also teases us by throwing obstacles in our way and maintains a tension between feeling free and wondering where one is."[5]

Today the internalized drama of the labyrinth, the folly, and the grotto is located predominantly in the black box of the cinema and the computer, that is, the virtual. Sitta's passion is not for the virtual; rather, his sketches broach the tectonic realities of construction, casting, hammering, and smoothing his fantasies into the third dimension.

3   Anthony Vidler, "History of the Folly," in B. J. Archer et al., eds., *Follies: Architecture for the Late-Twentieth-Century Landscape* (New York: Rizzoli, 1983), p. 10.
4   Monique Mosser, "Paradox in the Garden; A Brief Account of Fabriques," in Monique Mosser and Georges Teyssot, eds., *The History of Garden Design* (London: Thames & Hudson, 1991), p. 278.
5   Robert Harbison, *Eccentric Spaces* (London: André Deutsch, 1977), p. 6.

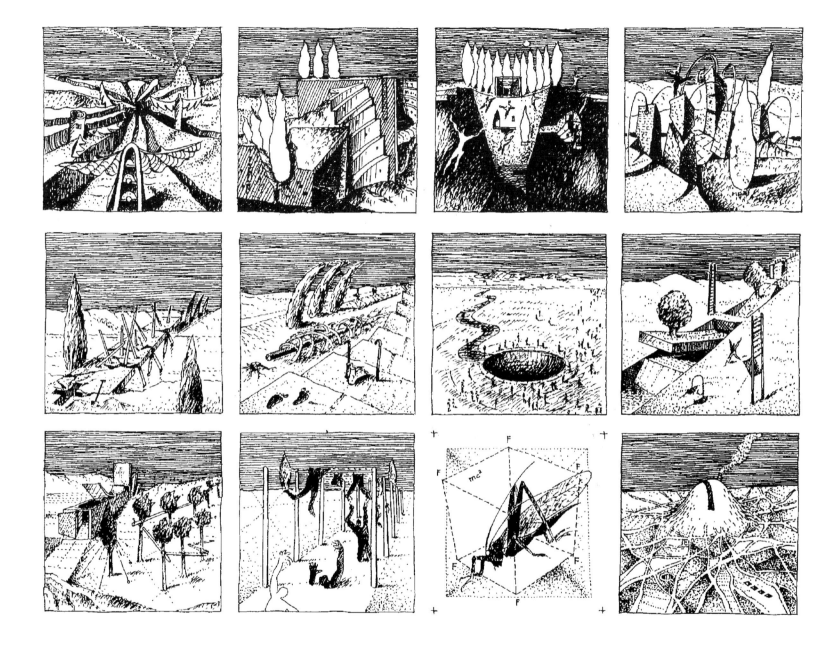

Nihilium

Chaumont-sur-Loire, France 1995

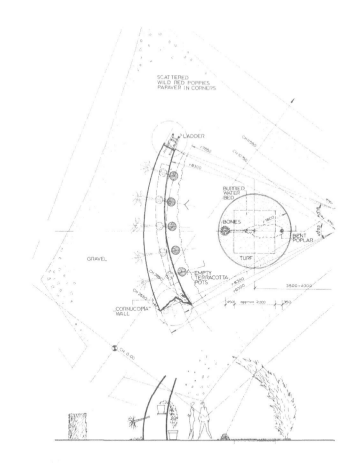

The Château Chaumont-sur-Loire Festival of Parks and Gardens in France commissions up to twenty or more small, ephemeral gardens each year in relation to a particular theme. This folly, entitled Nihilium, was selected in 1995 under the rubric of "Curiosities."

A one-meter-thick curved wooden wall operates as a warped cabinet of curiosities containing various elements that penetrate and emerge from it. From one side, tree roots jut out, while vegetation spills out from the other and falls toward empty pots on the ground. Peepholes reveal small perspex containers displaying various specimens such as insects. A ladder covered in duck feathers appears to pass through the cabinet before intersecting with a conifer. One end of the curved cabinet is blackened with bitumen, and inside a ticking metronome can be heard, as if this curiosity is about to either make music or explode. Standing opposite the cabinet, embraced by its curvature, is a single small poplar. A tension wire disappearing into a pile of bones bends the poplar.

As if all this is not curious enough, a covering of grass in front of the poplar conceals a buried waterbed, surprising approaching visitors with inexplicably unstable ground.

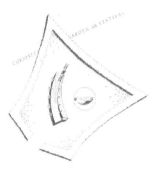

Seed Machine
New York 1992

As part of a competition for conceptual gardens for unspecified small spaces in Manhattan, we proposed a machine. The machine rotates an armature fitted with a rake. The rake moves slowly in a variety of patterns across the sandy ground plane of the garden so that a multitude of patterns can be traced into the garden's surface in the manner of Zen gardens. From the top of the rake's pivot is a container kept stocked with seeds. Wind randomly blows some of the seeds onto the sandy, moist surface of the garden. Seeds such as buckwheat propagate quickly in the ripples of the raked surface of the garden, enhancing its patterns, until the machine is reprogrammed and the seeds are plowed back into the ground as a new pattern takes form. Like Paley Park, the back wall is a waterfall.

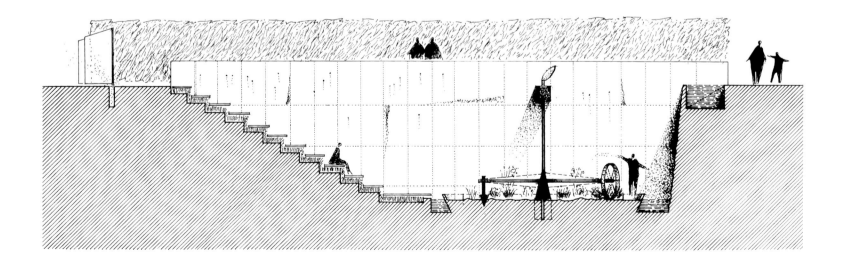

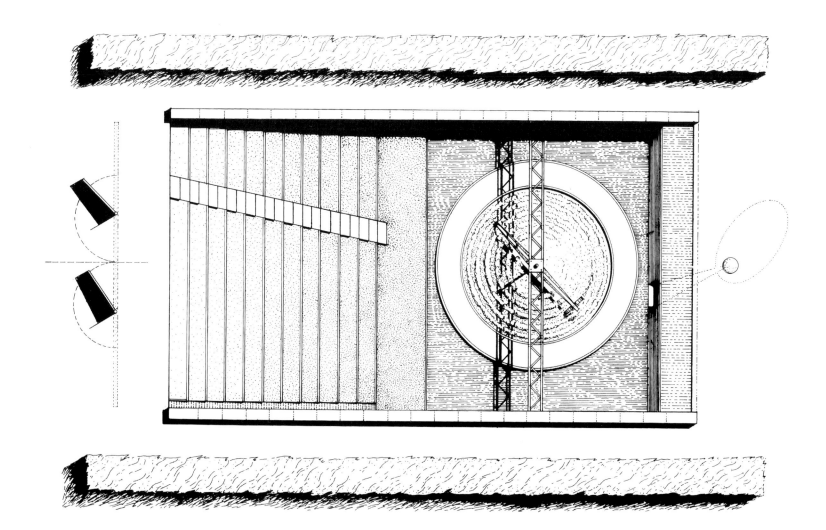

The Filmmaker's Garden
Sydney 1998

The technologies used in the installation $Z^2 + C$ (pages 106–109) are applied here to the vertical wall of a garden commissioned by a film producer. Beginning with the white screen of the industrial filter fabric, little rainforest plants in pockets, and a consistent flow of water, the whole screen slowly grows and decays into a dripping mass of different molds, lichens, slime, mosses, fungi, and plants. Initially horrified at the resultant growth, the client has since learned to appreciate this slow-motion scenography of a personal petri dish.

Fire Garden
Sydney 1999

Every summer, Australian cities are threatened by bush fires. For millennia, Aborigines managed and altered Australian ecosystems with fire. Much Australian vegetation now requires burning in order to propagate.

Remembering that the garden in history is a product and signature of the epochal shift from nomadic to settled cultures, then the use of fire as a feature in this suburban garden now invokes time, space and culture well beyond its boundaries.

At the head of the line of fire is a golden egg set upon a granite cross invoking both Eastern and Western mythologies of creation, orientation, and sacrifice. Fire is rich in associations and can mean many things, but in Australia fire is a phenomenon that threatens and often consumes property, so its appearance in a garden is simply to make that which is wild, domestic, which is, after all, what gardens do.

Water Garden
Sydney 1999

Vladimir Sitta's small gardens are status symbols in Sydney's salubrious eastern suburbs, a result he has no interest in. What does interest Sitta, and what he demands of his clients, is the right to experiment and push materials and craftsmanship to the limit. His skills are best tested in circumstances involving water, the material, which, as the Taoists say, can't be cut but cuts everything.

In this particular residential project, along the length of an entrance passage a brass grill is virtually invisible under the sheen of a millimeter-thin film of water. The water and the brass grill have considerable depth so as to create the illusion of a deep pool of calm, dark water. The water appears to have flooded the front of the property, making access to the front door impossible.

Seeing this for the first time, the client was furious and thought there had been a horrible mistake, until of course he discovered that he could walk on water.

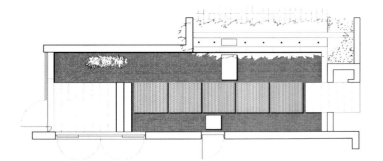

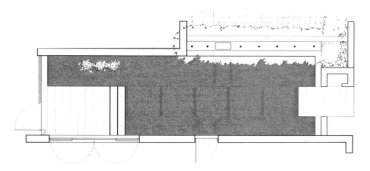

Plans showing the entrance passage from a street-front gate to the front door when the space is drained and when it is full.

Empty, the water garden reveals a bridge.

Full, the water garden appears to be a deep pool of dark water.

Terra Californius
Davis, California 1987

This project was submitted to a competition for themed gardens to be built on the campus of the University of California at Davis, in 1987. Entitled Terra Californius (after the British legal fiction of Australia as a *terra nullius*, "empty place") this submission of an "Australian Garden" represents a double displacement and colonization.

The garden is the size of a quarter-acre allotment, the most desirable parcel of land in Australian suburbia. Its surface is covered in a literal copy of a map of a large area of remote Australia. Enclosing the garden is a wooden fence typical of those in Australian suburbs. In the center of the site, a sunken burned wooden room is marked exactly by a suspended plumb bob. In the burned room is a pile of salt and a stand of *Xanthorrhoeas australis* ("Black Boys"), a plant synonymous with Australia's ancient and strange landscapes. These plants continue to elude botanists as to just how they survive in a range of adverse conditions and how they seem to thrive on being burned. Xanthorrhoea are a small wonder of natural history, whereas the salination of Australia's landscape is now a large cultural catastrophe.

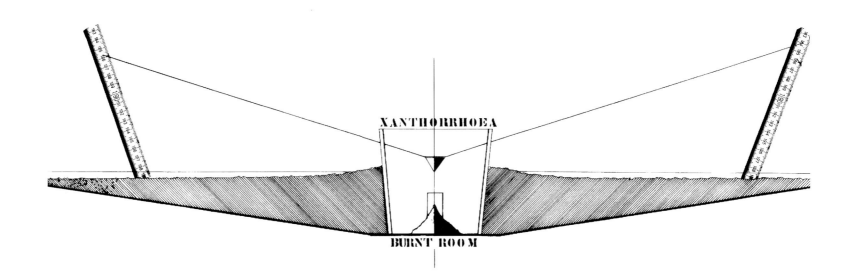

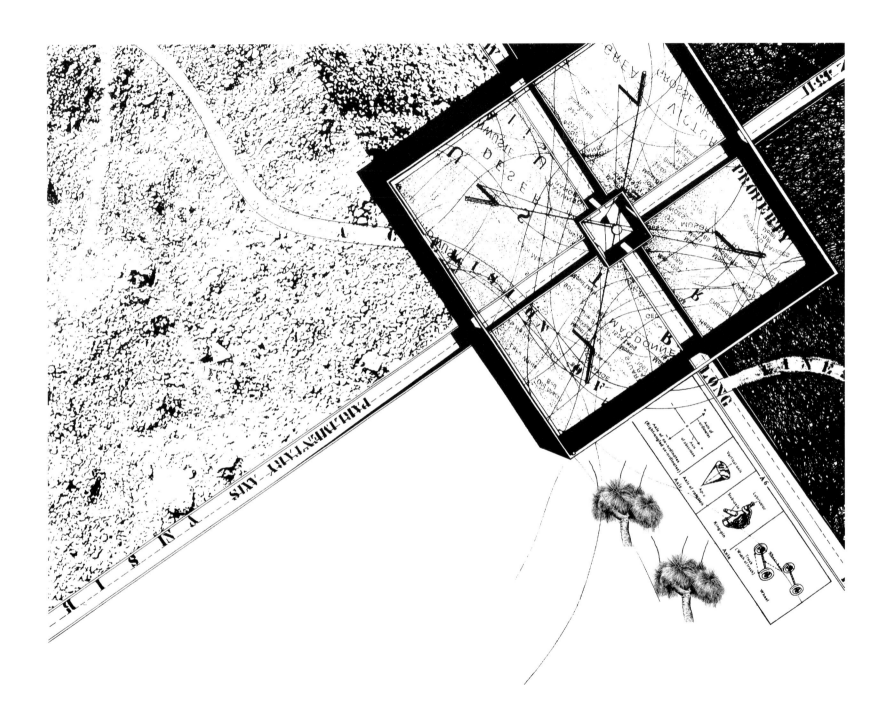

Geo-Semiotics

Paul Carter

The use of discursive signs is prominent in Room 4.1.3's practice. Conventional symbols used in cartography, as well as the letters of different alphabets, may be sculpted into the ground surfaces of their proposed gardens or parks. This device appears to treat the "ground" as a tabula rasa or white page—an odd, not to say perverse, position in what purports to be a material practice.

An inscriptive process that draws a veil over the ground in order to write its own name appears to recapitulate the opening move of the colonizer. It draws another map—an impression reinforced when Room 4.1.3's characteristic manipulation of maps is taken into account. The entire range of geo-graphics—ground plans, building profiles, geometrical figures—is transposed, overlaid, reoriented, and otherwise manipulated. The outcome is a pattern incorporating an edited cross-ply of geo-graphically derived lines, axes, points of punctuation, and expression.

In late eighteenth-century picturesque theory, gardens were said to be structured like language, but the analogy was left implicit. Room 4.1.3, by contrast, spells it out. Their ground writing is not allowed to disguise itself as artfully arranged seating or water: typography, longitude and latitude lines, contour lines, and, indeed, the reproduction of sections of maps, make it clear. *The ground invoked here is maps all the way down.*

Room 4.1.3 makes clear what most landscape design refuses to admit. A library can be assembled demonstrating the ideological design of geography as it is exemplified in maps. The discourse of landscape design is cognate with mapping. Yet landscape designers and their critics usually talk about something else. As if the template of enclosing lines were incidental to their practice, they behave like painters, disposing masses, adjusting textures and tones, arranging passages that guarantee the site's narrative legibility. At this point the negative critique of Room 4.1.3's representation of its own practice of representation comes into positive relief. The ground is not merely not given: in the art of garden-making, it is not even a consideration.

The significance of this is twofold. It lets back in "nature" or the wilderness. It materializes the line in a way that restores its "character." In fact, these two points are related. Landscape design discourse is picturesque wherever the designers talk about what their design represents—as if, instead of drawing another map, they were depicting a country. In this sense most contemporary design practice remains eighteenth century. Linear geometry is passed off as a jigsaw of physical shapes: a pseudo-Venetian chiaroscuro is caged inside a scheme of Florentine lines. Representing this enclosure act, Room 4.1.3 frees things up. The violent wildness of cultivation is disclosed.

The violence associated with cultivation goes back to the origins of Western city-making and gardening. There appears to be an etymological justification for this. The Greek words for *marketplace* and *wilderness*, and the Latin word for *field*, are all derived from a common root meaning to drive.[1] A desire to hear the orator drives the people to the agora. The hunter in the forest is the driver of animals. Finally, it is the responsibility of the cowherd and the shepherd to drive the herds and flocks out to the fields. Driving has two modalities. It drives people together: Canetti's "hunting crowd" is also the Kristallnacht mob. It drives people apart: the Dionysian procession through the streets of Thebes breaks up, and, as the crowd dissipates, it grows unruly. A scapegoat is found, tracked down, and his throat cut.[2] These drives have their technical counterpart in the cutting instrument the architect and the landscape architect use. They are ground scorers. Representational conventionalism has tamed their true significance. They are said to indicate edges. In fact, they commemorate acts of wounding, bloodletting, and incipient erosion.

A landscape design without picturesque veil has (perhaps particularly in Berlin) a history of violation written into it. The lines are not invisible. Nor are they merely intriguing folds and creases generally complicating the measurement of distances. They are a writing of the instincts; they indicate a history of driving tracks. It is the absence of this recognition that condemns most contemporary urban park and garden designs to death. They are arcadias without their Pan. They are arcadias from which the signature of death has been expunged. The danger of getting on the track of Pan is clear, but Jungian psychoanalyst James Hillman is prepared to take the risk: "Respect for life is not enough, and even love puts Pan down, so that the citizen cannot be re-educated through ways which are familiar. These all start with Pan dead."[3] Yet Pan's world "includes masturbation, rape, panic, convulsions and nightmares."[4]

Room 4.1.3's cartographically derived markings materialize a violent attack on mapping itself. They are not impositions on an innocent ground, but guerrilla raids on the spatial unconscious of imperial design, using techniques of blinding, asphyxiation, and cruel exposure to dramatize the violence of a place-making whose history is passed off as one of smooth (and soothing) progress. Swelling into materialized volumes, the arcana of linguistic and cartographic signs shrug off their conventional significations. They become traces of passage, plow marks, and aggressive ruptures. They are no longer even images, but aspire to negate their impression of abiding presence. Thinking of the tracker whose quarry always lies out of sight, Emmanuel Lévinas considers that the peculiarity of the trace "consists in signifying without making appear"[5]—a good description of a Pan-inhabited garden.

As thinking spaces, Room 4.1.3's designs look beyond themselves. Repressive enclosures yield to layered political disclosures. Their ability to indicate physically the traces of uneven power relations emerges ironically, from the modesty of the practice—from the point made before, that, instead of indulging in metaphysical descriptions of place, Room 4.1.3 presents a critical cartography. The overworked Borges fable retained a ground nostalgia: the joke of a 1:1 map depended on assuming that maps aspired to the condition of countries. But maps, if an admittedly dubious etymology can be believed, are essentially tablecloths, and the ground they cover is off-the-ground.[6] The flatness of maps embodies the same ideological bias evident in the rhetoric of sitting at the "negotiating table," so prevalent in First World-Last World negotiations. Like the "level playing field," always invoked in free trade discussions, it is a myth disguising a profoundly uneven and violated historical ground. Then to carve into that napkin of diplomacy, to score it and shred it, *should* induce panic.

Looking beyond the theatrical illusion, Room 4.1.3's practice reestablishes the materiality of the sign. Writing replaces textuality; and the treatment of drawn marks—whether calligraphic flourishes, Greek letters, or a dust-field of punctuation—is designed, I guess, to reveal their character. In the Garden of Australian Dreams, the three-dimensionalized calligraphy of Australia is not only mirrored to the north. Implicitly it is given another face. In my own practice a certain peripatetic charm is intended in the layout and scaling of lettering: walking as treading.[7] Room 4.1.3 operates differently, not peripatetic but Platonic in disposition—Socrates famously remarking that, in order to read the small print of an argument, it is best to print it in large letters first—and preferably on a wall! I am persuaded by the argument that the character of a letter (or other conventional sign) is derived not from its *skhema* but from its *rhuthmos*: "If *skhema* designates 'a fixed, realised form posited as an object' (a stable form, therefore a figure of Gestalt), *rhuthmos* Š is 'the form at the moment it is taken by what is in movement, mobile, fluid, the form that has no organic consistency.'"[8] Room 4.1.3, in contrast, is attuned to the irony of legible scale as such. At what point (distance or location in relation to the public space user) does writing become building, a path a calligram?

Materialized in built spaces, Room 4.1.3's interest in the semiotics of maps meets W. J. T. Mitchell's desideratum, that an adequate theory of representation must be able to represent the act of representation, in this way not only interpreting but changing its environment.[9] Here the field as cartographic palimpsest yields to the necessity of creating a map of maps. Jacques Bertin observes that carto-graphics offer a monosemic system (in which the meaning of the sign is preassigned by the legend). To employ it means that "all the participants come to agree on certain meanings expressed by certain signs, *and agree to discuss them no further.*"[10] In this case, it is necessary to make the legend *polysemic* again.

Here another classical anecdote occurs to me. Two stories are told about the famous ancient Greek poet and public sign-writer, Simonides. He devised four new letters for the Greek alphabet. He composed an inscription for the paintings of Polygnotos at Delphi and, when asked why, replied, "So that it might be conspicuous that Polygnotos had painted them."[11] I like to conflate these two stories: for how could text adequately represent image unless by inventing letters possessing form but no meaning? Upside-down, revolved, and mirrored letters are similarly disoriented.

Just as in fragments of maps it is impossible to distinguish creeks from hachures and roads from lines of latitude, so with Room 4.1.3's geo-semiotics. Focusing on the graphic arts used to represent the earth's surface, it underscores the need of further discussion. Maps are represented histories. The places they presume to locate outside themselves are the offspring of their projections. Other maps might disclose other places, or, better, dispensing with places altogether, lay the groundwork of something liker an ethics of tracking. In the meantime, excavating Room 4.1.3's designs establishes one principle: even if it is not maps all the way down, it is maps far further down than most imagine.

1   Raimo Anttila, *Greek and Indo-European Etymology in Action: Proto-Indian* (Amsterdam: Benjamins, 2000), p. 2.
2   Paul Carter, *Repressed Spaces: The Poetics of Agoraphobia* (London: Reaktion Books, 2002).
3   Wilhelm Roscher and James Hillman, *Pan and the Nightmare* (Zurich: Spring Publications, 1972), p. lxi.
4   Ibid.
5   Emmanuel Lévinas, *Basic Philosophical Writings*, ed. A. T. Peperzak, S. Critchley, and R. Bernasconi (Bloomington: Indiana University Press, 1996), p. 61.
6   Paul Carter, "Allotments: The Illusion of Ground," in Didier Bequillard, *Lotissements/Footings* (Ivry sur Seine: Le Credac, 2002), p. 3.
7   Paul Carter, "Arcadian Writing: Two Texts into Landscape Proposals," *Studies in the History of Gardens and Designed Landscapes* 21, no. 2 (April-June 2001), pp. 137–47.
8   Philippe Lacoue-Labarthe, *Typography: Mimesis, Philosophy, Politics* (Cambridge, Mass.: Harvard University Press, 1989), p. 200.
9   W. J. T. Mitchell, *Picture Theory: Essays on Verbal and Visual Representation* (Chicago: University of Chicago Press, 1994), p. 419.
10 Jacques Bertin, *Semiology of Graphics* (Madison: University of Wisconsin Press, 1983), p. 2, my emphasis.
11 Anne Carson, *Economy of the Unlost: Reading Simonides of Keos with Paul Celan* (Princeton, N.J.: Princeton University Press, 2002), p. 61.

Textuality and Tattoos

Jacky Bowring

On the ancient plains of Nacsa in Peru, enormous enigmatic geoglyphs were etched onto the surface of the earth. Only clearly visible from the air, the purpose of these signs and symbols is still uncertain, but the target audience appears to have been deities or aliens, with the landscape providing some kind of earth-to-space billboard.

At The Leasowes, an eighteenth-century English picturesque garden, literary quotations and Shenstone's poems were inserted strategically into the landscape. On urns, seats, and plaques, these literary allusions appealed to the erudite garden visitors and were like inlaid elements in the landscape.

And at the North Carolina Museum of Art in the 1990s the phrase "PICTURE THIS" was writ large in the landscape. A collaborative project between architects Henry Smith-Miller and Laurie Hawkinson, artist Barbara Kruger, and landscape architect Nicholas Quennell, the huge lettering was used as structure for outdoor theaters, gardens, playgrounds, sculptural works.

Three events in the intertwined relationship between text and landscape. Three contrasting scales of landscape texts. Three modes of engagement. Three diverse locations. Three audiences. Three textual encounters—language and landscape are old bedfellows, and in the work of Room 4.1.3 they cavort together everywhere from the evocative titles of projects, works on paper, projections on billboards, inlaid lettering, and colored concrete maps. Just as much part of this extensive legacy of mark making in the landscape, Room 4.1.3's works also manifest poststructuralism's destabilizing of text and concern with issues of representation.

Language allows strategizing; it facilitates speculation and invention beyond the particularities of visual expression. It demands that the reader/viewer participate, that they imagine. Room 4.1.3's oeuvre consists of both built works and speculative visions. These imagined projects with their interweaving of text and image become imagetexts, those "synthetic and dialectical composites that together contain and produce an array of striking and otherwise unpicturable images."[1] The imagetexts contain arcs and axes of lettering like some mystical diagrams, alchemist's charts, occultist's pentagrams. Laws and relationships are plotted, lunar cycles, the formula for the Mandlebrot set, the lifecycle of a forest. Webs of words in the Bestiary and the Herbal present compositions as concrete poetry. The prolific use of language in Room 4.1.3's imagetexts appears to evidence a concern with representation rather than abstraction. It seems to seek corroboration, offers pseudo-certainty, perhaps reveals a fear of not being understood. But the texts move in and out of focus, deferring from being a container of meaning, defying a singular interpretation. Language and landscape tease each other, dangling resolution then snatching it away. In $Z^2 + C$, the seemingly helpful text confounds by not referring to that very thing it defines—"nature." The human desire to resolve, decode, find closure, encourages the pursuit of these frustrating, tantalizing relationships between text and landscape.

Nig Heke in *Once Were Warriors*, New Zealand Film Commission.

Even more compelling is where the language leaves the page and arrives on ground, lettering the landscape. John Dixon Hunt refers to words in the landscape as verbal "supplements," "guid[ing] or even dictat[ing] how we experience sites."[2] Text appears in a number of Room 4.1.3's landscapes, fulfilling a range of roles and becoming central to the experience of the site. Like Nacsa, The Leasowes, and the North Carolina Museum of Art, the designs of Room 4.1.3 illustrate three modes of engagement between language and landscape: as (structure), in (insertion), and on (surface). Text masquerades as landscape structure in the Virtually Free Market's computer booths based on the words from Augustine's description of the eviction from paradise. In the German Institute of Standards courtyard, text is inserted into the landscape, like the literary allusions at The Leasowes, but is a destablized "nonsense" text that confounds as much as it elucidates. And as on the great plains of Peru, text is written onto the surface of the Garden of Australian Dreams and imagined on the landscapes of Melbourne's Docklands Waterfront and the Berliner Zimmer (Berlin Room), among many other works. The nature of the words, their embedded codes, their paradoxical elusiveness, and their presence as decorative surfaces represent a rich nexus of representation, landscape, and meaning. Conceptualizing these landscapetexts as tattoos is presented as a means to explore the practice of writing on the landscape.

If the landscape is a body, as one of the most pervasive environmental metaphors would have us believe, then to cover it with text is to tattoo it. For many, tattooing is an art form, a way of decorating the body to make it appear more beautiful, like corporal wallpaper. A tattoo can also be a sign of identity. This might be the voluntary decision to mark one's body with an identifying word or symbol, such as Nig Heke's gang-related facial tattoo in Lee Tamahori's film *Once Were Warriors*. Or the involuntary tattooing of numbers onto concentration camp prisoners by Germans in World War II. Related to identity are issues of ownership and intellectual property. Maori traditionally wore distinctive facial tattoos or *ta moko*, and the individuality of the patterns became a way of "signing" legal documents during the early colonial contact period. The indigenous New Zealanders would literally copy their facial tattoos onto documents as a way of making a unique mark or signature. Contemporary concerns over intellectual property relate to the ownership of the marks and the potential loss of their *mana* or prestige if they become commodities. Singer Robbie Williams' Maori tattoo on his upper arm illustrated the tensions bound up in cultural property. National M.P. Tony Ryall believed that Williams' Maori tattoo was something that New Zealanders should be proud of, while on the other hand Maori academic Dr. Pita Sharples sees it as an act of cultural appropriation–he says Williams has "my intellectual property on his shoulder."

Tattoos can be a mark of rebellion, of making a statement, love across one hand and hate across the other. They are culturally specific, a language of their own, and for some cultures tattooing is taboo. It is forbidden by the Jewish faith, and early Christian Europeans followed the Old Testament command, "Ye shall not make any cuttings in your flesh for the dead, nor print any marks upon you" (Leviticus 19:28).

They are also vehicles for meaning and can have narratives of their own. One of the most intriguing stories about tattoos is Christopher Nolan's film *Memento*, based on the short story *Memento Mori* by Jonathon Nolan. In the story, Leonard Shelby suffers from a form of amnesia that denies him short-term memory. In order to piece together a whodunit, he commits significant pieces of information to his body in the form of tattoos, an extreme version of the note on the back of the hand.

The process of tattooing is painful, meaning that tattoos are often worn as a badge of courage and have connotations of virility and machismo. There is also pleasure in the pain and the act of tattooing is described by many as compelling, with the feel of the needle becoming addictive. A less painful but also experiential form of marking the body is the sensuous body calligraphy of Peter Greenaway's film *The Pillowbook*. Both tattooing and body calligraphy represent a fetishizing of the body which is realized through the process of writing.

The textual works of Room 4.1.3 echo the practice of tattooing. The Garden of Australian Dreams is particularly analogous to a tattooed body. The smooth concrete surface is undeniably skinlike. The markings on the surface are in recognizable symbolic languages, including both text and other identifiable icons, such as the dotted white line of a road. The interpretation that the surface markings are for decorative purposes introduces one of the great debates in design–the role of ornamentation. In his seminal essay "Ornament and Crime" (1908), Adolf Loos used the analogy of tattoo to decry decoration in architecture. His statement that "the modern man who tattoos himself is either a criminal or a degenerate" expresses his belief that ornament is aesthetically unpure and debased.[3] This separation of ornament and function has been challenged by recent architectural theorists who present such a division as meaningless. In the context of a garden, the senselessness of the split is amplified–what *is* the "function" of the garden, and what is left if we take away the "ornament," remove its tattoos?

The garden's tattoos are powerful statements of identity. Just as emphatic as the gang member with Mongrel Mob tattooed across his face, the garden's markings make connections with cultures and subcultures. The references to locations, the multiple translations of the word *home*, the Edmund Barton signature, the red X, the "Australian" text, are all declaring identity. Just as the Maori *moko* was a form of signing, these contemporary landscape tattoos are decorations with significant cultural specificity, and they beg questions of intellectual ownership and cultural authority and authorship. The architectural setting of the Garden of Australian Dreams demonstrates the tension between a dissolution of any sense of authorship and the assertion of intellectual property rights. National Museum of Australia architects Ashton Raggatt McDougall incorporated a range of distinctive architectural quotations, with the most contested being the echo of Daniel Libeskind's Jewish Museum in Berlin as the Gallery of First Australians.

The process of using contextual texts to assemble a version of reality is also part of the scheme for the Berlin Room. Fragments of stories of the lives and deaths of the Potsdamer Platz appear to float in the water garden, pieces of information tattooed over the surface. The agrden and the Berlin Room are sites that operate as cultural aides-mémoire, like Leonard Shelby's need to constantly remind himself of the facts (which he constructed as he went), the markings are an attempt to avert cultural amnesia.

The process of marking has some implications for the "body" that bears them. This bearing of identity can be seen as a painful process–the sharp needle commits the words permanently to the skin of the site. Perhaps it is seen as a compelling act, a rite of passage for a nation celebrating its centenary of federation–a tattoo for its twenty-first birthday. Or the act of marking can be seen as more sensual, caressing, as in the projected images at Spreebogen, or in Room 4.1.3 collaborator Paul Carter's notion of tracings in Centennial Park Federation Garden, where the paths would be "written" with "calligraphic abandon." The relationship between text and body is critical: is the landscape "body" a macho character with a tattooed anchor, or the prevailing ideal of a female landscape, its surface caressed by the calligrapher's brush?

As part of the extensive legacy of language and landscape, this investigation of Room 4.1.3's work offers the metaphor of the tattoo as a fusion of the prevailing metaphors of landscape-as-text and landscape-as-body. It is a particularly fitting analogy for a body of work that seems more concerned with surface/text/meaning than space/form/light. Through conceptualizing design in this way, multifarious dimensions are excavated, revealing the work as mnemonic, iconic, rebellious, macho, sensuous, and, last but definitely not least, ornamental.

1   James Corner, *Recovering Landscape: Essays in Contemporary Landscape Theory* (New York: Princeton Architectural Press, 1999), p. 167.
2   John Dixon Hunt, *Greater Perfections: The Practice of Garden Theory* (Philadelphia: University of Pennsylvania Press, 2000), p. 116.
3   Quoted in Ulrich Conrads, ed., *Programs and Manifestos on Twentieth-Century Architecture* (Cambridge, Mass.: MIT Press, 1970), p. 19.

Room 4.1.3 and Australian Landscape Architecture

Julian Raxworthy

The search for an "Australian" landscape design sensibility is one that has permeated the development of landscape architecture in Australia.[1] During the late 1970s and early 1980s, when this quest for an embodiment of identity was at its peak, environmentalism was becoming a central mainstream concern. In the lead-up to and immediate wake of the proposed Franklin Dam (a conservation battle over the damming of one of Tasmania's "wild rivers"), the populace was engaged in a collective exercise in aesthetic imagining about the nature of their homeland.

This battle of signification was manifest in television at the time and was dominated by mini-series, such as "The Timeless Land." Such programs concentrated on colonial disjunctions between: English manners and impoverished criminals; between a Sublime landscape and one of extreme survival. Peter Dombrovskis' saturated transparencies of immaculate "messy" bush scenes entrenched a "sense" of the landscape, where the "real" qualities of the landscape became purely notional.[2] Wild landscapes were seen as truth and beauty incarnate, self-evidently beyond question. If it was there originally, it should be there now. Australian landscape architecture, like Australian painting eighty years prior, had found its ultimate model. Not only was the "bush" true and beautiful, it was ecological, and so landscape architects busied themselves manufacturing copies.

The doyens of this landscape aesthetic in Australia are Harry Howard[3] and Bruce Mackenzie.[4] Mackenzie's seminal work is perhaps Long Nose Point Park in Sydney.[5] Howard's most renowned project is the Sculpture Garden at the National Gallery of Australia in Canberra,[6] and it is fitting that twenty years later Room 4.1.3 would come to place their very different rendition of Australian identity on precisely the opposite side of the lake. Serious revegetation sites aside, of all the acres planted out with "indigenous bush" in the name of Australian landscape design, very little remains in any convincing form.

The next decade, pivoting around Australia's Bicentennial Celebrations in 1988, saw poor-quality mimicry of colonial period motifs, inevitably rendered in Sky blues and red brick.[7] This turn to culture instead of nature turned out to be at least as bereft as the commitment to the "indigenous" in terms of articulation, as the generic nature of these details became apparent. After all, Australia was just another penal colony, and correspondingly our formal elaborations comprised Victorian mail-order catalogue Whig mass productions. The 1990s saw any singular image of Australian identity abandoned, and a tentative, then gushing appropriation of international typological treatments ensued. In conceiving of and then selling their work, designers cited the "fine tastes" of Bernard Huet's Champs-Elysées, in Paris and picked whatever was at hand from the general, comprehensive redevelopment of Barcelona in the led up to the Olympics of 1992. This was manifest in a resurgence in "good taste" in urban design, in the form of Modernist proportion and detailing[8] with occasional wacky "liberated" postmodern moments.[9]

Apart from this generally gullible form of appropriation of the international, during the 1990s disgruntled practitioners and students increasingly turned to the enigma of cultural studies, according to which landscape was always a relative cultural construction. Under the aegis of theory everyone could appear scholarly while remaining polemical and even engage in aesthetic debate without ever having to actually draw or build anything.

As indigenous Australians brought pressure to bear on anyone that laid claim to the "bush," so too postcolonial scholarship focused deconstructive strategies on landscape structures and surfaces. Alternative histories, the quintessence of which is Paul Carter's Road to Botany Bay, established a range of processes of drawing on very personal and subjective connections to the qualities of the landscape.[10] The Manning Clarke generation of historians could not help find it interesting and relevant, although it gave them a headache.[11] Now, as befits contemporary multicultural Australia, the influence of the 1990s has resulted in the agreement to disagree that there is no inherent truth to either what the landscape is or what it means to be "Australian."

Rhetoric and Representation

Against this background, Room 4.1.3 emerges with a set of design methods for dealing with multivalent, subjective interpretation. These methods, notably reminiscent of those of Daniel Libeskind, immediately position the practice's work within the ubiquitous international designer super-series, whilst at the same time often engaging these methods as containers for Australian content. In Room 4.1.3, however, there is none of the paranoia about the local, which flows through other Australian practices. Vladimir Sitta and Richard Weller have always oscillated between old international design centers and the antipodean periphery as a matter of freedom and opportunity, following carefully selected projects wherever they might lead. Both are less "landscape architects" than "landscapes": travelers in Italo Calvino's "Invisible Cities," with the same naivety, wonderment, and, at times, an almost embarrassing romanticism. Room 4.1.3 is also arrogant enough to assume that the world is interested in hearing about their travels.

Plotting the global network of Room 4.1.3's practice is an interesting and telling statement on creative practice in Australia. Less a practice than an escape act, Room 4.1.3 is a flexible collaboration. Sitta and Weller are more like the Eureka Stockade[12] than anything else: fortifying themselves against the institution that is capitalist landscape architectural practice while clearly benefiting from the boundless condition that late capitalism makes possible. They are unified through their abhorrence of what passes for "landscape" architecture in this country and a similar belief in the transformative, analogous, and deeply poetic nature of the "landscape."[13]

Sitta's drawings combine aspects of the horticultural domestic garden with almost mystical senses of environments, drawing upon the historic/mythological associations that gardens have always had in their purest sense. Each drawing seems to relish the surrealism of this conjunction, and one has to pity the plants. For Sitta the garden seems a set of cabbalistic symbols that are presented with the same level of solemnity as one would turn over a Tarot card. Add to this a stinging wit and cross the whole equation with political caricature, and one begins to appreciate the complexity of these images. Although Weller's work is more concerned with language and less sensual and intuitive than Sitta's, the value given to the representational is similar.

In many of Weller's drawings geometry exists more as ancient markings and runic rulings than as actual formal or geographic notation. The map is more important than the land it describes.[14] Through simulated relationships, a dense patina of line work emerges that offers countless formal abominations to choose from, each unique. The truth of the work lies in the quality of that which is appropriated and brought to bear on this automatist's composition, not its final outcome. It has been brought to bear but does not necessarily speak, and this is the conundrum of design generation, generally, the difference between data and information. This is perhaps the most solid critique one could provide of Room 4.1.3's recent Australian work, and such a discussion would be more significant because Room 4.1.3 relies heavily on rhetoric to bring forth these buried meanings.[15]

It is also rhetoric that is welcomed by the international architectural design community, which demands abstract material rather than physical places to make its judgments of significance.[16] That said, the stuff is interesting, and perhaps there are not many built works from Room 4.1.3 because the world cannot accommodate icons of this degree of signification. Room 4.1.3's challenge remains: how to work outside the art market?

The Garden of Australian Dreams

The Garden of Australian Dreams is the culmination of Room 4.1.3's local interests and a dramatic and timely shift from the hypothetical to the real. It also represents a moment of change for Australian landscape architecture. This project treats a design exercise as a laboratory for the testing of unbuilt theories developed collectively over twenty years. Much of it works and some of it does not, but it is valiant. In an almost scholarly manner, it puts out all the methods and possibilities that Room 4.1.3 has hypothesized and looks to have the result evaluated. That all discussion has been oblique about this project has frustrated Room 4.1.3.[17] The work is a formal outcome and deserves a formal critique, except even Clement Greenberg would be hard pressed to do so.[18] The project lies shrouded in intentions and discussion that makes form almost invisible. The plethora of methods is easily navigated, though its actual content remains a sublime density of information, almost unintelligible, except to people with an interest in contemporary design, composed as it is of familiar "postmodern" operations: layering, collage, superimposition, blurring, scaling, tracing, and at every stage abstracting. Each operation relies on the interaction of graphic information where moments of frisson and tension appear between those things appropriated then made adjacent, and these are then utilized as found objects for material application. The work gains meaning through the selection of their material for transformation, which is why they are so representational—the material is only ever that: always graphic and inherently formal. Or is it? This is the single most important formal test the project undertakes, the site as a laboratory. The quality of design generation lies as always in their rendition—when it becomes a matter of taste, the artful articulation of the graphic into detail and materiality.

But this information is presented in a field condition, not a recognizable narrative structure of the landscape such as the articulated view of a choreographed path, the appreciable storytelling structure giving landscape languages understood through the Picturesque English landscape garden.[19] This is a language understood by the public, as it has provided the basis for the common municipal park and its recreational, perambulatory program. In contrast, the "field condition" of the Garden of Australian Dreams allows open movement which translates into open interpretation.[20]

The topographical surface with collaged maps on which flexible movement is possible is the most significant test in the project for this compositional method. With the Garden of Reversible Destiny in Japan (an acknowledged precedent), the Garden of Australian Dreams represents a major exercise in real, nonmodular surface manipulation, an interesting exploration of the field as a landscape form, somewhere between the openness of the plaza and the complete manipulation of the Picturesque.

The surface is concrete and gently undulates, although to a significant height at one point, across which text and markings flow. These notations allow an interesting registration of the actual form of the topography; however, their rendition ends up more like line markings in primary school, or possibly a weird 1970s external geography lesson. The sense of flexibility of movement is significant and quite disturbing; however, the text is quite irrelevant to this. So, did the text generate the topography, and, if so, how important is the map afterward? This would be a central issue to effective evaluation of the technique, however no specific moments of text-topography were immediately apparent. Certain moments of rendering of the map gain an independent worth as they are detailed beautifully, such as checker plate grid intersections.

While none of the stories implied through the relative texts and geometries is clearly appreciative, there are moments of peculiarly Australian spatiality. Moving from the highest part of the mapped topography of the garden across to the signature of *Australia* in the pond with the felled tree, enclosed by a wall, remains an experience of no other sort in a designed project in Australia, although it could be said to be operating more in a Japanese manner, reminiscent of the compositional methods and experiential modes of the Zen garden. This configuration though becomes reminiscent to me of a canyon in the Blue Mountains, outside of Sydney,[21] in which a tree has fallen, although obviously and pleasingly artificial. The tree provides a reality of scale that allows appreciation of the density of the space.

Landscape architecture is about a comprehensiveness of consideration, which ranges across all scales of experience and perception from the showy to the invisible. The landscape never stops, so nor should landscape architecture, but at the National Museum all the eggs are in one basket. No doubt a result of the designer's budgetary strategy, this leaves an impoverished site plan for a premier institution. Indeed, one enters through a long dull car park, and even if this is a joke, no one's laughing.

Beyond the spatial dynamic described above, the Australian-ness of the project seems undoubtably rhetorical, with the exception of the snapped ribbon axis to Black Mountain and presumably Ulurubeyond.[22] This one moment recalls beautifully the nature of Australia: a vast distance and mass that is more vivid from a distance than close to, when colors and forms merge to produce a particular gummy grayness. That this gesture is so strong is a testament to those aspects of landscape architecture that could be retained through avant-garde rebellion: precise siting and the facilitation of further relationships, bringing the rest of the physical world to bear.

Beyond the other numerous method-flexing moments of the project, which stand as valid experiments of ideas that have arisen from design studios for the last twenty years, the project's greatness and Australianness arises from the fact that it happened, and it happened now. The project firmly breaks the Australian mold of the invisible landscape that has become so recognizable to be nonexistent. It posits that the landscape is a significant medium of cultural expression, quite apart from its utilitarian importance. It also recognizes that the landscape is not silent, but is an active interpretive mechanism for dealing with meaning, so tied to the landscape of this country already. Australian landscape architecture will not be the same again, thank God.

1   Called by Weller "The Great Debate," the discussion on what was an appropriate design aesthetic for landscape projects is reflected in the first ten years of the magazine *Landscape Australia*, the official magazine of the Australian Institute of Landscape Architects. Citations from *Landscape Australia* will be used throughout this essay to reflect the direction of mainstream landscape architecture in contrast to which Room 4.1.3 have practiced.

2   Peter Dombrovskis photographed Tasmanian wilderness extensively until his death in 1996, producing numerous diaries and calendars for the Australian Conservation Society In his obituary for Dombrovskis, Tasmanian M.P. Bob Brown discusses the role of one photograph, in particular, of the Rock Island Bend in the Franklin River, that was reproduced a million times, in relation to a quote from William Blake that Dombrovskis was fond of: "The tree which moves some to tears of joy is in the eyes of others only a green thing which stands in the way." Bob Brown, "Quiet Recorder of the Landscape," *Habitat Australia* 24, no. 3 (June 1996), pp. 26–27.

3   Harry Howard passed away on September 9, 2000.

4   Citing himself in an article in 1985 (Bruce Mackenzie, "Artstry, Relevance and the Landscape Architect," *Landscape Australia* no. 4, [1985], p. 311) from 1966, Bruce Mackenzie notes "a unique opportunity exists for achieving a cohesive and powerful theme for landscape design throughout this country by realising and promoting the potential of the indigenous environment."

5   Described and discussed by Bruce Mackenzie, "Alternative Parkland," *Landscape Australia* no. 1 (1979), pp. 19–27.

6   This project is described upon its design by Harry Howard in "Landscaping of the High Court of Australia and the Australian National Gallery—The Sculpture Gardens," Landscape Australia no. 3 (1982), pp. 208-215. In his obituary for Howard, James Weirick describes this project as "one of the great works of the imagination in Australia" (James Weirick, "Obituary: Harry Howard," *Landscape Australia*, 22, no. 4 [2000], p. 343).

7   Perhaps the clearest example of work from this period is Sydney's Bicentennial Park. Public Works Department of New South Wales, "Bicentennial Park, Sydney," *Landscape Australia* no. 2 (1990), pp. 173–183.

8   Canberra, then Harvard, graduate Garth Paterson, with Anne T. Pettus, and their firm Paterson + Pettus, developed a range of projects that notably engaged with American "postmodern" landscape architecture, in the manner of Martha Schwartz and Peter Walker, notably their Box Hill TAFE project (Erica Muetzelfeldt, "At a Glance," KERB, 5 [1998], pp. 80–82).

9   This form of treatment was probably pioneered, and then stylized, by Denton Corker Marshall, a Melbourne-based architecture practice that has been responsible for many of the larger civic architecture and landscape projects undertaken in Australia during the last ten years. An example of this approach is Sydney's Pyrmont Point Park (Adam Hunter, "Making a Point: Pyrmont Point Park and Giba Park, Sydney," *Landscape Australia*, no. 3 [1997], pp. 244–249).

10 Paul Carter, *The Road to Botany Bay* (London: Faber & Faber, 1987).

11 Manning Clarke was a pivotal Australian historian who, in his four-volume *History of Australia* (Melbourne: Melbourne University Press, 1962), used a chronological approach that emphasized facts at the expense of interpretation, and in doing so, for example, glossed over the existence of indigenous Aboriginal culture prior to white invasion.

12 The Eureka Stockade is an important incidence of civil disobedience on the Goldfields of Victoria in the 1860s, which, like Ned Kelly, the Bushranger, emphasizes the fundamental respect given by the Australian public to individuals who resist authority on the basis of principle.

13 It is interesting to note the similarity of this interest to that of Mackenzie, differentiated, however, by the embracing of contradiction by Room 4.1.3, in contrast to the passivity of the Bush School.

14 This interest in the interpretive relationship that representation has with cultural constructions of place is one that links Weller to Paul Carter, as well as landscape theorist James Corner.

15 This is best typified by Weller's own discussion of the Garden of Australian Dreams, which concerns not the physical space of the design, but rather the source of the layers that are appropriated to create it.

16 One has only to look at numerous *Architectural Design* titles to see the fascination that architectural publishing has had with design process rather than constructed form.

17 The published work about the landscape aspects of the project has to date concentrated on the nature of its location, in the context of Griffin & Mahoney's Canberra work, and where form is discussed, it is as "a vortex of madness so horrible that it is wonderful" (James Weirick, "Landscape and Politics: The Museum and Its Site," *Architectural Review* 75 [March 2001], p. 63).

18 Referring here to Greenberg's call for purely formal critiques of works of art, devoid from the automatic substantiation provided by art history.

19 The choreography and characterization of landscape form to ensure the imparting of meaning is one discussed well in relation to theories of association and the picturesque by Edward Harwood, "Personal Identity and the Eighteenth Century Landscape Garden," *Journal of Gden History* 13, nos. 1-2 (1993).

20 Notably articulated in the landmark essay by Rosalind Kraus, "Sculpture in the Expanded Field," from H. Foster, ed., *The Anti-Aesthetic: Essays on Postmodern Culture* (Seattle: Bay Press, 1983).

21 The Blue Mountains is a long sandstone massif that stopped early settlers from colonizing the inland of Australia, now preserved as national parks.

22 Uluru, previously Ayers Rock, is the enigmatic rock massif in the center of Australia, outside Alice Springs, in the Northern Territory.

Cowboy Critical: The Antipodean Practice of Room 4.1.3

Peter Connolly

Never underestimate the importance of compelling imagery.
—Michael Sorkin

Broad dissemination of the design work of Room 4.1.3 raises the stakes in landscape architecture. This essay, however, argues that the presentation of design in such a publication champions a problematic international style of landscape architecture design. This style has become, without any discussion, a design approach with its own language, attitude, and even tradition.[1] The chief characteristics seem to be crudely borrowed from architecture, the most obvious being the presumption that landscape design difference is produced almost wholly within the space of representation itself: and if not wholly, then what preceded representation is very often simply not affirmed. Hence I term this approach the "architectural" approach to landscape architectural design. Such work often appears graphically and formally forceful, yet tends to be highly uncritical and passive. The results commonly seem restricted to the scenographic and have distinct tendencies to deny what is particular about landscape architectural design.[2] The scenographic in this sense is, however, not just restricted to the scene or the visual, but denotes a whole Western cultural way of understanding, thinking, and acting. "It" tends to see the world as a collection of separable objects in a neutral space.

While locating the recent built work of Room 4.1.3 within this admittedly nebulous international category of scenographic production, this essay shields its eyes from the glare in order to see beneath the surface and uncover what is meant by the significant claim that Room 4.1.3 is a "critical" practice.[3] The importance of this critical ambition probably equals the general landscape architectural vagueness about what a critical practice might be. Past attempts at a theory of criticality have agreed that it involves a superior form of practice, some authority.[4] Such authors agreed most practice was not "critical." It just so happens that there is a precise theoretical model of criticality associated with the recent built work of Room 4.1.3.

Using this theory as a convenient departure point, this essay presents an alternative notion of what a critical landscape architectural practice might look like. This is followed by an attempt to show how the theory and presentation of the recent work of Room 4.1.3, in particular the National Museum of Australia, does not capture the propensities of their practice. This provides an opportunity to present an alternative account of what Room 4.1.3 actually does, why it may be critical and, as suggested, "antipodean."

Room 4.1.3's Theory of a Critical Practice: Simulacra

Amy Thorpe's reading of the architects Ashton Raggatt McDougall's (ARM)[5] "extension" into landscape provides such an entry point.[6] Thorpe effectively presents the work of Room 4.1.3 as an extension of the ideas of ARM. An accompanying account by Richard Weller varies little from Thorpe's account. Thorpe considers that the "architectural strategies of appropriation previously developed by ARM are now extended into landscape." She says that ARM have for some time set about an examination of an object's relationship to an original "as a means to develop a more critical practice."

Thorpe cites Gilles Deleuze and Jean Baudrillard's notion of the simulacrum, which they borrow from Plato.[7] For Plato the copy is superior to the simulacrum, as it resembles the "idea," an "idea" being the kind of ideal essence of any particular thing, such as a table or "justice." The copy resembles this essence, whereas the simulacrum underhandedly does not. The inauthentic simulacrum, in contrast to the copy, exists independently of the "idea." ARM articulate an interest in exploring affects related to the difference between the copy and the original.[8] Thorpe says that "images have for some time been 'borrowed' to inflect upon them some new meaning"; "to provide a critique of both standard modes of representation and the objects they represent." The simulacrum is a copy without an original, an effect without a cause. Baudrillard terms the condition of the simulacrum the "Hyperreal," a kind of weightless exchange of images or signifiers.

Baudrillard's notion of the simulacrum has been especially popular in architecture. His idea of a simulacrum ambiguously asserts a commonly assumed reference and takes it away at the same time. Polemically associated are the attendant postmodern paradoxes of how to act if we do not seem to have any secure referents. The ARM/Room 4.1.3 collaboration seem to creatively rerun this "eighties" theoretical ambiguity, with localized variation. ARM is quoted as exploring the "illegitimacy" of sampling originals in a manner "where the antipodes could be turned against the centres . . . we are the rude bits, the bits that bite back." It is the rude manner with which ARM (and Room 4.1.3) borrows that is said to be antipodean. To explore this "illegitimacy," ARM is presented as appealing to the legitimacy of the theory of Deleuze and Baudrillard.

Thorpe presents Room 4.1.3 as championing simulacra yet interested in the potential of appropriation for "sociopolitical discourse outside mere "design issues." ARM appropriates from the architectural canon. Room 4.1.3, with a "social conscience," is said to recycle clichés, instead. The increasing detachment of the reference means that "meaning and association become easier to attach." "No-one has the final say." Hence such work is presented as resonating with the legitimacy of being "democratic." Despite affirmation of a sort of freedom and democracy of the "Hyperreal," Thorpe-ARM-Room 4.1.3 cannot, like Baudrillard, do without the original for legitimacy.

Following others, the author would like to suggest that the notion of the Hyperreal may be useful in under-standing the functioning of mass media and image and text, however, landscape architectural design is not merely about the appropriation of a set of interacting images or signifiers in some image-ether.[9] This is also not what Room 4.1.3 practices. To proceed we need a stronger notion of simulacra and authority.

A More Useful Variant: Deleuzian Simulacra

As opposed to the Baudrillardian notion of the simulacrum I would like, for this purpose, to consider the Deleuzian version. Thorpe assumes them the same. They are instead radically opposed. Where in Baudril-lard there is a rigid distinction between original and copy, actual and virtual, Deleuze argues that the real is always actual-virtual. Simulacra are simultaneously actual and virtual. What is scenographically actual, obvious, present, and visible is only so because of what is virtual–the interaction of "invisible" forces and relationships. Such forces and relationships are connected and connective. They are only force-ful because of the connections.[10] "The (Baudrillardian) idea of copy presupposes some original model and Western thought has been dominated by the figure of the copy: the idea that there are originals that can be used to measure and judge claimants."[11] Authority via originals. The Baudrillardian idea that all we have are mere representa-tions or constructions of the world seems to suggest some real world that is lost or unavailable. The simulac-rum is not, for Deleuze, "the loss or abandonment of the real; it is the real."[12] Connections replace origins, but these connections are certainly not limited to the Hyperreal play of images. This suggests a very different notion of a landscape than that suggested by Baudrillard.

ARM/Room 4.1.3 seek a difference found in the affects of variations through repetition, and/or through the liberating affects of the Hyperreal.[13] Both involve difference through variation on what is repeated, repetition being, in this sense, repetition of the "same," of something that has been. This is the commonly understood notion of the relationship between repetition and difference. Anything beyond this exclusive relation bet-ween original and copy or between copies themselves is ignored.

However, repetition in the Deleuzian sense does not work in this commonly understood way. Origins are replaced by connections. Simulacra are connections of differences. According to Deleuze, repetition only occurs because of differences. Repetition occurs because of the interaction of differences.[14] Such repetition is an "act of God," a "miracle" according to Deleuze. Such "miracles" are simply a normal part of life and tend to be obscured by common sense, "natural vision" and practice. Simulacra just do this. The world just does this. Space and time are "not homogeneous, composed of separated objects in a neutral field, or pure chaos.[15] Instead, space and time are "repetitive milieu." Landscape is a repetitive milieu.[16] This notion of landscape is radically different from a scenographic field, whether it is involving the movement of signifiers or not. The Universe or Nature is, as recent scientists attest, "self-organizing."

As true repetition is the product of the interaction of forces and relations, it is therefore not about resemblance to some original. Resemblance, as that which is the obvious scenographic aspect of repetition, is a by-product of this repetition. True repetition, as this interaction, involves an affect. This is the source of the "new." This affect is also simultaneously a signal of the interaction of forces and relations and allows exploration of these forces and relations. This affect may then be intensified through such "learning." Hence repetition is produced by difference as well as being an entry point to exploring difference and the new. This repetition, as an act of God, is the source of criticality. Previous theorists have suggested all sorts of criteria for criticality. However, criteria are very secondary. The world instead itself provides the critical device—an authority of the world. The obviousness of this equals the obscurity of it. A repetition that is "discovered" is like an entry point, to be followed, and developed upon—a regulating moment in the discovery of what produces such newness—and this discovery opens up connections to other affects and newness, just because it does. This affect provides a way to move beyond the scenic and the scenographic. To consider what this specifically means for landscape architecture will also require considering the unique function that representation plays in landscape architecture, which will returns us to the problematic model of much international work circulated through publication to the global landscape design community.

REPRESENTATION

To employ a useful fiction, in terms of representation, landscape architectural design is made up of two types of design, the "landscape architectural" and the "architectural." Both are "proper" to landscape architecture, and they always connive together in various mixtures of the two. Various found conditions and practices privilege one more than the other. The "landscape architectural" approach involves the transformation of representational material which has been appropriated in relation to the found differences of the landscape. In contrast, the "architectural" approach to landscape design does not involve an appropriation of something, in relation to the differences of landscape, which exists prior to representation. This "architectural" approach occurs when what that which is transformed is of a material constructed wholly within the space of representation. The "landscape architectural" approach involves a much more radical notion of appropriation than that conceived of by Baudrillard et al. However, this form of appropriation is strangely unaffirmed in landscape architecture. The "architectural" is central to the productivity of landscape architecture, yet the "architectural" has strong tendencies to deny found difference.[17]

The National Museum of Australia seems an exemplar of this "architectural" approach. It is presented as wholly to have been constructed within the space of representation, with little regard for "found differences." From the draft version of this publication, it can be seen that as the project progressed the garden became increasingly isolated from the surrounding landscape. The landscape was taken inside, into another condition. The rest of the site—bar the Uluru Line, which is presented more or less as a separable object with only a visual relation to a nonaxis–became strongly deemphasized. Was this a fear of the sublimely unrepresentable and difficult difference of nature and the world in preference to the safety, security, and familiarity of the "architectural"? Once fixed in the sanctity of an architectural container, landscape sets about familiar fabrications indulging only an "architectural" freedom–an "architectural" dreaming where graphic and/or borrowed difference seems privileged over found difference. The resultant "text" consists of suggestive discussion of prominent antipodean themes in cliché form. The interlacing of the ideas is also homologous to the interlacing of the forms. Exclusive of everything else, the attention of the presentation is almost exclusively on the relationship between form and "meaning," image and text, and the resonance between the two.

The Baudrillardian theory of simulacra promotes and supports this exclusivity. However, this is relatively easy to point out. The "architectural" is problematic for more than not appropriating found difference. It is problematic because the "architectural" puts its own intense "spin" on the general uncriticality of landscape architecture. To put it simply, the "architectural" borrows much from architecture, yet almost universally fails to borrow something useful from the corresponding critical practices of architecture.[18]

Repetition

It is only recently[19] that architecture has developed critical practices that allow an exploration of the intertwining of the actual with the virtual, the relation between what you see and what invisible forces and relations are inseparable from it. Such practices involve architectural repetitions, architectural "acts of God," chiefly explored through the practices of typology. The affectual dimension and consequences of any act can be referenced through the affectual nature of typology to the world. Landscape architecture has had little disciplined practice of such a critical device.[20] So, what if we consider, speculatively, some of the more architecturally related "landscape" repetitions that may be relevant to the museum project, which could be identified in the following questions. How to connect into the demands of a national capital car-tourist day? Should I go here or there? What makes a photo opportunity? What scale of space and regime of detailing make it generously "public" (and on budget or not)? What amount of stretching of space is needed to encourage a participant to enter and when do you stop stretching? Is the garden the ultimate experience of the museum or inconsequential? What type of orientation and "reading" has the museum-machine set up that the garden may reorient?

Any of these connect to the others and to wider "assemblages" (as Deleuze says) and any of them may be "botched." Such typological questions are decision-machines of this repetitive milieu. The difference of the milieu, "architectural" difference, is inseparable from and radically different from "landscape architectural" difference. "Landscape architectural" found difference involves connections of multiple other realms of repetition and difference with a bias to orders and disorders outside that constructed in representational space.

It could be said with confidence that landscape architectural critical practices are loose and *haphazard* at best. Strong intuition, clever decision making, and inspired design acts are always connected with repetition, yet these will remain unaffirmed and isolated without disciplined practices. Landscape architecture *most definitely* has not developed critical practices related to found difference. What would such critical practices be like?

Landscape Architectural Criticality

To answer this we could consider the following question: If it can be accepted that representation functions radically differently in landscape architectural design, how should it function if the medium is a repetitive milieu? This double radicality is, it is suggested, the predominant condition of landscape architectural practice. What happens when these two unaffirmed but very landscape architectural particularities are brought together? What tasks would be involved?

To begin with, it could be said that appropriation from the found differences of a landscape would be an appropriation guided by repetition-difference, by affects,[21] discovered "in" the landscape. This is more than doubly radical, but as yet it is not whole enough. What would a fully critical landscape practice involve, which critical appropriation is part of? To answer this it should first be acknowledged that there has been some general theorizing about landscape criticality.[22] Beth Meyer identified that a landscape is inseparable from a "situation" it is part of and that this "situation" is central to criticality. A "situation" is, after Deleuze, of the order of an "event," involving an interplay of differences repetitively.[23] A situation is not a form with qualities; it instead demands a response, according to James Corner.[24] To this it would be added that the situation is engaged in many ways: through a "hunch"; in interpretation, judgment, or speculation; in the imaginative leap; through the emergence of a problem; through a proposition; through acts of appropriation; through engaging in typology and "events"; and through design acts themselves. These are repetitive acts, involving repetitive moments. Such design acts also involve a "propositional moment," which Deleuze terms the "possible." It is when the development of the possible develops upon the virtual simultaneously that the "new" results. Without an exploration of the virtual the exploration of the "possible" will collapse, as it tends to in the "architectural," into the "actual or scenographic," the look of the new.

In concrete practice it is the connection between any act and the repetitive that makes sense of any act, makes it resonate, gives it force. It is the resonance between these that nurtures them all and the whole of design. The repetitive involves an affect that makes instant connections across different dimensions, concrete and abstract. The fascination of the scenographic obscures the affectual, "intuitive," and connective nature of repetition. Without a "disciplined practice," design and intuition only have a *haphazard* relation to the world.

COWBOY CRITICALITY

However, disciplined practices occur only through actual practices, and the actual practices of Room 4.1.3 seem to exceed the theories and tendencies of the "architectural" presentation. This excess reflects what could be called a type of "cowboy critical" that occurs through a unique intensity and style of design development—involving conceptual brainstorming, parallel formal and graphic development, an inseparable wider art of practice, and, in the case of the National Museum, a productive alignment with ARM. This involves a discipline where the intensity and endless creativity of it seem to transcend some of the common deficiencies of the haphazard and the volunteered theory. The *haphazard* starts to hum through intensity.

In terms of simulacra it might be fair to say that the Baudrillardian notion of simulacra misses entirely the value of Room 4.1.3's work. Deleuze's notion of the "*artificial*" would be more apt. "The artificial is always a copy of a copy, which should be pushed to the point where it changes its nature and is reversed into the simulacrum."[25] The garden surface seems to achieve, to use Weller's words, a kind of "uncanny virtual reality." Using copies of supposed clichés, Room 4.1.3 seems to have built the affect of the image, thus achieving a foreignness that is little about clichés. Almost unmentioned is that this seems achieved through connecting to other connections already made, already "appropriated," largely "through" the architecture, including the choice of the detached interior condition of the Garden of Australian Dreams, which turns its back on the "attraction" of the lake outside.

This detachment is central to the rigorous construction of a faux-Hyperreal condition. This is a kind of space abstracted from the world, thus connecting with more abstracted aspects of the world, including inseparably, the image-world. The lowness of the surrounding buildings and sharp horizon line blocking out the middle and distant landscape thus connect the unusually expansive and open ground plane to the vast sky. This openness is accentuated by the lack of the normal microclimatic and vegetal comfort of a courtyard. The scale of the map space and the up-buckling of the ground plane intensify the body-sky and scenic relation to the ground plane further, and the sun-sky in return intensifies the virtual-look of the ground. The intensity of the ground plane graphic is further intensified by a restraint in the detailing. This apparent rigor goes way beyond the notion of the Hyperreal.

There is something "antipodean" about the style of the design development of Room 4.1.3: a playfully serious and skeptical disregard for the ponderousness of authority which, strangely enough, does not exist anywhere else in built landscape architecture, yet also reflects a wider local ethos. The positive energy of this local skepticism has been distilled into an ambition and discipline seemingly brought on by having to build. The weakness of the Room 4.1.3 antipodean theory is its exclusivity. A fully antipodean landscape would be one where the image-world is but one dimension and is transformed by the others.

1   Its lineage no doubt goes back to the scenic side of the pre-twentieth-century picturesque, and can be traced through such things as site-planning techniques, Gordon Cullen's Streetscape, the "art" landscapes of 1980s Americans, the famous La Villette schemes, the Dutch in general, and recent digital landscape design. Something of this model is central to virtually all landscape architecture.

2   Martin Jay, *Downcast Eyes: The Denigration of Vision in Twentieth-Century French Thought* (Berkeley: University of California Press, 1993). Similarly, the "actual" is the Deleuzian term that signifies the component of the world that we already know/assume/see/remember, etc. Things, clichés, etc.

3   Amy Thorpe, "Version to Version: Ashton Raggatt McDougall's Architecture Revisited for a New Landscape," *KERB: Journal of Landscape Architecture* no. 5 (1998), p. 33.

4   Margaret McAvin, et. al. "Landscape Architecture and Critical Inquiry," introduction by Margaret McAvin; papers by Elizabeth K. Meyer, James Corner, Hamid Shirvani, and Kenneth Helphand; responses by Robert Riley and Robert Scarfo, *Landscape Journal*, 10, no. 2 (fall 1992), pp. 155–172. Richard Weller reminded me of this piece.

5   Collaborators with Room 4.1.3 on the National Museum of Australia.

6   Thorpe, "Version to Version," pp. 23–33.

7   Deleuze regards Plato as starting the whole Western history of representation through being interested in distinguishing the copy from the simulacrum.

8   Whether an original and Plato's notion of the idea can be regarded as equivalent is questionable.

9   Deleuze is critical of "signifier enthusiasts." For Deleuze the Hyperreal is a "mundane amorphous atmospheric continuum" where what carries the signifier is only a medium for the signifier. Such a model is based on linguistic ideas, and "it appears difficult to analyze semiotic systems in themselves: there is always a form of content that is simultaneously inseparable from and independent of the form of expression, and the two forms pertain to assemblages that are not principally linguistic." "There is such diversity in the forms of expression, such mixtures of these forms, that it is impossible to attach any particular privilege to the form or regime of the signifier.'" The regime of the signifier is only one amongst others and "not the most important one." Gilles Deleuze and Félix Guattari, *A Thousand Plateaus* (London: Athlone Press, 1988), pp. 111–115. Also Claire Colebrook, *Gilles Deleuze* (London: Routledge, 2002), pp. 97–99.

10 As Deleuze says "Nature is not attributive, but rather conjunctive." Gilles Deleuze, *The Logic of Sense*, trans. Mark Lester (New York: Columbia University Press, 1990), p. 267.

11 Ibid., p. 257.

12 Colebrook, *Gilles Deleuze*, pp. 97–99.

13 Even if the Hyperreal is disconnected from some lost origin, it shares the characteristic of a denial of the "virtual" within the "actual."

14 As discussed extensively in Gilles Deleuze, *Difference and Repetition*, trans. Paul Patton (London: Athlone, 1994).

15 Space and time are inseparable, and once we move beyond the conventional and modern theoretical separation of them, the reintroduction of time produces what Deleuze terms the "spiritualisation of space." Time is not expressed as dynamism or movement, as most architectural theorists–and some landscape architects, such as Tschumi–seem to understand the notion of "event."

16 Beth Meyer identified that landscape difference involved a complex of relationships, and that engaging in relationships was central to criticality. However, relationships are infinite by definition, and she was unable to say how to engage in such relationships in design.

17 The "nineties" was valuable for being the era of privileging the productivity of the "architectural."

18 Architectural practice has its own unique ways to engage with found difference through the "narrowness" of architectural construction via typology.

19 Rossi is instrumental in bringing typology back, from its functionalized obscurity within modernism, into the architectural spotlight. It would appear that the Deleuzian emphasis on the mutually entwined nature of the actual and virtual has much to offer a theory of typology. However, Deleuzian inspired architectural theorists, such as Sanford Kwinter, seem to privilege events over type, not foregrounding that type only functions eventmentally, through time.

20 The most publicized notion of typology in landscape architecture, that of Patrick Condon, is hopelessly essentialist and says very little about difference. It assumes that just by repeating the supposed form of a type, some sort of "golden glow" follows. The graduate program at the Royal Melbourne Institute of Technology under the author has developed an alternative model of typology that escapes the limitations of such a model.

21 Brian Massumi notes that recent cultural theory does not have very developed means to engage in the affectual and that it may be that this so-called postmodernity is distinctly affectual, despite the theoretical inclination having been distinctly on the significatory, identity, and meaning. Refer to Massumi's essay in Paul Patton, Deleuze: *A Critical Reader* (Oxford: Blackwell, 1996).

22 McAvin et al., "Landscape Architecture and Critical Inquiry."

23 See Deleuze's discussion of the problem in *Difference and Repetition*. For Deleuze a problem is not something you solve with a received set of tools, but is a repetitive phenomenon, where the "conditions" that produce a problem are also the source of the new, of solutions.

24 Corner identifies that criticality "arises, responds, and adapts in relation to specific situations and needs." James Corner, "Critical Thinking and Landscape Architecture," in McAvin et al., "Landscape Architecture and Critical Inquiry," p. 161.

25 Richard Weller, "Mapping the Nation," in Dimity Reed, ed., *Tangled Destinies: The National Museum of Australia* (Melbourne: Images Publishing, 2002), p. 134.

VII. LANDMARKS

Voss's Garden
Centennial Park, Sydney 1998

Centennial Park is Sydney's premier public park. In 1900 the picturesque park was the setting for the inaugural celebrations of the birth
of Australia, a nation formed from an amalgamation of the colonies
of Western Australia, Victoria, New South Wales, Queensland, and
South Australia. In 1998 an open design competition called upon
landscape architects to symbolically commemorate the nation's
centenary at its ceremonial birthplace and simultaneously improve a
degraded corner of the park.

In addition to using the languages of landscape design to edify the
nation, competitors were also asked to address the site's ecology as
the head of a large water catchment. Our solution to these symbolic
and pragmatic conditions was to locate a 50-by-50-meter enclosed
garden (hortus conclusus) as a rarefied, allegorical space in the midst
of an island, around which the entire site was devoted exclusively
to an artificial wetland designed to filter the water from the park's
larger catchments.

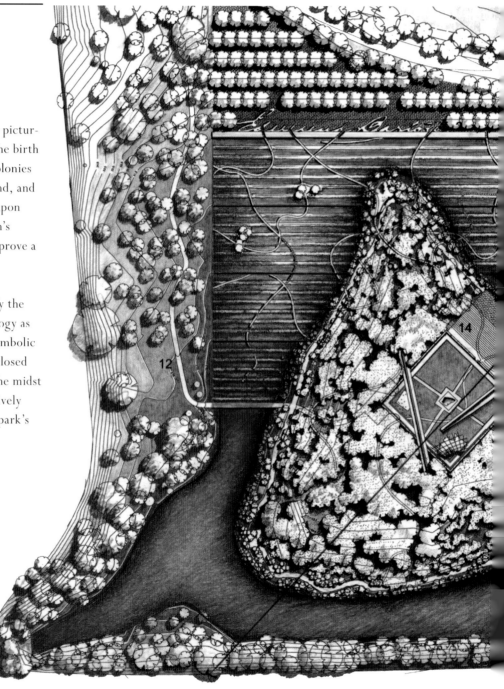

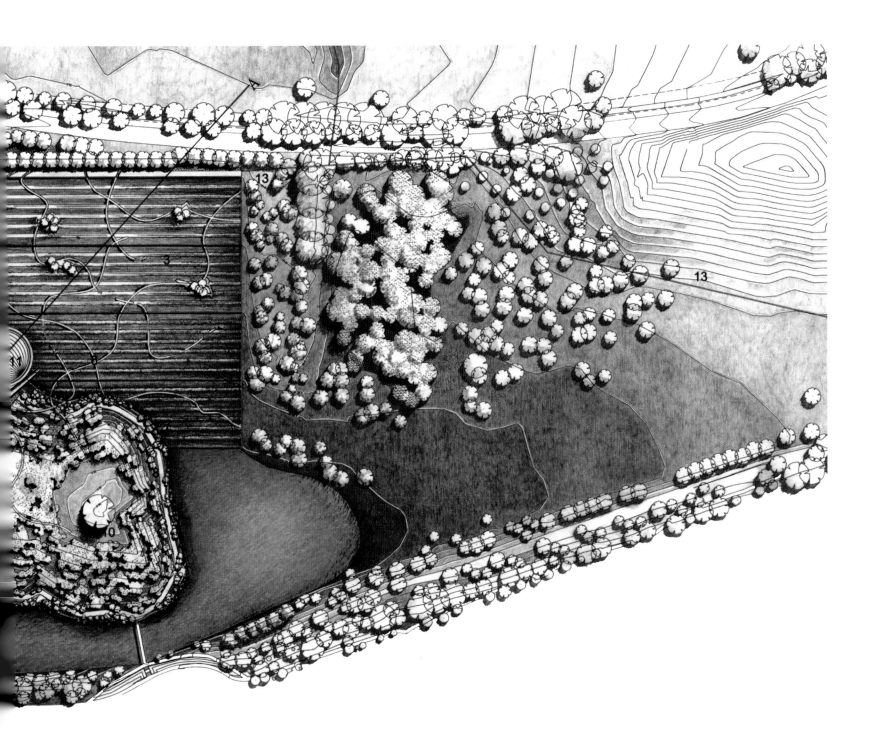

The Garden

In Australia, an enclosed manicured garden is a potent symbol of Christian colonialism and contemporary suburbia. In trying to embody the contradictions of Australia through the agency of the garden, we wanted first to build a perfect and puritanical version of a western European Christian garden, and then undermine it. That is, after setting out the traditional locus of an orthogonally organized and clearly framed garden, rather than placing a fountain or a tree at its center, we have carved out an 8-meter-wide hole.

The hole in the center of the garden is a finely stepped sculptural form made from an accurate CAD (computer-aided design) contour model of a part of the ranges in the real, central Australian landscape. The landform from central Australia has thus been scaled and inverted beneath the surface area of the garden, so as to leave a negative impression. The hole in the center of the garden can be understood as an absence, even a grave, but so, too, it is a crucible.

In this sense the broader sublime landscape is folded into the confine of the garden within the park. Symbolically this is to carve out a space in Christian accounts of Genesis as personified by the garden, eroding it with the forms of a landscape that indigenous people perceive as traces of a different creation.

This new *axis mundi* of the garden is formed in raku clay and fired in situ for three days so that a rich array of glazes is baked into its surface. The hole can contain a shallow pool of water or be drained and used as a fireplace.

In the expectation that this well-turfed open space in the center of the island becomes a destination, the garden includes an outdoor kitchen and wooden banquet table. The table is 72 meters long, specifically so as to comfortably seat 273 people–the number of different cultures currently coexisting in Australia. At the table, the big, abstract themes of national identity that this design competition expected us to negotiate are placed into the laps of strangers, who, even if at opposite ends of the table, will have trouble ignoring one another. Additionally, to satisfy the brief's desire for botanic representation, a long planting bed contains a transect of species endemic to this landscape.

The *giardino segreto* of the project is a soundscape, an aural landscape architecture, orchestrated by the artist and writer Paul Carter. Along anastomotic paths that wander with calligraphic abandon out of the garden into the wetland, Carter proposes to weave site-specific sounds and texts which offer subtexts to the official tones of Federation celebrations.

Finally, the garden draws its name from the novel *Voss* by the Australian writer Patrick White, who lived directly adjacent to the site in question. Also, Voss, the central character of the book, which is based on the life of the explorer Ludwig Leichardt, makes an epic journey from the Australian coast into the desert and ultimately to his own psychological and physical oblivion.

MODEL BY STEPHEN VIGILANTE.

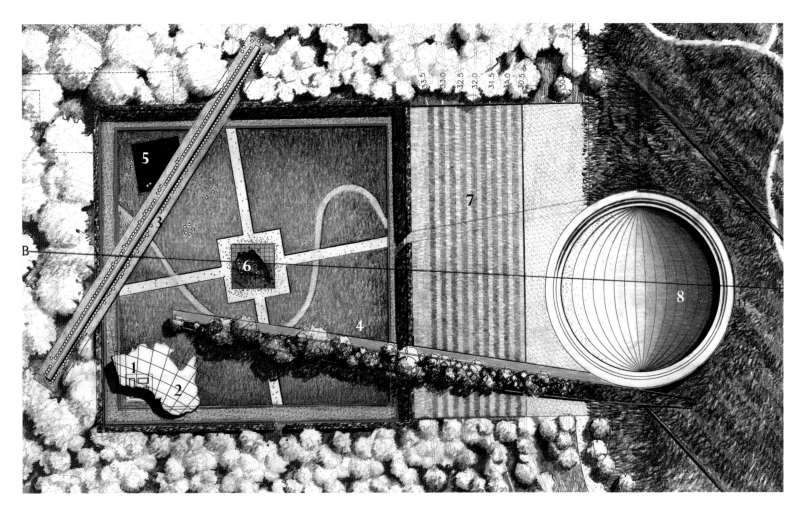

1. Kitchen
2. Shade Structure
3. Pine Banquet Table
4. Botanic Time Line (Ha Ha)
5. Xanthorrhoea australis
6. Fireplace
7. Grass Terraces
8. Tidal Pool

THE WETLAND

The wetland surrounding the island is formed by cut, and the island is formed by fill. Following specifications from the University of Western Australia's Centre for Water Research, the wetland is a serious attempt to design a landscape system that would effectively cleanse the water before it leaves the site and enters Botany Bay, an area already suffering high levels of water-borne pollutants.

Along the northern edge of the design, the water from the park's broader catchment is collected and then dispersed along a 350-meter trough. According to an even distribution, the water slowly filters out and begins to trickle over undulating linear earthworks in which formal bands of wetland plants are cultivated. Viewed from surrounding park, the grasses of the wetland appear en masse as a naturalistic swampland, recalling the original character of this site. From side and interior views, however, the design reveals itself as a mechanistic filter.

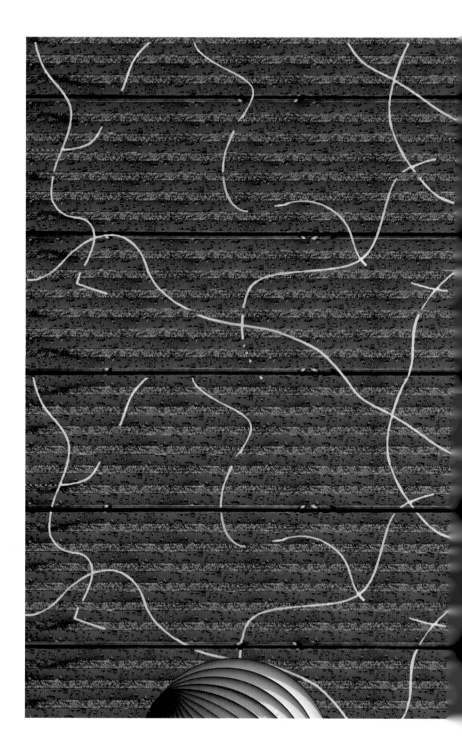

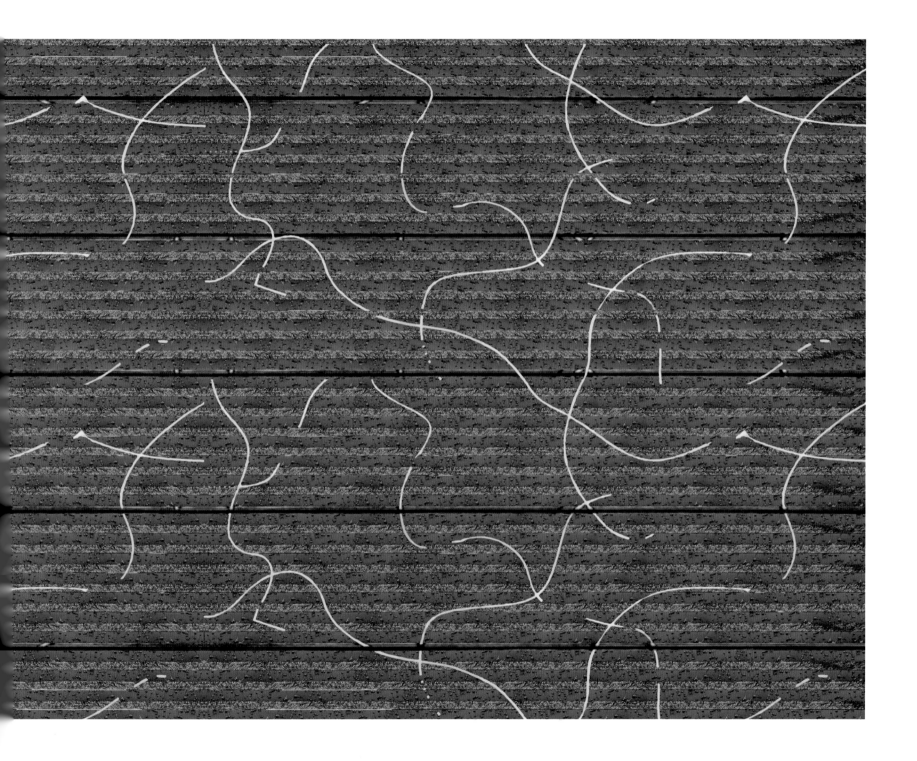

The Tidal Pool

In the wetland, at the edge of the island, is also proposed a water feature based on the lunar calendar. This embodiment of the moon and its cycles is something we have wanted to build for a long time and appears in other projects (see the Memorial to Fallen Bodies, page 124). The terraced pool mimics the appearance of the moon in the sky by an ebb and flow of water over its elliptical terraces. It is a gravitational point in our overall scheme, heralding water as the site's most distinctive feature.

But what has it to do with Australian Federation? The moon landing was perhaps this century's most humbling and ennobling event—not only because of the technological prowess needed to get there but because of the views back to our earth, views of a fragile ecosystem transcending nationalism. So while our work is specific to Australian history and identity, the water body implies global culture. Indeed, this project is saying that a nation that celebrates its founding, both by focusing on its own internal contradictions and simultaneously transcending its national boundaries, is surely a nation suited to the twenty-first century.

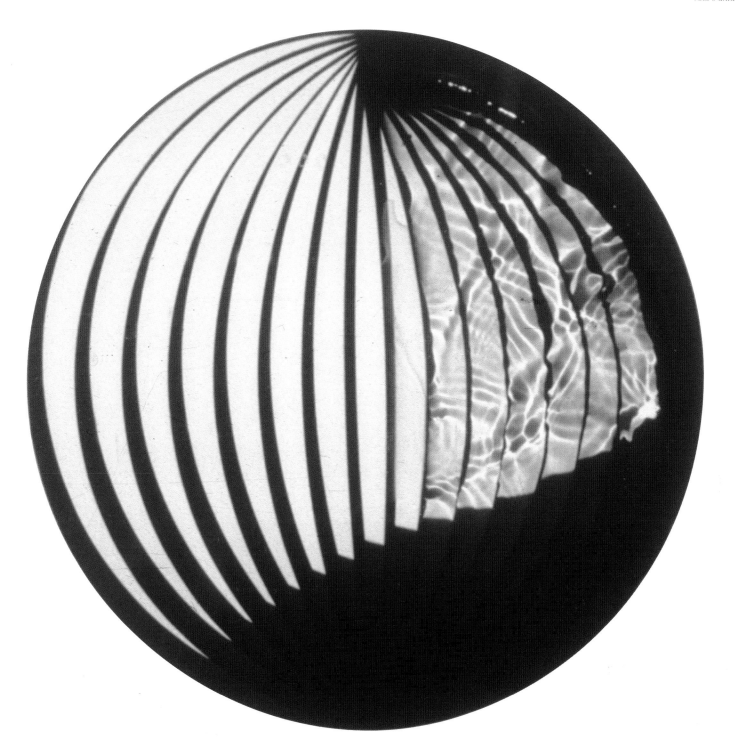

RECONCILIATION PLACE

CANBERRA 2001

"Reconciliation" is the rubric of race relations in Australia. As a historical theme and a political process, reconciliation is the most vexed issue in Australian cultural life today, an issue fraught with shame, misunderstanding, and fundamental political differences. It seems the nation's sense of self depends upon how, or even if, reconciliation unfolds.

Reconciliation Place, a design competition in Canberra (the nation's capital) for the creation of a place that would be part of this unfolding, was quickly criticized as mere symbolism. True enough; yet, in the nation's capital, on the grand, main axis to its Parliament, adjacent to the High Court, the National Library, and the National Art Gallery, symbolism matters.

Fundamental to the complex process of reconciliation is the simple fact that both indigenous and nonindigenous cultural histories are passionately vested in the land and that the nation's moral, spiritual, and ecological future depends largely on its shared management. In wanting to provide a profoundly simple and resonant embodiment of the land as common ground, we found ourselves returning to our propositions for the Potsdamer Platz and the Spreebogen.

That is, set out in a space 30 meters wide and 130 meters long across the main axis of Canberra are samples of the 150 different soils that make up the landmass of Australia. The soils, sands, and gravels are mixed with a polymer to form a durable, secure, and multifunctional surface. The rich array of textures and colors presents an ecological and cultural spectrum, the bedrock and topsoil of a nation. The spectrum of earth concludes at either end with coastal sandstone and limestone as is the case if one takes a geological transect across Australia.

As is also the case with the Australian landmass, in this designed microcosm the spectrum shifts to deep red earths in the center. There a preordained ramp from the recently constructed Commonwealth Place on Lake Burley Griffin arrives at Reconciliation Place. Our scheme neatly represents a semantic shift from Commonwealth Place to Common Ground, a shift from colonial to postcolonial. The proposed Common Ground *must* be traversed no matter which of the several circulation routes one takes through the site in order to reach the adjoining National Library, High Court, and National Gallery. Two long, dark axes lead to Reconciliation Place from either direction.

The process of collecting the soil samples is to be a rich story of reconciliation in itself. All Australians are represented by the samples, and every sample *must* only be gained with permission from traditional Aboriginal custodians and negotiated as to where the earth is best taken from and in what manner this is done. In this sense the nationwide process necessary to make Reconciliation Place symbolically reproaches a history of taking and abusing land. The process of making Reconciliation Place will be documented and exhibited in two pavilions at either end of the site.

This design for Reconciliation Place is potentially rich in story and simple in form.

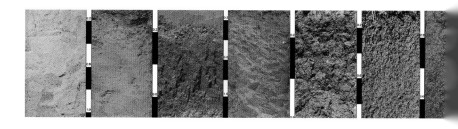

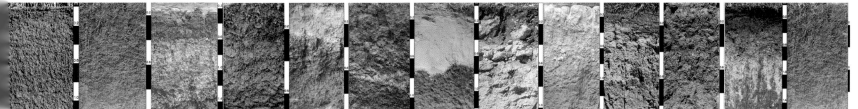

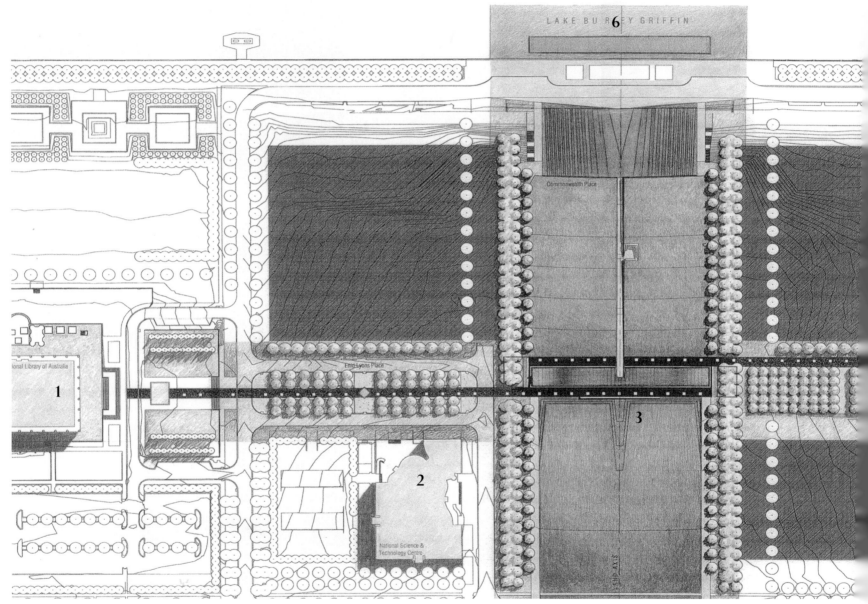

LAKE BURLEY GRIFFIN

1. NATIONAL LIBRARY OF AUSTRALIA
2. NATIONAL SCIENCE AND TECHNOLOGY CENTRE
3. RECONCILIATION PLACE
4. HIGH COURT OF AUSTRALIA
5. NATIONAL GALLERY OF AUSTRALIA
6. LAKE BURLEY GRIFFIN

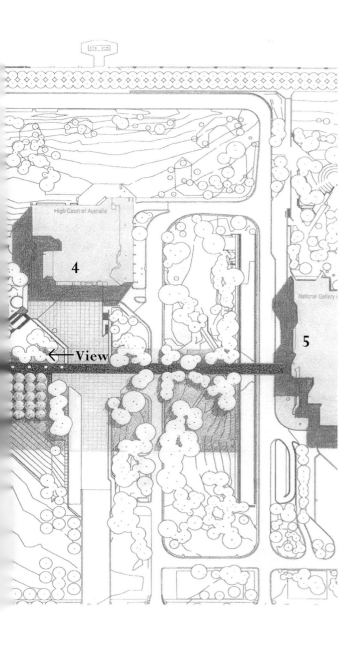

Federation Garden

Sydney 2001

On the occasion of Australia's Federation celebrations and commissioned by the New South Wales Historic Houses Trust, this design competition called for landscape designs which would not only express Australia's sociopolitical history but also reorganize a neglected area of the hallowed grounds of Sydney's Government House, the residence of the governor of New South Wales.

The winning idea is this.

The scheme threads a new picturesque circuit through the site. Interrupting this picturesque route is a large granite slab tilted up out of the ground. From under the slab a fine rill of water flows off into the distance and disappears behind some trees and shrubs. Upon the surface of the slab is a brass plaque explaining that visitors should follow the flow of water and that it will lead into a secret garden.

The secret garden is a simple "green room," 8 by 8 meters square, made from high, thick hedges. Parts of the room's green walls can be adjusted, and fiber optics convert it into a luminous lantern at night.

At the entrance to the room are two large (Grecian) urns; one is full of black pebbles and the other full of white ones. The plaque invites visitors to select a black or white pebble and enter the green room. The plaque suggests they throw their chosen pebble into a large pool of water, as in a wishing well. The water from the rill that leads to the garden spills into this pool.

The plaque also briefly explains that the simple action of selecting a pebble recalls the ancient Greek method of voting on the issues of the day. One might also note that the urns containing the black and white pebbles sit in squares of terra-cotta fragments. These fragments (ostroika) are the same as those upon which the Greeks would inscribe the name of a political figure to be ostracized from the polis.

For those wishing to stay after they have "cast their vote," there is a 7-meter-long solid stone seat. The seat is made by selecting the highest quality stone from each state and territory of Australia and then joining them exactly according to the shapes by which the states and territories are joined on a map of Australia. Visitors then leave the garden by a small gap in the hedges and continue on their picturesque circuit.

This small intervention in Sydney's Government House not only recalls Western political traditions and reminds visitors that Australia was formed mainly by the vote, not violence, but it is also mindful of the fact that indigenous Australians were ostracized from the political processes of much of the history of our first hundred years of Federation. Moreover, the design continues a tradition of classical references in gardenesque antipodean follies and revisits the garden as a site of moral coding and choice.

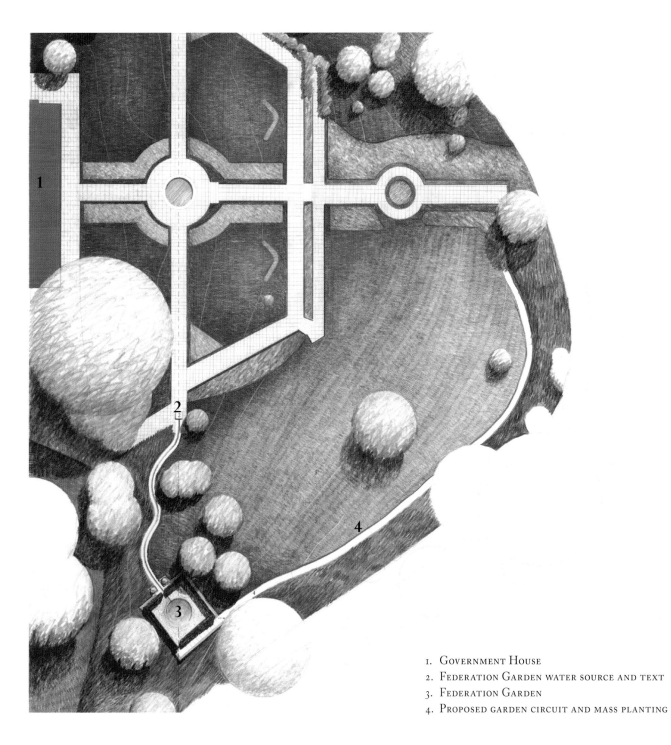

1. GOVERNMENT HOUSE
2. FEDERATION GARDEN WATER SOURCE AND TEXT
3. FEDERATION GARDEN
4. PROPOSED GARDEN CIRCUIT AND MASS PLANTING

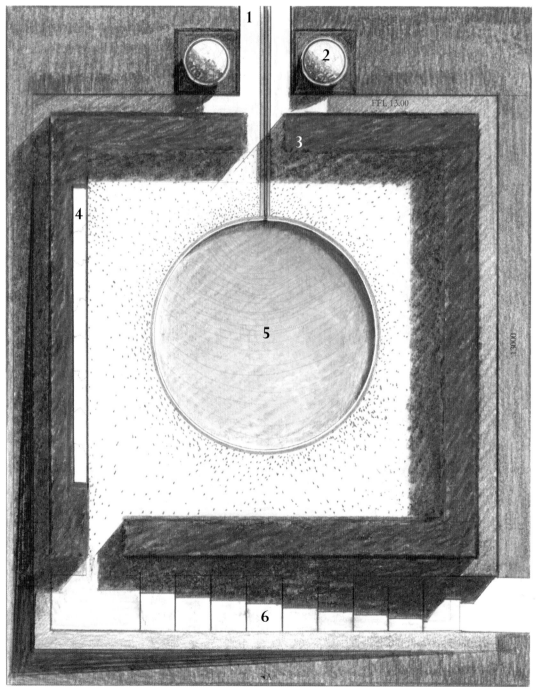

1. Bronze water rill set in stone in decomposed granite path
2. Bronze urns containing black and white pebbles standing on sandstone pedestals in squares of terracotta fragments
3. Mature hedge walls
4. Seat comprised of stone from each Australian state and territory
5. Bronze and black granite wishing well
6. Steps to broader garden circuit

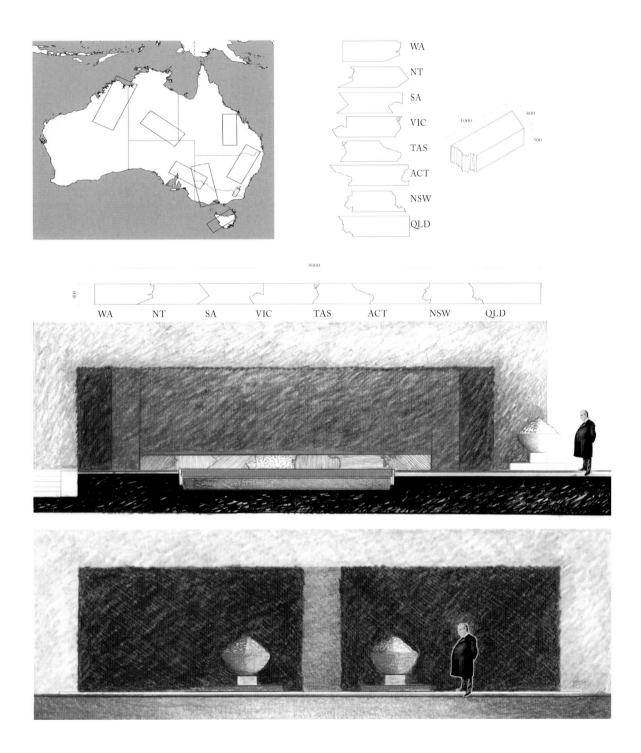

The National Museum of Australia
Canberra 1997–2001

In association with the architects Ashton Raggatt McDougall (ARM) and Robert Peck von Hartel Trethowan, Room 4.1.3 won the competition for the National Museum of Australia and the Australian Institute of Aboriginal and Torres Strait Islander Studies (AITSIS) sited on the Acton Peninsula in Canberra, in 1997. Completed on budget and on time, the project was opened in May 2001 by the prime minister of Australia, John Howard. The project has caused considerable controversy.

Introduction

Prominent projects such as national museums are expected to be educational narratives, tourist attractions, academic texts, and crystallizations of contemporary design discourse. Something for everyone, they are also self-consciously set down for posterity and must at some level engage with the aesthetic and ideological risks of national edification.

This national museum's thematic trinity is Land, People, and Nation. In popular culture, economy, and the fine arts, Australians have drawn on landscape as the prime referent for their identity. How this will continue to be so is dependant upon the landscape(s) Australians decide to construct in the light and shadow of rubrics such as postcolonialism, environmentalism, and globalism, an emergent triad that will surely dominate the next century of Federation. In short, the landscape is no longer a given—it is by design. Landscape architecture then should be expected to speak to us of these shifting conditions. Indeed, Land, People, and Nation can no longer be approached reductively.

View of the National Museum of Australia sited on the Acton Peninsula, Lake Burley Griffin, Canberra, Australia.

In retrospect, we have learned that the creation of Australia began not with seamless mapping, but with an almost impossible super-imposition of old world landscape mirages on strange terrain. For some, the strange was not sublime or noble, but monstrous. Hence the Aborigines, in resisting the impossible social contract they were presented, were cast outside the economy of salvation. Eyes versed in the picturesque simply could not "see" the landscape and its origi-nal people.[1]

The project of European modernity suddenly and violently collided with the deep time and vast space of Australia in 1788. Ever since, compromises have been hard won. Now, insofar as Australia is tech-nologically managed and aesthetically known, it has been made into a garden, that is, domestic space. It follows, then, that the popular Australian euphemism for blissful ignorance "not in my backyard" is not a model of twenty-first century citizenship, something a trip to the museum will confirm.

Not only is Australia domesticated in the sense that technology can scan all terrain, but more so in the sense that the domestic is a con-dition characterized by repression or fear of the other. Indigenous culture, guardian of a vast ancient archive of maps interweaving every detail of Australia into a flow of spirit, was temporarily written out of history, effectively banished from the garden. This uncanny reenactment of Christian lore coincides with the notion that there must have been a second creation, for otherwise how could Australia possibly have been so monstrously different from Europe. Now the mute, blank page of *terra nullius* (the legal doctrine of an empty place prior to British colonization) suddenly becomes blotting paper, and the bloodstains of history take form.[2]

In the vernacular the land is simplified and mythologized as beach, suburbia, city, bush, and outback. However, recent maps show com-plex mosaics of bioregions while others show the wandering lines of more than three hundred Aboriginal nations. Both significantly complicate the nation's relatively simple cartographic self-image. Furthermore, contemporary Australia is an amalgam of more than two hundred cultures which have coalesced here in greatest numbers during the calamitous course of the twentieth century.

At the close of this century in a nation of such exemplary diversity, networked into a global sense of the local, one wonders to what extent the Australian landscape can continue as a stable or preemi-nent register of immigrant identities? Nonetheless, all immigrants adopt the new country and therefore inherit its cultural and natural history, which is to say they inherit the landscape and its meanings. Even if the land is no longer a stable reflection of our progress and fewer people actually work the soil, the nation's grounding in eco-logical and metaphysical terms will remain considerably landscape based for several reasons.

First, the presence of landscape no matter where one is in Australia is strong. It leaks through large gaps in most Australian efforts at town planning. This presence also bears deep time and its ghosts.

Second, Australian history is, if not a sociopolitical epic, then cer-tainly a monumental collision of modernity and environment, so any future history is constructed upon that ubiquitous ecological condi-tion. This is also aesthetic, for the shrapnel is everywhere. Austra-lian developments seem out of place, unlike in Europe where culture and nature appear on the surface to have resolved their differences in the acquiescence of the garden.

Third, much of Australia's ways of life are bound into the vigorous use of open space. It is an outdoors nation with a healthy disrespect for architectural enclosure and its authority, with a love of its more picturesque settings only surpassed by the devotion applied to its private gardens. Indeed, many mistakenly think a backyard is a birthright.

Fourth, Australia's ecosystems are ravaged, its farms exhausted, and its cities have spread too far to make sense. The equation of people to place is now unbalanced. It is well known and well documented that the Australian landscape mocks settlement and quietly destroys those who break its rules. Environmental metaphors tend to victimize "nature" or see it fighting back, but in Australia the land simply salinates and slips into oblivion.

Finally, white and black Australia can reconcile only where land is involved.

Thus the nation's fate will continue to be bound up in how it legislates, manages, and represents its various landscapes and built environments. The manner in which this is conducted is in no small part dependent on how the nation represents and confronts its history. If the landscape is to be an honest register of identity, then the ground needs to be constantly scrutinized and rewritten. Shifting cultural constructions of landscape need be ongoing, for otherwise lies become truths. The design for the landscape and architecture of the National Museum of Australia has been concerned to creatively embody shifting cultural constructions of landscape and identity.

CANBERRA

Canberra is affected by two landscape styles, both of which are key signatures of power. One is traceable to the British picturesque, whereby the small prototypes of places like Stourhead have been writ large in the artifice of Lake Burley Griffin and the placement of buildings within landscape "scenes" that mark out a nationalist narrative. The second style is that of the Cartesian, whereby strict axial structures such as found in Versailles and Washington literally direct the city of Canberra toward major local landscape features. Not only that, the axes emanating from the Federal Parliament (Capitol Hill) in Canberra were also intended to align with the nation's other far-flung state capitals (Perth, Sydney, Adelaide, Melbourne, and

MAP OF ABORIGINAL AUSTRALIA ACCORDING TO THE LINGUISTIC BOUNDARIES OF INDIGENOUS AUSTRALIANS PRIOR TO WHITE SETTLEMENT. THIS MAP IS LARGELY BASED ON THE RESEARCH OF NORMAN B. TINDALE. MAP CREATED BY DAVID R. HORTON, PUBLISHED BY ABORIGINAL STUDIES PRESS, AIATSIS, CANBERRA. (THIS MAP INDICATES ONLY THE GENERAL LOCATION OF LARGER GROUPINGS OF PEOPLE, WHICH MAY INCLUDE SMALLER GROUPS SUCH AS CLANS, DIALECTS, OR INDIVIDUAL LANGUAGES IN A GROUP. BOUNDARIES ARE NOT INTENDED TO BE EXACT. FOR MORE INFORMATION ABOUT THE GROUPS OF PEOPLE IN A PARTICULAR REGION CONTACT THE RELEVANT LAND COUNCILS.)

DIAGRAM SHOWING THE AXES OF WALTER BURLEY GRIFFIN'S MASTER PLAN RADIATING OUT FROM CAPITOL HILL TOWARD THE NATION'S STATE CAPITALS.

Hobart), in this sense inscribing a (meta)physical geomancy out from the nation's prosthetic heart.

If Walter Burley Griffin sought the best of British in elevation, and the best of the French in plan, then he was also obsessed with the indigenous landscape, although it was to remain as a backdrop to Australia's continued allegiance to the Crown (England). Griffin's Canberra, set out in 1912, is a stiff but nonetheless grand attempt at a synthesis of the three, an inspired effort to interweave the warps and wefts of urban structure with the existing topography.[3]

For Griffin this may have constituted a grand dialectic with a view to achieving a higher synthesis between culture and nature, the nation and its landscape, the old world and the new. But now, at the beginning of the twenty-first century, the awesome Australian landscape, which he wanted the nation to kneel before, is somewhat harder to romanticize as capable of redeeming modernity's spiritual exhaustion or correcting its technological excesses.

BENDING THE RULES

The brief for the design of the National Museum provided a neat diagram of how one could symmetrically extend Griffin's existing mandala so that it would provide straight guidelines for the new developments on the Acton Peninsula. As an initial design generator, these axes have been playfully bent, stretched, and knotted into one another.[4]

The notion of the knot, or just the idea of a single straight line being turned into a tangle, lends itself to metaphor and rhetoric. Indeed, a line looping back onto itself can be understood as denoting a condition of *feedback*, a process crucial to the self-organizing of complex systems. This is contrary to the linear logic of *trajectory* described by the mechanics of ballistics which organized landscape designs such as the infamous Versailles. Furthermore, as Howard Raggatt, architect and principal of ARM, has elsewhere commented, a knotted line

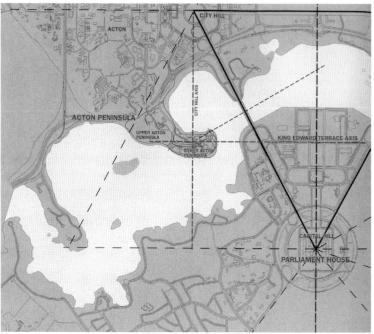

THE GUIDELINES FROM THE INITIAL BRIEF FOR THE MUSEUM WHICH EXTEND GRIFFIN'S GEOMANCY SO AS TO CROSS THE ACTON PENINSULA.

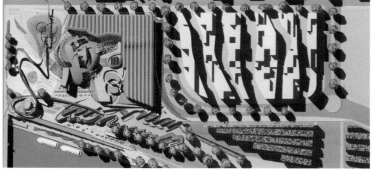

FEDERATION SQUARE. ASHTON RAGGATT MCDOUGALL IN ASSOCIATION WITH ROOM 4.1.3. COURTESY OF ASHTON RAGGATT MCDOUGALL.

returning and bending back upon itself traces a dance rather than the straight line's march of progress. This teasing of intersecting axes is also to approach modernity at its profane center, the intersection of X and Y axes, the graticule that binds the Cartesian matrix.

If this manipulation of straight lines into wandering tangled forms posits architecture as *knot* then it follows that landscape can be thought of as an extended fabric, a conversation ARM and Room 4.1.3 began back at Federation Square in 1997. To think of architecture as *knot* and landscape as *fabric* is to reimagine architecture and landscape as coextensive rather than emblems of culture and nature juxtaposed.[5] It is common parlance to speak of urban fabric, and so designed places, especially cultural clots like museums, can be understood as complex knots (built and semiotic), intensifications emerging from the material and immaterial fabric of the broader landscape. The metaphors of knot and fabric also served our purposes of moving beyond the normative Canberran typology of architecture as a monumental modernist object set in an aloof spread of grass and trees, a forlorn apologia for arcadia, something not dissimilar to what one finds in Washington, D.C.

The warp and weft of these metaphorical moves also sidestep the Australian vernacular impasse of architecture and landscape cojoining only in the form of well-crafted hut lightly poised in a bush setting, a previous and, for many, a more appropriate symbolic incarnation of this national institution.[6] Indeed, it is the kangaroo-like master of "touching the earth lightly," Glenn Murcutt, who generically represents Australian design internationally; yet it is ARM and Room 4.1.3 who, in building this museum, make "Australia" somewhat harder to package.

The weaving of axes that underpins the site planning of the National Museum generates a series of loops that become guidelines to configure the buildings and landscape spaces for the new institutions to be sited on the Acton Peninsula. These curving, interwoven lines,

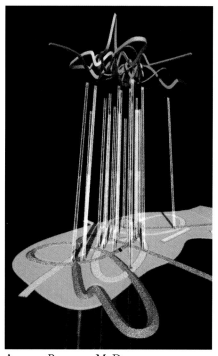

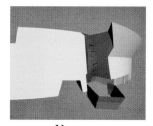

ASHTON RAGGATT McDOUGAL, THE ARCHITECTS OF THE NATIONAL MUSEUM, USED BOOLEAN THREADS TO ORGANIZE AND CARVE THROUGH ARCHITECTURAL BLOCKS. COURTESY OF ASHTON RAGGATT McDOUGALL.

VIEW INSIDE THE GREAT HALL, THE ENTRANCE SPACE TO THE NATIONAL MUSEUM OF AUSTRALIA. COURTESY OF ASHTON RAGGATT McDOUGALL.

1. National Museum of Australia
2. Garden of Australian Dreams
3. Gallery of First Australians
4. Australian Institute of Aboriginal and
   Torres Strait Islander Studies
5. Wetland
6. Carpark
7. Uluru Axis

now a consistent part of Ashton Raggatt McDougall's repertoire, are, at face value, naïve swirls, but when manipulated to create solids and voids in computer-aided design programs, they become difficult Boolean configurations. The wandering lines of the scheme, then, are not crafted mimicry of some visible aspect of nature, nor tracings of Hogarth's Line of Beauty; rather, they are generated and knotted by the algebraic logic of computation that is used to model non-Euclidean geometry.

The negative spaces and scars left by the movement of the Boolean threads through solid blocks of architectural matter are, in some moments, beautiful (if such a word can apply to this project). To enter the museum's Great Hall is to enter an extraordinarily grotto, one that owes its construction to the computer. The creation of space by such subtraction positions architecture as a trace of larger invisible forces, a traditional Western fantasy but also a distant

reminder that, for indigenous Australians, the actual landscape is a sculpted residue of events played out by mythic beings.

Calligraphy of the In Between

At Versailles, the main axis connected monarch and infinity; in Griffin's Canberra the axes connect the nation's state capitals with the federal center. As if to write further into Griffin's orientations, we have inscribed a new axis 6 meters wide and 300 meters long across the Acton Peninsula. This new axis is orientated toward Uluru, known otherwise as Ayer's Rock, a geological tourist attraction marking the metaphoric center of Australia.[7] Operating across a range of levels, Uluru operates in contemporary culture as a potent shared symbol. Uluru, a cliché for good reason, is a powerful carrier of meaning, a site of pilgrimage, politics, and taboo.

This inscription of an axis to what was otherwise turbulence leads the imagination along well trodden historic and contemporary quests

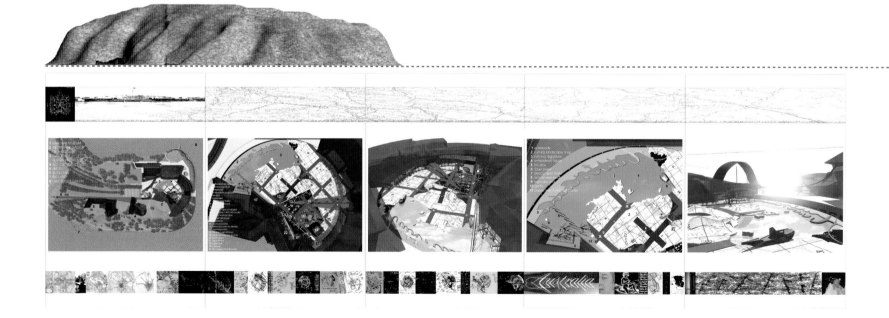

to find the heart and soul of Australia.[8] More than just a parched romance with Australia's interior, the Uluru axis brings the ancient center of the country into conversation with the nation's coastal political and bureaucratic headquarters, the icon of which is Parliament House. The dialectical conditions, which the axis refers to, are simply that Canberra is culture and the desert is nature. Canberra is monumental architecture and the desert is monumental geology. Canberra is political center and Uluru is political periphery. Canberra is, in fact, constitutional monarchy and the desert is Aboriginal law. Canberra is reason and the desert is mysticism. Canberra is picturesque and the desert is sublime. Uluru can signify a dream(ing) of spiritual kinship, and Parliament House can signify the dream of democratic modernity. Uluru cannot be seen from the site, so one expects the axis to gain a reputation and to incite by name the association of the nation's two most significant natural and cultural monuments.

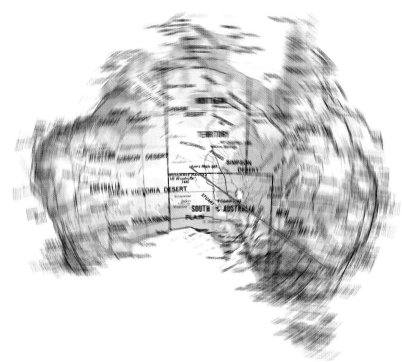

The Uluru axis (in red) links Canberra near the coast and the central Australian deserts.

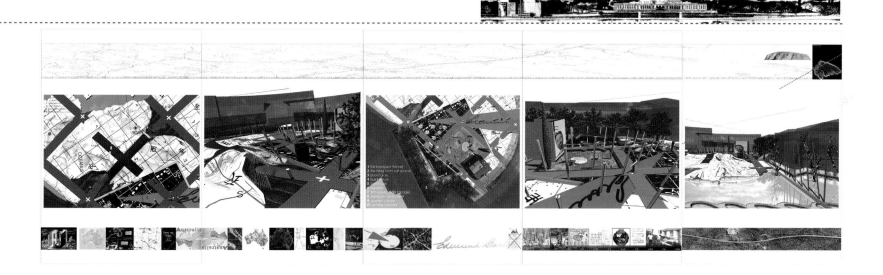

However, while linking opposite ends, an axis only really ensures a duality making nothing of it. To look at the master plan for the peninsula is to notice that the axis is partially effaced and explored by the invisible and visible Boolean threads, which guide the whole project. In plan the whole museum complex can be seen as a knot in the midst of the axis which reaches from the end to the beginning of the peninsula, from Uluru to Parliament House. The two institutions, the National Museum and the AIATSIS, that share the peninsula are thus positioned as occupying a physical and conceptual space enframed by dialectics but increasingly hybridized and emergent. In this sense, the Uluru axis, and the knotted configuration of buildings over and across it, symbolically tease out a path of Australia's introspection upon the cultural contradictions of its own history, an introspection now overshadowing the dialectic of colony and motherland, which framed much of Australia's previous history.

The most obvious signature of all this is the logo of the project, a 30-meter-high pixelated loop designed by the architects as the entrance feature of the museum. This giant loop, one of many Boolean threads that carve out the museum's architectural spaces, aligns with and can be read as an extension of the Uluru axis. After completing its carnivalesque loop, the Boolean thread hints at its larger abstract role by slicing off a portion of the main entrance and then literally disappearing into the sky. From then on we see only the leftovers of its flight through the blocks of architecture that house the museum. Unlike normal axes, which fade into perspective or fix a monument, the other end of the Uluru axis, while oriented toward the heart of the country, rises up and peels back on itself.

The Uluru axis aligns the Australian Institute of Aboriginal and Torres Strait Islander Studies. The AIATSIS building personifies the architect's reputation for appropriation and reference by copying the façade of Parliament House and attaching to that a black copy of Le Corbusier's Villa Savoye. ARM has long argued that a valid, indeed critical, method for making architecture from the periphery

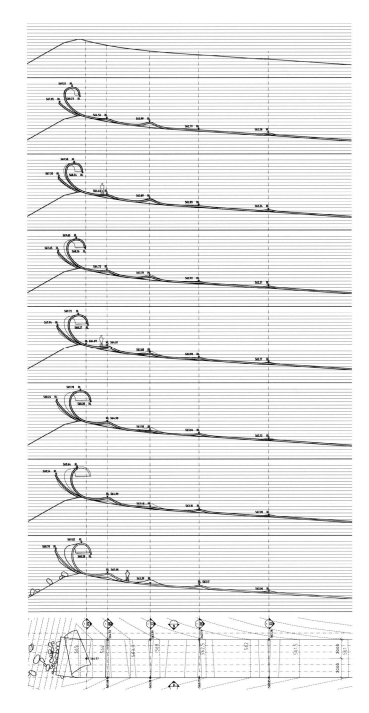

of the design world is to appropriate masterpieces and conscientiously morph and misread them in the process. Suddenly, AIATSIS is part of twentieth-century highbrow architectural history and also waves a red flag at conservative white Australian politics. Most controversially, ARM has also used Daniel Libeskind's extension to the Berlin Museum (known colloquially as the Holocaust museum) as a base map for a building entitled the Gallery of First Australians, a part of the National Museum containing the world's best collection of indigenous Australian artifacts. This black and somewhat distorted version of Libeskind's Berlin Museum constitutes almost half of the National Museum's floor space and demarcates one side of the Garden of Australian Dreams, to which we will shortly come. Reported variously as a scandalous conflation of European history with the history of Australia's race relations such loaded symbolism is not so interested in stirring journalistic controversy as it is in testing the limits of authorship, originality and architectural signage. Amy Thorpe reads it correctly when she explains that, although based on appropriation, "the resultant works are still in a sense original, creative, and authentic, but not in the traditional definition. Originality and authenticity are replaced by a reworked originality and authenticity of manipulation."[9] For its part, the landscape architecture of the National Museum utilizes similar techniques, invoking a tangle of referential connections, which tie together in the museum's central open space, the Garden of Australian Dreams.

The Garden of Australian Dreams

The Garden of Australian Dreams is not a verdant horticultural design, nor is it a set design of a "dreamscape." It is a map of Australia upon which the public can walk and read interwoven layers of information. The surface of the Garden of Australian Dreams is a richly patterned and written concrete surface, made to look like folded paper or printed fabric.

Pensively linked buildings devoted to white and black histories of Australia surround the garden's elliptical domain, and the map sur-

face stretches across to connect the two. Consequently, the garden takes on the allegorical role of representing and interweaving both the "Great Australian Dream," the ideal of acquiring a cornucopian suburban property, with the Aboriginal "Dreaming," a mystical system of mapping and a comprehensive set of creation myths vested in landscape. Both are landscape-based mythologies concerned with defining boundaries and kinship. Both are profound systems of orientation.

The garden does not, however, just accumulate artifacts that represent these two worldviews; rather, it makes a claim for a shared national cartography by overlaying and interweaving Aboriginal and English maps of the country. The two main maps used are a standard English-language map of Australia (which reveals virtually no traditional Aboriginal presence) and David Horton's map of the linguistic boundaries of indigenous Australia, which reveals Australia as a complex mosaic of more than three hundred Aboriginal tribes or nations but bears no evidence of contemporary Australia.

Instruments of power seminal to the colonial project, maps are currently Australia's most contested symbolic terrains, and politicians have been seen waving them in frustration on national television as Australia fights to reconcile its history by undoing the legal fiction of *terra nullius*, the fallacious yet convenient doctrine that Australia was an empty place upon British settlement, and work through the consequences of recognizing native title to land.

Other mapping information used to form the surface of the garden includes vegetation, soil and geology maps, electoral boundaries, maps of Australia's history of exploration, a weather map taken from Australia Day 1998, a Japanese tourist map, and various cartographic oddities such as the Dingo Fence and the Pope's Line. The Dingo Fence is the world's longest continuous structure and runs from the South Australian coast to the Queensland Coast—a few thousand kilometers of fencing to prevent wild dogs moving east. The "Pope's

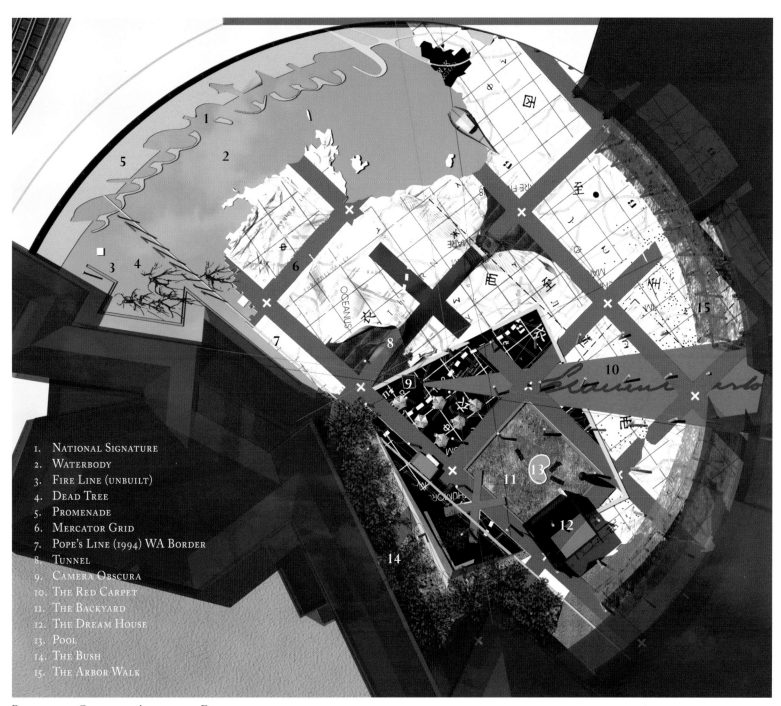

1. NATIONAL SIGNATURE
2. WATERBODY
3. FIRE LINE (UNBUILT)
4. DEAD TREE
5. PROMENADE
6. MERCATOR GRID
7. POPE'S LINE (1994) WA BORDER
8. TUNNEL
9. CAMERA OBSCURA
10. THE RED CARPET
11. THE BACKYARD
12. THE DREAM HOUSE
13. POOL
14. THE BUSH
15. THE ARBOR WALK

PLAN OF THE GARDEN OF AUSTRALIAN DREAMS.

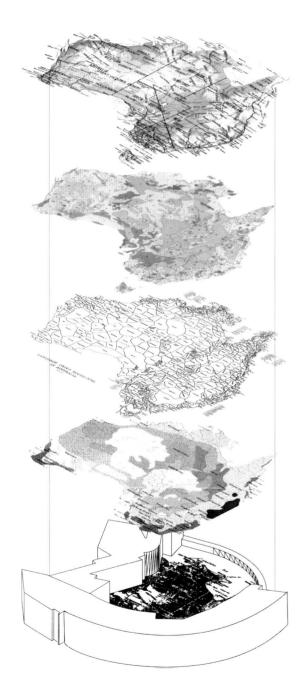

Line" is the colloquial expression for the Western Australian border, traceable to a line inscribed on a globe by the pope in 1494 to divide Spanish and Portuguese interests in world trade.[10] Some information from sites distant from the actual landmass of Australia such as a map of Gallipoli, where Australian blood was sacrificed to nationhood in World War I, is also included. Laid over all this information are two grids: the Mercator, binding the Australian continent to the world, and a local survey grid binding design ideas to design construction. Finally, in addition to maps, the word *home* has been translated into the many languages spoken in contemporary Australia and written intermittently across the surface of the whole map.

The notion of making a landscape design as a map obviously suits the idea of a garden at a national museum within the context of the nation's political and bureaucratic center, since it abstractly compresses all of Australia into its paper trails. Our interest in maps, however, stems from their representational agency, their enigmatic location between the real and the virtual. Denis Cosgrove, who, along with James Corner, has focused our attention on this enigma explains that "maps are troubling. Their apparent stability and their aesthetics of closure and finality dissolve with but a little reflection in to recognition of their partiality and provisionality, their embodiment of intention, their imaginative and creative capabilities, their mythical qualities, their appeal to reverie, their ability to record and stimulate anxiety, their silences and their powers of deception."[11]

The mapped surface provides a continuous ground sheet, but it is not always flat. In part, the ground rises up as a landform stretching the map over its topography, encouraging visitors to break from a passive walk through a museum and clamber up the map's slopes and folds to gain panoramic views in all directions across the garden. This landform also affords a tunnel underneath, so that in one brief passage visitors can pass under the layers of information which otherwise riddle the entire surface of the space. In being other to the written surface, the tunnel under the map lends itself to an aural interpreta-

PLAN OF THE GARDEN OF AUSTRALIAN DREAMS REVEALING THE COMPLEXITY OF THE FINAL MAPPED SURFACE.

tion of place and was designed with a soundscape from the writer and composer Paul Carter in mind. To date the tunnel under the map remains incomplete. Due to typical but unforeseen constraints, the map's topology and the tunnel entrances are also far from the complex, fluid folds that we originally designed. The topography of the garden was originally derived and abstracted from the landform of Shrapnel Valley in Gallipoli, a site of bloodletting and one often referred to as the birthplace of Australia as a nation.

The scale of the map is crucial, for to build a map at this size is to bring the virtual convincingly into the real and conflate the two. One footstep in this garden equates to 50 kilometers in the actual landscape, and the map stretches for almost 80 meters across the space of the garden, from Australia's southern coast to its northern interface with Asia. Inside the bubble of the equally graphic architecture, the garden space offers an uncanny virtual reality. The garden's aesthetic is intentionally one that tries to retain the artificiality of the computer images produced prior to construction.

Although there are organic elements and materials, such as some trees and water, the Garden of Australian Dreams is careful to mark itself off from much landscape design by making no mimesis of unmediated landscape. Rather, the garden re-presents copies of cultural artifacts, simulacra. It is concerned with the ways in which we come to know and perceive landscape, rather than copying the visual quality of real landscape. In this manner the garden turns attention to the cultural construction of landscape, bringing modes of seeing, mapping, and imaging the country into play.[12]

Signatures

A nation's map is an official document, a kind of social contract, and so it will often bear signatures of authority. Accordingly, the signature of Australia's first prime minister, Edmund Barton, is writ large on one arm of a large bright red X. It is (un)common knowledge that many Aboriginal people signed (and still do sign) documents with an

THE X SIGNATURE, UPON WHICH IS ALSO A COPY OF EDMUND BARTON'S SIGNATURE, THE FIRST PRIME MINISTER OF AUSTRALIA.

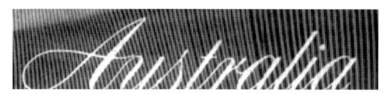

X. The X is a contradictory mark, an emblem of negation, but on a legal document it suffices as a mark of agreement. Yet, if affirmative, it is the signature of a nonidentity, one who most likely could not read or write.[13]

The X is also a mark made by all Australians when they participate in the democratic process and are asked to approve or deny a proposition being put forward by national referendum. The X is a "No" vote, a denial of change, as has most often been the case in Australian political history, although it was a "Yes" vote that formed the Australian Federation which the construction of this museum com-

memorates. Not only that, the other great "Yes" was in answer to a referendum in 1967 when white Australians overwhelmingly agreed that Aborigines, the owners of the country, should be allowed to vote so as to determine its future.

Written across 70 meters of promenade at the northern water's edge of the garden is another signature, the word *Australia*. An "n" has been added to Australia to imply a question or at least a difficult adjective, and the word has been written in mirror image, half in and half out of the water. The word has been forged from our

SIDNEY NOLAN (1917–1992), *DEATH OF CONSTABLE SCANLON* (NED KELLY SERIES), 1946, GIFT OF SUNDAY REED 1977 NATIONAL GALLERY OF AUSTRALIA, CANBERRA.

VIEW TOWARD THE CAMERA OBSCURA.

Gordon Bennett, *Myth of the Western Man (White Man's Burden)* (1992)

Detail of *The Dome* (1997) by Jeffrey Smart (Sussan Corporation).

national currency, extending a laconic tradition of Australian creativity based on forgery. Notably, Australia's first government architect, Francis Greenway, and early colonial painters such as Thomas Whatling and Joseph Lycett were convicted of forgery and hence banished to Australia. Here their art remained at least derivative, the latter straining to find the Claudian picturesque in the unruly scribbles of the Australian landscape—a landscape that, as the poet Marcus Clarke quipped, seemed to have been made by a nature just learning to write.

And so, from the museum's entry concourse people can look down at the water's edge and read the word *Australian* reflected, whereas shifting ground-level perspectives will offer oblique visions of nonsensical scribble fading in to the distance. The capital letter A that begins the nation's title is scrawled across Cape York, the northeastern landmass of Australia. Here on the map a large black chunk of concrete bearing only the legal file number QC94/3 is extruded. This land belongs to the Wik people and has been subject to the nation's most controversial legal arguments testing whether Aboriginal native title over land can coexist with pastoral leases. For now, white Australia has decided its identity and its land cannot be confused by dual occupancy.

To further the themes of culturally constructing the landscape, a camera obscura is situated in the center of the map near the tunnel. The camera obscura is located where Uluru would appear on the map, the megalithic icon to which the site planning of the museum is directed in the real geography beyond the garden. The camera obscura is designed as a metallic cubicle inside of which is a small image of the outside view inverted on a screen, exactly what happens on the human retina. To enter the camera obscura is, as René Descartes would have it, to enter one's own head. The camera obscura is one of the garden's heavier elements, symbolically carrying five hundred years of European vision and its associated dreamss of objectivity and truth.

From the outside, the camera obscura cubicle is designed to look like the armor of Australia's most infamous and beloved criminal, Ned Kelly, who wore a metal mask to withstand sprays of police bullets. The camera obscura has been modeled on the Australian painter Sydney Nolan's Kelly famous series of paintings, where we see through Ned Kelly's black helmet to clear blue sky. Not only that, in Nolan's series, the police are often painted upside down.

In addition to this, the garden contains references to several significant Australian painters. For example, Arthur Boyd's penchant for eucalyptus forests can be imagined in a stand of ghost gums planted

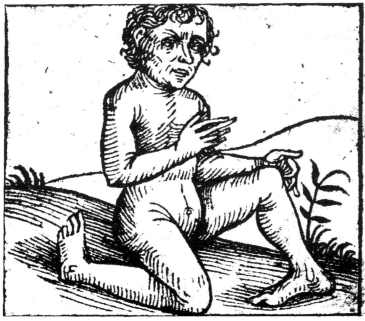

Hartmann Schedel, "Antipode" (1493). Woodcut from *Liber Chroni-carum* (Nuremberg Chronicle). Courtesy of Mitchell Library, State Library of New South Wales.

in one corner of the garden. Similarly, we are reminded of Arthur Streeton's fascination with lumber by a massive dead tree that has fallen into the water. A grid of red and white surveyor's poles intimates Jeffrey Smart's spartan industrial landscapes, and the whole map surface is reminiscent of Gordon Bennett's postcolonial paintings, wherein similar strategies of appropriation are deployed.

Looking in a different direction, one notices an area of well-kept grass, a small swimming pool, and a *Phoenix canariensis* (Canary Island palm tree), lovely clichés of Australian suburbia. More than just exhausted signs, these icons of suburbia can, to the educated eye, connote a *hortus conclusus*, the paradise Australia was hoped to be. The X signature cuts from the stand of ghost gums into the crisp grass yard, marking a tension between indigenous identity and suburbia, crossing between the three paradises one finds in Australia:

The Honorable Gough Whitlam, AC, QC, former Australian Prime Minister, in the Garden of Australian Dreams.

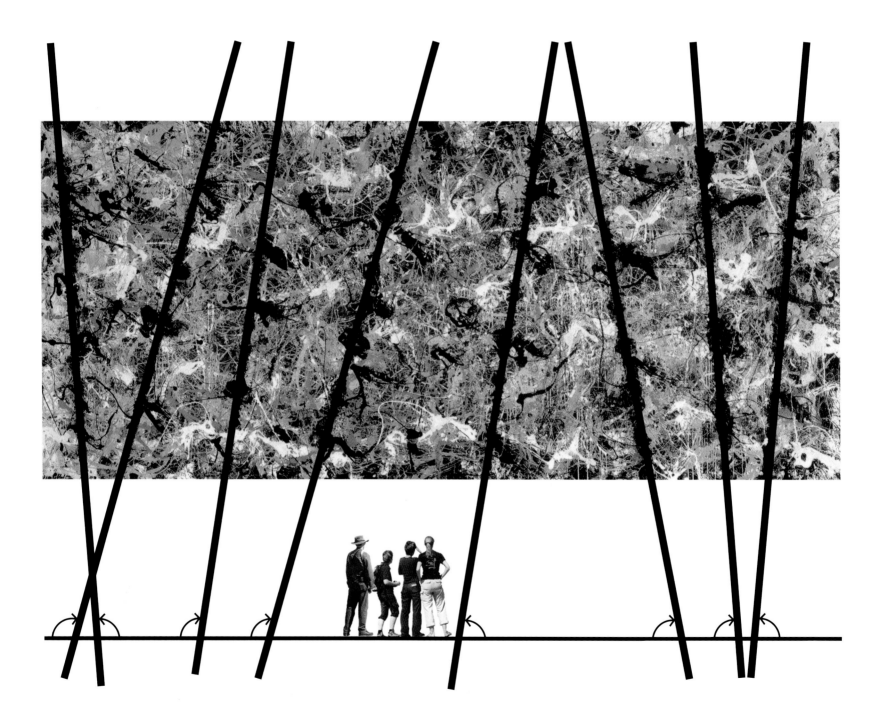

BLUE TELEGRAPH POLES ANGLED EXACTLY AS POLLOCK'S LINES IN HIS INFAMOUS PAINTING *BLUE POLES*.

VIEW OF THE DREAM HOME, WITH A CUT CORNER SERVING AS AN ENTRANCE.

the one the indigenous Australians lost, the one imposed, and the one we still imagine.

Fronting this grass allotment is a large white cube, an empty room that we entitled the Dream Home. The client expected a roof and therefore a function space, but the home is devoted to emptiness. The Dream Home is obviously not a copy of a typical red-brick Australian suburban home; rather, it is the living room (family and dining room) of the interior of a typical house stripped bare. It is also homage to Magritte, James Turrell, and Luis Barragan's Garden of the Trough in Mexico City.

The 8-meter white cube has an enormous door and a cut corner, a monument to "cutting corners"–an Australian propensity for taking shortcuts in whatever task is at hand. Inside the "living Room," soft furniture, not unlike that found in a padded cell, invites one to lie down and daydream, taking in an unmitigated view into the monumental Australian sky. Looking up, with all peripheral vision blocked, one can imagine falling into the sky. Confounding its Euclidean order, fractal clouds float into the frame of the white cube.

Laughing at all this, on a small porch high on the façade of the Dream Home is the garden's proverbial gnome, an "Antipodean," a caricature of the monstrous creatures thought to populate the antipodes, a figment of the medieval European imagination.[14]

Eight blue painted poles, set according to the angles of Jackson Pollock's painting *Blue Poles*, animate the space around the Dream Home. Controversially, the painting by Pollock was acquired for a small fortune by the Australian (Labor) government on behalf of the taxpayer for the National Gallery in the early 1970s. For some, the purchase was a sign of that decade's resurrected cultural patronage, for others it was an obscene amount of money wasted on an incomprehensible mess painted by a drunkard.

Amid the fray one remembers Jackson Pollock's exclamation that he did not paint nature because, rather, he *was* nature. It is along these lines that our landscape architecture for the National Museum of Australia is different from that of the National Gallery of Australia on the other side of Lake Burley Griffin, where Pollock's original painting remains.

Apparently, during the design process of the National Museum of Australia, some political figures were unimpressed by the Garden of Australian Dreams and the blue poles in particular. The latter were thought to be a clandestine monument to Gough Whitlam, the prime minister at the time of the controversial purchase of the Pollock painting.

A Controversial Garden?

Since opening in March 2001, the buildings and landscape of the National Museum have created controversy and divided Australia's design community. While many appreciate the project's vigilance toward narrowing the gaps between concept and construction, they also tend to recoil from its garish tones, its difficult composition of incongruous elements, and its excess of signification.

Surprisingly, many intellectuals from across the arts and sciences seem confused that the design mixes high and low culture and philosophy with humor. They know it is no fool, but they worry whether it is a clown or a scholar; whether it is beauty or the beast? And what if it is both? These intellectual guardians also worry for the public, who they say cannot possibly understand the esoteric Esperanto that surrounds them. They worry that the poor souls seem to like it and boisterously explore it.

We remain shocked that conservative critics so feverishly slander the appearance of both the buildings and the landscape with almost no regard for the serious and in parts beautiful ideas underpinning them. Where critics' expressions of fear and loathing shift to admonish the museum's rough grain and use of ignoble materials, they are, however, correct. Built too quickly and too cheaply, the museum is decidedly better in photographs. Even in the third dimension much of it appears to remain in the second, as if the graphics on the ground and the façades prefer the flatland of magazines and computer screens—the realm of paper tigers from whence no one expected us to escape.

For Australia's design establishment, flabby in mind and body from years of having it all to themselves, the architectural and landscape architectural outpourings at the National Museum are a travesty and a good reason not to hold open competitions. More specifically, because the Garden of Australian Dreams refuses to pay mimetic homage to the authentic landscape of this continent—the godhead of nearly all work done here—it sits like a satanist in a church. For those who can think their way out of romanticism's landscape entrapment and stomach its strange fruit, the whole museum is an unlikely looking masterpiece of critical regionalism perched precociously at the edge of the international design world. Others, particularly younger designers, draw strength from just the fact that a design team could break through the labyrinth of bureaucratic checks and measures to brazenly graffiti Canberra's soporific shores.

Something had to happen in Australia.

As the "flagship" for Australia's centenary of federation, the museum's provocative design came at a bad time. Just when everyone had worked so hard during the Sydney Olympics to emit images to the world of a reconciled nation set in nature's wonderland, this refugee wreck washes up on Lake Burley Griffin and begins transmitting mixed messages. A golden bow in the day and a spectral dazzle at night, it blinds those on the other side of the lake who cannot bear to think they not only commissioned but approved it.

For the government and its intellectual apologists, the form of the National Museum is one problem, but the content is another. The exhibitions, which purport to tell the stories of Australia, cannot withdraw into abstraction like buildings and landscapes, and so they stand charged directly with political bias. Since its opening the National Museum has been accused of political correctness and historical inaccuracy. The debate in the "culture wars" of Australia at large has centred on the question of the degree to which white culture made concerted efforts to destroy indigenous culture—a debate that used the National Museum as its battleground and found its most pertinent and pained metaphor in the fact that the architects had quoted Daniel Libeskind's Berlin Museum to house the museum's indigenous content. That the Garden of Australian Dreams was based on a map of contested terrain has not helped.

In efforts to establish its illegitimacy, the government has commissioned two reviews of the National Museum—one for each year of its short life. In respect of the question of political and historical bias, both have been inconclusive, but the most recent review recommended changes to the landscape design, terrain it had no mandate to move into. Despite having no qualifications in design, the review panel—consisting of a sociologist, a palaeontologist, a corporate director, and a curator—concluded that the existing garden was too abstract for the public, too uncomfortable, and in any case not "a real garden." They proposed that it be replaced with trees, grass, rocks, sundials, painted copies of traditional Aboriginal rock art, and educational exhibits related to Australia's natural history. They say a team of scientists should be engaged as the design consultants of the new garden. As the president of the Australian Institute of Landscape Architects, Noel Corkery said in a press release urging the Museum Council to reject the review, it would be funny if it were not so alarming.

Indeed it is alarming that a designer's moral rights can be so blatantly disregarded and that landscape architecture is not thought equivalent in stature to the disciplines represented by this project's politically appointed reviewers. It is also alarming, though perhaps not surprising, that the image of a "real garden" remains so firmly entrenched in the nineteenth century.

All this is not to say that we would not welcome a qualified review of the Garden of Australian Dreams; in fact, as Julian Raxworthy points out in his essay in this volume, we crave serious discussion. However, surely a proper review would consult the original authors and look to the museum's exit polling, which add up in the garden's favor. A serious review would recognize that the design satisfies its brief for a low-maintenance, multipurpose event space, but that, due to diversion of funds committed to its construction, the original design remains incomplete.

Regardless of reviews, what is finally of some importance for the landscape architectural canon is that the source and subject of this design is the cultural construction of landscape, not the landscape itself.

1   I am grateful for Sister Veronica Brady's brief yet resonant account of psychological and theological tensions between white and black Australia. See Veronica Brady, *If These Bones Could Live* (Sydney: Federation Press,1996).

2   The High Court of Australia's 1992 decision in *Mabo v. Queensland [No 2]* recognized a limited right of community native title over land where its indigenous inhabitants could prove a continuous traditional connection with the land and where no inconsistent grants of interest in the relevant land had been made. As well as the obvious effect on property law concepts in Australia, *Mabo* was significant because it repudiated the historical belief that Australia was settled *terra nullius*. Where land was deemed *terra nullius* ("no one's land") or without civilized inhabitants, it could be occupied and held in the sovereign power of the settlers. In 1996 the Wik people of northern Cape York gained legal recognition that their native title could coexist with pastoral lease interests in the area. This decision and its misinterpretation by politicians, media, and vested interests caused a hysteric government reaction. Amendments were passed to native title legislation to severely curtail legitimate Aboriginal interests in land. The issue of land rights remains as one of the major impediments to reconciliation between Australia's indigenous peoples and its European settlers.

3   The original indigenous landscape of Canberra is primarily used as a backdrop to the artificial lake and its eclectic edge planting scheme. Christopher Vernon (University of Western Australia) and James Weirick (University of New South Wales) are both Griffin scholars who have explained aspects of Canberra which we found useful at the sketch design stages of this project.

4   It should be noted that the main figure of the master plan was gesturally established by the architects in a stage one submission and emerged from their recent research. The landscape architects (Room 4.1.3) then entered the scheme, interpreted it, and extended its abstract ideas. I do not claim to speak authoritatively for the architects. Readers could begin to pursue this in Howard Raggatt, "Howard Raggatt," in *Fin de Siecle? and the Twenty-First Century: Architectures of Melbourne* (Melbourne: RMIT Publications, 1992), pp. 113–173.

5   Toying with the metaphor of landscape as fabric and building as knot began at Federation Square when ARM invited Room 4.1.3 to contribute to their finalist scheme in 1998. See image on p. 208, where the strands of an implied ground plane fabric become, literally, writing, and thus landscape and architectural design become forms of calligraphy and hieroglyph written into the text of the city.

6   The National Museum of Australia had been designed some years back by other consultants in a vernacular style and sited in a bush setting on another part of Lake Burley Griffin. Not only has the design been started and stopped several times, but so too the actual collection has been in storage for at least twenty years while different governments prevaricated and procrastinated.

7   Uluru is a site to which most Australians believe they must travel. The mystique of this geological anomaly is well documented in Barry Hill, *The Rock: Travelling to Uluru* (London: Allen and Unwin, 1994).

8   Upon Federation in 1901, artistic attention was drawn toward the bush as the seat of Australia's uniqueness. Throughout the course of the latter half of the twentieth century, as the bush has been poetically exhausted and literally cleared, the "real" Australia has been relocated to the country's vast interior deserts. R. Haynes, "Seeking the Centre," comprehensively documents this; see his *Australian Desert in Literature, Art and Film* (London: Cambridge University Press, 1998).

9   Amy Thorpe, "Version to Version: ARM's Architecture Revisited," *KERB: Journal of Landscape Architecture* (1998), p. 23.

10   Robert Hughes, *The Fatal Shore: A History of the Transportation of Convicts to Australia 1787–1868* (London: Collins & Harvill, 1987), p. 575.

11   See Denis Cosgrove, ed., *Mappings* (London: Reaktion Books, 1999), p. 2.

12   The expression "singing the country" refers to Aboriginal techniques of aurally invoking the meaning of the landscape and the location of its significant features. These "songlines" are thought to interconnect like a series of maps across the whole of Australia.

13   I am grateful to Kevin Williams for this anecdotal information.

14   The figure was sculpted by Karl Valerius.

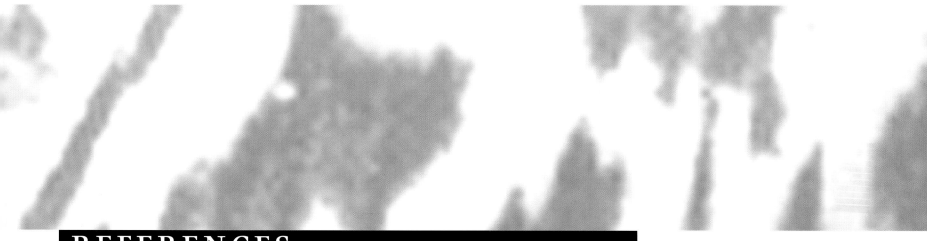

REFERENCES

Project Details

I. Dialectical Geographies

Vertigorium

Brief: Unsolicited conceptual project marking the geomancy of Berlin
Site: Kreuzberg to Tuefelsberg, Berlin, Germany
Date: 1991
Project Team: Richard Weller

The Satellite's Garden

Brief: Unsolicited conceptual grotto in response to the question: What is a cathedral of the twentieth century?
Site: Fehrbelliner Platz (an existing park at the midpoint between Teufelsberg and Kreuzberg), Berlin, Germany
Date: 1991
Project Team: Richard Weller

No-Man's-Land

Brief: Unsolicited polemic concerning the future of No-Man's-Land
Site: Perimeter of former West Berlin
Date: 1990–1994
Project Team: Richard Weller

Potsdamer Platz

Brief: Invited Urban Design Ideas Competition for landscape design ideas for the redevelopment of the Potsdamer Platz
Site: Vicinity of the Potsdamer Platz and Leipziger Platz, Berlin, Germany
Date: 1991
Client: Berlin Senat für Stadtentwicklung und Umweltschutz
Project Team: Jan Wehberg, Cornelia Müller, Kamel Louafi, Richard Weller
With: Daniel Libeskind (architect), Müller Knippschild Wehberg (landscape architects)

The Park on Potsdamer Platz

Brief: Unsolicited conceptual project regarding infrastructure for an urban park in former No-Man's-Land
Site: Vicinity of the Potsdamer Platz and Leipziger Platz, Berlin, Germany
Date: 1991
Project Team: Richard Weller
Status: Later adapted to suit a site in Gelsenkirchen for the 1997 Bundesgartenshau (National Garden Show)

Trans-European Songline

Brief: Invited Urban Design Ideas Competition for landscape design ideas for the redevelopment of the
                    Potsdamer Platz
Site: A line joining Paris, Berlin, and Moscow
Date: 1991
Client: Berlin Senat für Stadtentwicklung und Umweltschutz
Project Team: Richard Weller, Jan Wehberg, Cornelia Müller, Kamel Louafi
With: Daniel Libeskind (architect), Müller Knippschild Wehberg (landscape architects)

Bundesgartenshau '97 (National Garden Show)

Brief: Open competition for a master plan for the Annual National German Garden Show
Site: Decommissioned coal mine and associated postindustrial landscape, Gelsenkirchen, Ruhrgebiet,
                    Germany
Date: 1992
Client: City of Gelsenkirchen
Project Team: Richard Weller, Jan Wehberg, Cornelia Müller, Kamel Louafi, Lutger Engel, Tobias Micke
With: Müller Knippschild Wehberg (landscape architects)
Status: Second prize

Das Berliner Zimmer (The Berlin Room)

Brief: Open competition entitled "Zwei Parks am Potsdamer Platz" (Two Parks on Potsdamer Platz).
                    Proposal for two small parks within the redevelopment of the Potsdamer Platz, of which only one is
                    documented herein
Site: Triangular open space adjacent to Berlin's Tiergarten and Sony Corporation, Bellevuestrasse, Berlin,
                    Germany
Date: 1995
Client: Berlin Senat für Stadtentwicklung und Umweltschutz
Project Team: Richard Weller, Jan Wehberg, Cornelia Müller, Constanza Bitzageio, Tatum Hands
With: Müller Knippschild Wehberg (landscape architects)
Status: Third prize

Eyelands

Brief: International competition calling for designs to connect the two Diomede Islands
Site: Diomede Islands, Bering Strait, Russia and America
Date: 1987
Project Team: Richard Weller and Vladimir Sitta

II. Infrastructures

The Farm

Brief:	International competition for the design of a park in an agricultural landscape including a World War II internment camp
Site:	Carpi, Fossoli, Italy
Date:	1988
Client:	Town of Fossoli
Project Team:	Vladimir Sitta, Richard Weller, Dib Dib, Conny Kolmann, Peter Ireland
Status:	Not taken further (lost in the mail)

Bloodlines

Brief:	International Ideas and Design competition for the planning of the Gallipoli Peninsula as a Peace Park
Site:	Gallipoli Peninsula, Republic of Turkey
Date:	1997
Client:	Turkish government
Project Team:	Richard Weller, Lorne Leonard, Keli Harrison, Karl Kullmann, Lizzie Burt, Daniel Firns, Julien Bolletter
Status:	Commendation

New Singapore City

Brief:	Urban design ideas for a 372-hectare extension of Singapore City
Site:	Marina South landfill site, Singapore
Date:	1987
With:	Creative Design and Technology (CDT)
Client:	Singapore government
Project Team:	Vladimir Sitta
Status:	Not taken further

Sun City

Brief:	Unsolicited speculation regarding sustainable infrastructure for the Perth Central Business District
Site:	Perth Foreshore, Perth Central Business District, Western Australia
Date:	1995
Project Team:	Richard Weller, Simeon Glasson, Karl Kullman, Daniel Firns, and Tom Griffiths
Status:	Not taken further

Future Generations University

Brief: International competition regarding the theory, practice, and form of a university devoted exclusively to the issue of sustainability

Site: Wyong, Central Coast, New South Wales, Australia.

Date: 1996

Client: Future Generations Alliance

Project Team: Vladimir Sitta, Richard Weller, Des Smith (architect), Simeon Glasson (architect), Ian Weir (architect), Oui Chantarachota (architect), Craig Burton (environmental designer), Peter England (set designer), Nigel Westbrook (architect), Shaun Tan (artist), Dr. Paul Collins (theologian), Marni Shepherd (physicist), Tatum Hands (political theorist), Kevin Williams (lawyer, indigenous consultant), Anthony Rose (information systems designer), Victor Bossell (engineer), Rosemary King (education consultant), Dr. Robert King (biologist), Andrew Marsh (architectural scientist), Bob Sinclair (architect), Elwyn Dennis (composer), Anne Davis (librarian), Rosanna Blackett (architect)

Status: Selected finalist. Project delayed indefinitely

III. Event Spaces

A-Political Project(ions)

Brief: Open European competition for the landscape architecture the new government quarter of Berlin

Site: The Spreebogen, (arc of the Spree River), Berlin, Germany

Date: 1996

Client: Berlin Senat fur Stadtentwicklung und Umweltschutz

Project Team: Vladimir Sitta, Richard Weller, Karl Kullmann, Pavol Moravcik, Eva Wagnerova, Elke Morneweg

Status: Finalist

The Women's Rooms

Brief: Open European competition for the design for an urban park and surrounding environs

Site: Park Monbijou, Oranienburgerstrasse, Berlin, Germany

Date: 1993

Client: Berlin Senat für Stadtentwicklung und Umweltschutz

Project Team: Jan Wehberg, Cornelia Müller, Frank Kiessling, Richard Weller

With: Müller Knippschild Wehberg (landscape architects)

Status: Second prize

The Esplanade

Brief: Limited competition to design the public domain, with particular emphasis on the waterfront espla-
                   nade for the new development of Melbourne's Docklands
Site: Melbourne Docklands, Victoria, Australia
Date: 1998
Client: Docklands Authority
Project Team: Richard Weller, Vladimir Sitta, Ian McDougall, Daniel Firns, Luca Ginoulhiac, Simeon Glasson,
                   Maren Parry
With: Ashton Raggatt McDougall (architects)
Status: Winning submission

Namesti Miru

Brief: Open European competition for the design of an urban square in Prague
Site: Namesti Miru, Central Prague, Czech Republic
Date: 1995
Client: City of Prague
Project Team: Vladimir Sitta, Peter Ireland
Status: Third prize

The Field

Brief: Urban waterfront park
Site: Chaffers, Wellington, New Zealand
Date: 2002
Client: Wellington City Council
Project Team: Richard Weller, Vladimir Sitta, Jacky Bowring, Tom Griffiths

IV. Denatured Ecologies

$Z^2 + C$

Brief: An exhibition of Room 4.1.3's environmental design work in the Museum of Contemporary Art in
                   Sydney
Site: Museum of Contemporary Art, Circular Quay, Sydney, Australia
Date: 1998
Client: Museum of Contemporary Art
Curator: Linda Michael
Project Team: Vladimir Sitta, Richard Weller, Lizzie Burt, Karl Kullmann, Maren Parry, Tatum Hands, Daniel
                   Firns, Oleg Putilin, MCA staff
Status: Seppelt Art Award. Selected finalist. Three-month installation

Decomposition

Brief: Invited competition for a new office complex and landscape design
Site: Wiesbaden, Germany
Date: 1992
Client: City of Wiesbaden
Project Team: Jan Wehberg, Cornelia Müller, Kamel Louafi, Richard Weller
With: Daniel Libeskind (architect), Müller Knippschild Wehberg (landscape architects)
Status: First prize. Not built

The Amber Room

Brief: Landmarks and processes for the open cut, brown coal mines of Dessau
Site: Dessau, Germany
Date: 1993
Project Team: Richard Weller
Status: Project emerged from teaching a studio at the Bauhaus with Hinnerk Wehberg of Braunschweig University

The Bestiary and the Herbal

Brief: Noncommissioned conceptual project regarding the use of parts of former No-Man's-Land concerning the theme of ecological crisis
Site: Potsdam, No-Man's-Land, Berlin, Germany
Date: 1992
Project Team: Richard Weller
Status: Later adapted to a postindustrial site in Oberhausen for an invited competition in association with Müller Knippschild Wehberg

Animale Ignoble

Brief: International ideas competition seeking alternatives to the privatization of a postindustrial island in Sydney Harbor
Site: Cockatoo Island (Biloela), Sydney Harbor, Australia
Date: 1995
Project Team: Richard Weller
Status: Commendation

V. Memoria

The Virtually Free Market and the Memorial to Fallen Bodies

Brief: International ideas competition for a "Justice park" and "Memorial to victims of violent crime" in
                    central Los Angeles
Site: Criminal Courts, Los Angeles Civic Center, California, United States
Date: 1995
Project Team: Richard Weller, Simeon Glasson, Craig Akhurst, Jenny Marschner, Tatum Hands

The Twentieth Century Monument

Brief: Unsolicited project proposing to relocate or split the test foundation of Albert Speer's Great Hall of
                    the German People
Site: Dudenstrasse, Berlin, Germany
Date: 1992
Project Team: Richard Weller

Place de la Révolution

Brief: Inventer '89, international competition for landmarks to commemorate the bicentenary of the
                    French Revolution
Site: Not sited
Date: 1989
Client: French government
Project Team: Richard Weller, Vladimir Sitta
Status: Finalist. Not taken further

Pentagon Memorial Sky Garden

Brief: Open international competition
Site: Pentagon periphery at point of impact, Washington, D.C.
Date: 2002
Client: U.S. government
Project Team: Richard Weller, Vladimir Sitta, Jacky Bowring, Peter England, Martin Musiatowicz, Tatum Hands,
                    Maren Parry, Robert Faber, Tom Griffiths, Sid Thoo, Andrew Nugent
Status: Finalist

Ground Zero

Brief: International competition for the design of the World Trade Center site and memorial
Site: World Trade Center, Manhattan, New York
Date: 2003
Client: Lower Manhattan Development Corporation
Project Team: Richard Weller, Vladimir Sitta, Tom Griffiths, Martin Musiatowicz, Tatum Hands

VI. Gardens
DIN A4

Brief:	Commission to design the garden for the courtyard of the German Institute of Standards
Site:	Deutsche Institut Normen, Kurfurstenstrasse, Berlin, Germany
Date:	1991-1993
Client:	Deutsche Institut Normen (German Institute of Standards)
Project Team:	Richard Weller, Cornelia Müller, Jan Wehberg
With:	Müller Knippschild Wehberg (landscape architects)
Status:	Sketch design only by Richard Weller. Design development and documentation by Müller Knippschild Wehberg. Garden opened in 1993

ETA Hoffmann Garden

Brief:	Landscape fit out for a sunken outdoor space entitled the ETA Hoffmann Garden as designated by Daniel Libeskind's original plan for the extension to the Berlin Museum
Site:	Jewish Museum, Berlin, Germany
Date:	1991
Client:	Berlin Museum
Project Team:	Richard Weller
With:	Müller Knippschild Wehberg (landscape architects)
Status:	Not built

Nihilium

Brief:	Open competition for interactive, ephemeral gardens based on the theme "Curiosities"
Site:	Château Chaumont-sur-Loire Garden Festival, France
Date:	1995
Client:	Chateau Chaumont Garden Festival
Project Team:	Vladimir Sitta
Status:	Selected and constructed

Filmmaker's Garden

Brief:	Novel and symbolic garden design in tiny urban space
Site:	Private inner-city courtyard, Sydney, Australia
Date:	1998
Client:	M. Fink
Project Team:	Vladimir Sitta, Maren Parry
Status:	Constructed by Above the Earth Landscape Constructions

Fire Garden

Brief:	Novel and meaningful small garden design
Site:	Private, suburban backyard, Sydney, Australia
Date:	1999
Client:	B. and P. Rooke
Project Team:	Vladimir Sitta, Maren Parry
Status:	Constructed by Above the Earth Landscape Constructions

Terra Californius

Brief:	International competition for environmental art and themed gardens
Site:	Campus of University of California, Davis, United States
Date:	1987
Client:	University of California, Davis
Project Team:	Richard Weller
Status:	Commendation

The Seed Machine

Brief:	International competition for gardens concerning the theme of paradise in New York City
Site:	Imaginary pocket park for a small vacant lot in Manhattan, New York, United States
Date:	1992
Project Team:	Vladimir Sitta
Status:	Selected entry; not built

VII. LANDMARKS

Voss's Garden

Brief:	National competition for the redesign of the southwest corner of Centennial Park celebrating the centenary of Australia's Federation
Site:	Centennial Park, Sydney, Australia
Date:	1998
Client:	Centennial Park Authority
Project Team:	Richard Weller, Vladimir Sitta, Karl Kullmann, Lizzie Burt
With:	Dr. Paul Carter (artist, writer, Australia Centre, Melbourne University), Dr. Caroline Oldham (reconstructed wetland designer, Centre for Water Research, University of Western Australia), Kevin Willams (indigenous lawyer and artist)
Status:	Second prize

Reconciliation Place

Brief:	National competition for a landscape design regarding reconciliation between indigenous and nonindigenous Australians
Site:	Land axis, Parliamentary triangle, Canberra, Australia
Date:	2001
Client:	National Capital Authority
Project Team:	Richard Weller, Vladimir Sitta, Lisa Shine
With:	Julie Dowling (artist)
Status:	Commendation

Federation Garden

Brief:	National competition for design of a garden to celebrate the centenary of the Federation of Australia
Site:	Grounds of Government House, Sydney, Australia
Date:	2001–2002
Client:	New South Wales Historic Houses Trust
Project Team:	Richard Weller, Vladimir Sitta, Nathan Greenhill, Tom Griffiths
Status:	First prize, not built

National Museum of Australia

Brief:	National competition for the design of the National Museum of Australia, including the Australian Institute of Aboriginal and Torres Strait Islander Studies
Site:	Acton Peninsula, Canberra, Australia
Date:	1997–2001
Client:	Department of Communications and the Arts, Australian Government
Project Team:	Vladimir Sitta, Richard Weller, Maren Parry, Lizzie Burt, Kioshi Furuno, Luca Ginoulhiac, Scott Hawken, Silvia Krizova, Pavol Moravcik, Daniel Firns
With:	Ashton Raggatt McDougall, Robert Peck von Hartel Trethowan (architects)
Status:	First prize. Construction completed May 2001

Awards and Prizes

Room 4.1.3
Richard Weller and Vladimir Sitta

The following list of competition prizes refers to open competitions unless otherwise stated. Open competitions allow anyone to enter and be anonymously judged, whereas invited competitions often involve a relatively small number of participants and the work is generally not received anonymously.

2003   **National Concrete and Cement Association of Australia Awards Overall Winner:** Room 4.1.3 for the National Museum of Australia

2002   **AILA (Australian Institute of Landscape Architects) President's Award** for "Contribution to Culture of Landscape Architecture in Australia," to Vladimir Sitta

           Finalist: 1 of 6 selected from 1,126 entries. Pentagon Memorial Competition, Washington, D.C.

           First prize: Federation Garden, Government House, Sydney, Australia

2001   **Honorable mention:** Reconciliation Place, Canberra, Australia
Consultants: Sister Veronica Brady (Department of English, University of Western Australia); Julie Dowling

2001   **Final selection:** Rabin Peace Forum, Tel Aviv, with C. Elliott

1999   **Second prize:** Garden to Mark the Centenary of Federation, Centennial Parklands, Sydney, Australia

           Final selection: Nanning China, the Square of Metamorphoses, in association with Peddle Thorpe Walker Architects

           First prize: Docklands Esplanade, Melbourne. Winner in limited competition with Ashton Raggatt McDougall, Melbourne

1998   **First prize:** National Museum of Australia, Canberra, Australia.
In association with Ashton Raggatt McDougall (project architects)

           Finalist: Seppelt Australian Art Awards, Museum of Contemporary Art, Sydney, Australia. Final three selected from more than two hundred nominations from Australia and New Zealand to exhibit in Sydney's Museum of Contemporary Art

           Honorable mention: Gallipoli Peace Park, Ankara, Turkey

FINALIST: Federation Square, Melbourne, Australia, in association with Ashton Raggatt McDougall (architects) (ARM selected initially and Room 4.1.3 invited to participate)

FIRST PRIZE: Giba Park, Pyrmont, Sydney, Australia. Invited and limited competition

FIRST PRIZE: Shade structure designs for Pyrmont, Sydney, Australia. Invited and limited competition

1996   **FINALIST:** Future Generations University, New South Wales, Australia

1995   **THIRD PRIZE:** Namesti Miru (Peace Square), Prague, Czech Republic

THIRD PRIZE: Two Parks on Potsdamer Platz, Berlin, Germany. In association with Müller Knippschild Wehberg

Honorable mention: Cockatoo Island, Sydney, Australia

HONORABLE MENTION: "Landschaftspark Munchen-Riem," New Town and Landscape Park on Former Munich Airport Site, Munich, Germany. In association with Müller Knippschild Wehberg

SELECTED AND CONSTRUCTED ENTRY: Festival International des Jardins, Garden of Curiosity, Chaumont-sur-Loire, France

1994   **FOURTH PRIZE:** Helmholzplatz, East Berlin, Germany, in association with Müller Knippschild Wehberg

SECOND PRIZE: Urban Furnishings, Frydek Mistek, Czech Republic

1993   **SECOND PRIZE:** Park Monbijou: The Women's Rooms, Berlin, Germany, in association with Müller Knippschild Wehberg

FIRST PRIZE AND HONORABLE MENTION: Residential Design, Uncommon Ground (ASLA) Landscape Architecture magazine

1992   **FIRST PRIZE:** Corporate and government office complex, Wiesbaden, Germany, in association with Müller Knippschild Wehberg, and Daniel Libeskind. Invited competition

SECOND PRIZE: National Garden Show, Gelsenkirchen, Ruhrgebiet, Germany, in association with Müller Knippschild Wehberg

1991   **Second prize:** Moabiter Werder; parkland and residential development, Berlin, Germany, in association with Müller Knippschild Wehberg

           Commended entry: Perth Foreshore Urban Design Competition, Perth, Australia

1989   **Finalist:** Fountain for Airport Centre, Sydney, Australia

           First prize: Slavic Square, Brno, Czech Republic

1988   **Commendation:** Anatomy Garden, Ingolstadt, Germany. Annual Young Landscape Architects competition series (Arbeitskreis Junger Landschaftsarchitekten)

1987   **Commendation:** Five gardens for the University of California, Davis: Australian Garden, Seed Garden, Moss Garden, Palm Garden, Rust Garden

           Selected entry: Garden of Emergence, Inventer '89, monument to commemorate 200th anniversary of the French Revolution, Paris, France

           Selected finalist: Landscape design to commemorate Governor Arthur Phillip's landing site in Sydney, Australia

1986   **Lenne Prize:** Work titled A Cemetery in the City, West Germany

1985   **First prize:** Blacktown City Bicentennial Monument Competition, Sydney, Australia

           Commendation: Queens Square Competition (with Victor Allen) Sydney, Australia

           Special prize: Parramatta Road Design Competition, Sydney, Australia

           First prize: Australian Institute of Landscape Architects National Student Award. Project presented at the 1985 International Conference of Landscape Architects, Kyoto, Japan

1983   **Second prize:** Biohouse for Garden Show, Berlin, West Germany

1981   **Third prize:** National Garden Show Hamm, West Germany (with Rose Herzmann und Partner)

1980   **Lenne Prize:** Proposal for Treatment of Façades with Biologically Active Surfaces, West Germany

1978   **Selected project of the year:** Czechoslovakian Institute of Architects, category Open Space, Playground Slapanice Brno, Czechoslovakia

1977   **Selected project of the year:** Czechoslovakian Institute of Architects, category Urban Design, Forecourt of SS Zelesice, Brno, Czechoslovakia

Merit award: Reconstruction of Historical Park, Paskov, Czechoslovakia

1976   **Third prize:** Plaza, Dortmund, West Germany

Second prize: Hermannplatz (Plaza), Berlin, West Germany

1974   **First prize:** LUVA Essen, West Germany

1973   **Second prize:** Forecourt, Baumschule Hoemann, Haan, West Germany

Room 4.1.3 Publications and Media

Book Chapters and Essays

Weller, R., et al. (eds.). *Hope: Art, Design, Ecology*. Perth: School of Architecture and Fine Arts, University of Western Australia, 1994, pp. 13–75.

Weller, R. "Mapping the Nation." In D. Reid (ed.), *The National Museum of Australia*. Melbourne: Images Publishing, 2002, pp. 124–137.

———. "An Art of Instrumentality: Landscape Architecture and the City Now. A Polemic Regarding an Art of Planning in Current Theory and Praxis." In C. Waldheim (ed.), *Landscape Urbanism: A Reference Manifesto*. New York: Princeton Architectural Press, in press.

———. "Re-scapes: A Retrospective of Room 4.1.3." In L. Van Schaik (ed.), *The Practice of Practice*. Melbourne: RMIT Press, 2002, pp. 244–257.

———. "Room 4.1.3 @ RMIT." In P. Connolly and R. Van Der Velde (eds.), *Technique*. Melbourne: RMIT Press, 2002, pp. 112–117.

———. "Four Projects in Berlin and Australia." In V. Bird and H. Edquist (eds.), *The Culture of Landscape Architecture*. Melbourne: Edge Publishing, 1994, pp. 222–239.

Articles

"Peter Joseph Lenne Preis 1978." "Magdeburger Platz, Berlin." Schriftenreihe Peter–Joseph–Lenne–Preis. Der Senator fuer Wissenschaft und kulturelle Angelegenheiten mit der Technischen Universitat Berlin, pp. 58–59, 64, 65.

"Peter Joseph Lenne Preis 1983." "Lebendes Haus." Schriftenreihe Peter–Joseph–Lenne–Preis. Der Senator fuer Wissenschaft und kulturelle Angelegenheiten mit der Technischen Universitat Berlin, pp. 20, 21.

"Peter Joseph Lenne Preis 1985–1986." "Der Friedhof in der Stadt." Schriftenreihe Peter–Joseph–Lenne–Preis. Der Senator fuer Wissenschaft und kulturelle Angelegenheiten mit der Technischen Universitat Berlin, pp. 54–64.

"Peter Joseph Lenne Preis 1980." "Die wesentlichen Faktoren die fuer or gegen Fassadenbegruenung sprechen." Schriftenreihe Peter –Joseph–Lenne–Preis. Der Senator fuer Wissenschaft und kulturelle Angelegenheiten mit der Technischen Universitat Berlin, pp. 52–86.

Sitta, V. "A Nature Film: The Film Producer's Paradise." *Landscape Australia* no. 3 (1998), pp. 299–301.

———. "Inverted Topographies." *Landscape Australia* 3/1999, pp. 192–196.

———. "Landscape of Guilt." *Landscape Australia* 2/1993, 123 –124 (Transcript of the lecture given at Macquarie Galleries, Sydney in July 1992.

———. "Living Epidermis for the City." *Landscape Australia*, 4/1983.

———. "Renewal of a Square in Brno" (Czech Republic). *Topos: European Landscape Magazine* (Callwey Munchen) 5/93, pp. 14–22, (English/German).

———. "Sketches." *Garten und Landschaft* 10/1995, pp. 23–28.

———. "Stretching the Space." *Landscape Australia*, 4/1994, pp. 324–329.

———. "The Highway – Landscape Treatment and Security, Ecological Principles." DT Prerov, 1975, 30 pp. (in Czech).

———. "A Particular Case – Notes About Design of One Country Garden." *Landscape Australia*, 3/1991, pp. 226–233.

———. "Landscape Australia Looks Abroad - Czechoslovakia." *Landscape Australia*, 1/1992, pp. 37–41 and 2/1992 pp. 180–182.

———. "Nekolik zastavení v hledání australské zahrady" (1), *Domov* 6/97, pp. 41–43 (Czech Republic).

———. "Nekolik zastavení v hledání australské zahrady" (2), *Domov* 7/97, pp. 36–39 (Czech Republic).

———. "Nekolik zastavení v hledání australské zahrady" (3), *Domov* 8/97, pp. 36–39.

Weller, R. "A-Political Project-ions." *Land Forum* (California), no. 6 (2000), p. 65.

———. "A-political Project-ions: A Response to the New German Government Citadel in Berlin." *KERB: Journal of Landscape Architecture*, no. 4 (1997), pp. 13–16.

———. "Between Hermeneutics and Datascapes: A Critical Appreciation of Emergent Landscape Design Theory and Praxis Through the Writings of James Corner, 1990–2000—Part I." *Landscape Review* 7, no. 1 (2002), pp. 3–24.

———. "Between Hermeneutics and Datascapes: A Critical Appreciation of Emergent Landscape Design Theory and Praxis Through the Writings of James Corner, 1990–2000—Part II." *Landscape Review* 7, no. 1 (2002), pp. 25–44.

———. "Centennial Park Competition" *Landscape Australia*, 22, no. 85, (1999) pp. 32–38.

———. "Cryptic Perspectives." *Review of the Inaugural Australasian Landscape Architecture Workshop* (Queensland University of Technology Press, Brisbane, July 1996), pp. 31–34

———. "Fabrications: Federation Square and the Australian National Museum from a Landscape Position." *KERB: Journal of Landscape Architecture*, no. 5 (1998), pp. 29–33.

———. "Flotsam and Jetsam: A UWA Studio." *KERB: Journal of Landscape Architecture* no. 7 (2000), pp. 44–50.

———. "For God 'n Country: Rethreading the Mythic Terrain of the Master Plan." *Transition: Discourse on Architecture*, no. 59 (1998), pp. 110–113.

———. "Hoc Vile Animale: Design Proposal for Cockatoo Island, Sydney." *KERB: Journal of Landscape Architecture*, no. 3 (1996), pp. 82–84.

———. "In Between the Lines: One Project in Concrete and One in Ink." *Landscape Australia*, 17, no. 2 (1995), pp. 157–161.

———. "Ink Fields and Paper Gardens: Landscape as Logo." *UME: Journal of Architecture & Design*, no. 5 (1997), pp. 55–59.

———. "'Is It Landscape Architecture' A Review of Some Recent International Design Competitions." *Landscape Australia*, no. 4 (1989), pp. 358–363.

———. "Lebensraum: the Life and Death of the Potsdamer Platz" *Transition: Discourse on Architecture*, nos. 50-51 (1996), pp. 40–52.

———. "Making Australia a Better Place in Which to Live?" *Landscape Australia*, no. 1 (1996), pp. 37–39.

———. "Mapping the Nation and Writing the Garden." *Landscape Australia* 23, no. 3 (2001), pp. 40–44.

———. "Millenarianism" *KERB: Journal of Landscape Architecture*, no. 4 (1997), pp. 68–69.

———. "National Museum of Australia, Canberra." *Garten + Landschaft*, no. 10 (2001), pp. 30–33 (translated by Gesa Loschwitz).

———. "No Man's Land: Stitching the Void at Potsdamer Platz." *Land Forum* (California), no. 6 (2000), pp. 66–71.

———. "Ogni Pensiero Vola: Wandering Through Vladimir Sitta's Sketchbook." *Landscape Australia*, 17, no. 3 (1995), pp. 242–250.

———. "Pentagon Memorial." *Landscape Australia* 25, no. 1 (2003), pp. 8–10.

———. "Poetic Places: Other Arenas." *Arena Magazine: The Australian Magazine of Left Political, Social and Cultural Commentary*, no. 27 (1997), pp. 13–16.

———. "The Future Generations University." *Landscape Review* 6, no. 1 (1998), pp. 62–74.

————. "The Garden of Intelligence. Re:Forming the Denatured." *Transition: Discourse on Architecture*, no. 59 (1998), pp. 114–131.

————. "The Heart of America." *Transition: Discourse on Architecture*, no. 48 (1995), pp. 44–49.

————. "The Landscape of the National Museum of Australia." *Landscape Architecture* 92, no. 6 (2002), pp. 66–96.

————. "The National Museum and Its Garden of Australian Dreams." *Studies in the History of Gardens and Designed Landscapes* (London) 21, no. 1 (2001), pp. 66–85.

————. "The Rubric of Place: A Discussion of 'Sense of Place.'" *KERB: Journal of Landscape Architecture*, no. 5 (1998), pp. 2–3.

————. "The Satellite's Garden." *Transition: Discourse on Architecture*, no. 42 (1993), 44–63.

————. "The Site of Reversible Destiny." *Landscape Australia* 25, no. 3 (2003).

————. "Toward an Art of Infrastructure. A Critical Survey of Contemporary Landscape Architectural Theory and Practice." Keynote address to the MESH International Landscape Architecture Conference, July 2001. *KERB: Journal of Landscape Architecture*, no. 10 (2001).

————. "Weaving the Axis—The National Museum of Australia, Canberra." *Landscape Australia* 20, no. 1 (1998), pp. 10–17.

————. "Critical Opinion: The Competitive Edge" 25 (4) *Landscape Australia* (2003) 48–50.

————. "Lean and Hungry like and Architect" *BEEP – The Journal of the RAIA Student Organisation* (2003) 3.

————. "Outside the Square: UWA students win the Beresford Square Design Competition" (2003) *Landmark: Newsletter of the Australian Institute of Landscape Architects*.

———— "Pentagon Memorial Sky Garden: An American Elysium" (2003) 5 BE: *The Disaster Issue* (Faculty of the Built Environment, University of New South Wales) 4–5.

————. "The Art of Disorientation." *Landscape Australia* 25, no. 3 (2003), pp. 46–48.

————. "The Best and Brightest – Resurrecting Perth's Foreshore." *Landscape Australia* 25, no. 2 (2003) p. 24.

————. "Windows of Opportunity – University of Western Australia." *Landscape Australia* 25 no. 2 (2003) p. 22.

WORK IN DESIGN ANTHOLOGIES AND PUBLISHED ILLUSTRATIONS

Aitken, R., and M. Looker. *The Oxford Companion to Australian Gardens*. New York: Oxford University Press, 2002, pp. 553–555.

Archer-Wills, A. *Water Power*. London: Conran Octopus, 1999, p. 77.

Billington, J. *New Classic Gardens*. London: Quadrille Publishing, 2000, pp. 48, 119.

Bradley-Hole, C. *The Minimalist Garden*. London: Mitchell Beazley, 1999, pp. 16–17, 60–61.

Bull, C. *New Conversations with an Old Landscape*. Melbourne: Images Publishing Group, 2002, pp. 142–147.

Cantor, S. L. *Contemporary Trends in Landscape Architecture*. New York: Van Nostrand Reinhold, 1997, pp. 141, 168–184.

Conran, T., and D. Pearson. *The Essential Garden Book*. London: Conran Octopus, 1998, pp. 70, 121.

Cooper, G., and G. Taylor. *Paradise Transformed*. New York: Monacelli Press, 1996, pp. 98-107.

Cooper, P. *Living Sculpture*. London: Conran Octopus, 2001, pp. 103, 111, 146, 147.

The Garden Book. London: Phaidon Press, 2000, p. 417.

Hobhouse, P. *The Story of Gardening*. London: Dorling Kindersley, 2002, p. 452.

Holden, R. *New Landscape Design*. London: Laurence King, 2003, pp. 142–147.

Johnson, C. *Greening of Sydney*. Sydney: Government Architect Publication, 2003, pp. 186–188.

Jones, L. *Chaumont*. London: Thames & Hudson, 2003.

Jungmann, J.-P., and H. Tonka. *Inventer 89*. Champ Vallon/AGH–La Villette, France, 1988, p. 101. (Garden of Emergence).

Oslzly, P. *Jan Simek - Pribehy soch*. Brno, Czech Republic: Atlantis, 1998, pp. 21–36.

Pigeat, J.-P. *Festival de Jardins*. Paris: Editions du Chene, 1995, p. 118.

Segall, B. *Gardens by the Sea*. Sydney: Random House, 2002, p. 122.

Stevens, D. *Garden Design*. London: Conran Octopus, 2000, p. 37.

———. *Small Space Gardens*. London: Conran Octopus, 2003, pp. 34–37, 82–85.

———. *Water Features*. London: Conran Octopus, 2000, p. 77.

Sydney Spaces. Sydney City Council, 1995, pp. 62–63.

"Uncommon Ground"–"Horse Farm and Estate Garden." *Landscape Architecture* (USA), no. 4 (1994), pp. 82–83.

Weller, R. "Community." *Arena Magazine: The Australian Magazine of Left Political, Social and Cultural Commentary* 26 (1996), p. 37.

———. "Machine Elysium." *Arena Magazine: The Australian Magazine of Left Political, Social and Cultural Commentary* 33 (1988), p. 16.

Wilson, A. *Influential Gardeners*. London: Mitchell Beazley, 2002, pp. 143, 156–159.

EXHIBITIONS

"Future City – Parasitic Architecture." Installation in collaboration with Anne Graham, Sydney 1992 (Catalogue).

"International Exhibition Public Spaces Brno." 1998 (Czech Republic).

"Minimalist Gardens-Architektur Aktuell." Travelling exhibition. March 2001, Freising Oberhaus, May 2001 Hamburg.

Seppelt Contemporary Art Awards, 1998. Museum of Modern Art, Sydney Australia.

REVIEWS AND DISCUSSION

Beck, H., and J. Cooper. "The Role of Landscape Design as 'Other': The Work of Richard Weller." *UME: Journal of Architecture and Design*, no. 5 (1997), p. 54.

Bolt, C. "Recording Life, Remembering Lives." *Australian Financial Review* (November 2002), p. 62.

Bowring, J. "Theories at the Bottom of the Garden." *Landscape New Zealand* (March–April 2002), pp. 10–13.

Bull, C. "One Year on at the NMA: Landscape at the National Museum of Australia." *Architecture Australia* 91, no. 2 (2002), pp. 64-65.

———. "The Landscape of the National Museum of Australia." *Landscape Architecture* 92, no. 6 (2002), pp. 60–65.

Burger, H., and A. Gebhard. "Landschaftspark Munchen-Riem." *Garten und Landschaft* (German Society for Landscape Architecture), 12 (1995), pp. 9–12.

———. "Zwei Parks am Potsdamer Platz." *Garten und Landschaft* (German Society for Landscape Architecture), 12 (1995), pp. 17–25.

Burt, L. "Pinched Landscape-Delving into the Details." *Landscape Australia* no. 4 (2000), pp. 371–373.

Casey, D. "History with a Larrikin Touch." *Daily Telegraph*, March 13, 2001, p. 20.

Cronin, D. "Love It or Hate It." *Canberra Times*, March 10, 2001, p. 6.

Droege, P. "Australia's Hyper-Museum in Context." *Architectural Review* 75 (2001), pp. 60–61.

Farrelly, E. "Thinking Outside the Paddock." *Sydney Morning Herald*, April 7, 2001, pp. 8–9 (Spectrum).

Firth, D. "Room 4.1.3's Design for the National Museum of Australia." *Landscape Australia*, 23, no. 3 (2002), pp. 45–46.

"Garden of Walls." "Film-maker's Garden." *Via arquitectura* (Spain) (April 2001), pp. 74–77.

Gibson, G. "Australian Rules." *Blueprint*, no. 183 (May 2001), pp. 48–54.

Griffin, R. "A Garden to Commemorate the Centenary of Federation." *Australian Garden History* 14, no. 4 (2003), pp. 4–6.

Hamann, C. "Enigma Variations: The National Museum of Australia and the AIATSIS Centre." *Art Monthly Australia* 138 (2001), pp. 5–9.

Hawken, S. "Suburban Alchemy." *Landscape Australia* no. 4 (2001), pp. 83–85.

"Ideen fur Berlin: Stadtebauliche und Landschaftsplanerische Wettbewerbe von 1991–1995." Berlin: Senat für Stadt Entwicklung und Umweltschutz, 1996

Jackson, D., and M. Keniger. "Radar: Museum of Australia." *Architecture Australia*, 87, no. 1 (1998), pp. 12–13.

Jackson, D. "Radar Landscape Belmore Park." *Architecture Australia* (1998), p. 24.

Jacobs, G. "Bambus in Licht und Nebel." *Garten und Landschaft* 3 (2001), 22–23.

Jencks, C. "The Meaning of Australia." *Domus*, no. 837 (2001), pp. 96–115.

Jones, R.S. "Breaking New Ground." *Gardens Illustrated*, 74 (2002), p. 106.

Kearney, C. "A Room of Their Own." *UNSW News, Alumni Edition* (2003).

Keniger, Michael. "Taste Over Analysis: The Garden of Australian Dreams." *Architecture Australia* 92, no. 5 (2003), pp. 34–36.

Macarthur, J. "Australian Baroque: Geometry and Meaning at the National Museum of Australia." *Architecture Australia* 90, no. 2 (2001), pp. 48–61.

McGrath, A, C. Bull, P. Carter, P. Droege, and L. van Schaik. "Troubled Dreams." *Architectural Review* 85 (2003), pp. 24–28.

Michael, L. (ed.). *Seppelt Contemporary Art Awards 1998*. Catalogue, Museum of Contemporary Art, Sydney, Australia, November 27, 1998–February 28, 1999. Exhibit curated by MCA senior curator Linda Michael.

Müller, C. "Gartenhof Des Din-Instituts, Berlin." *Topos: European Landscape Magazine* (Callwey Munchen), no. 11 (1995), pp. 19–24.

Neale, R. "Small Garden." *Landscape Australia* no. 1 (1997), pp. 41–44.

O'Brien, G. "Grounds for Inspiration in the State's Premier Home." *Sydney Morning Herald*, June 2002.

Perlman, I. "Contested Ground." *Australian Financial Review*, November 2002, pp. 78–84.

————. "Museum for a PlayStation Generation." *Sydney Morning Herald*, March 19, 2001, p. 16.

Pickersgill, S. "Magill Estate." *Architecture Australia* (July–August 1996), pp. 45–50.

Pickette, S. "East Meets West." *Pol Oxygen* 4 (2003), pp. 130–141.

Poblotzki, U. "Ein Ort Der Zehnten Muse." *Topos: European Landscape Magazine* (Callwey Munchen, Munich), no. 4 (1993), pp. 74–80.

Rooke, B. "Convergences." *Landscape Australia* no. 3 (1999), pp. 200–202.

Simon, K. "Sky Garden--184 Black Box Life Recorders." *Architecture Australia* 92, no. 2 (2003), pp. 70–75.

Tonkin, C. "Hope Against Hope." *D2Ecod* (Sydney, Ecodesign Foundation), vol. 3, no. 3(1995), pp. 8–9.

Ward, P. "Triumph of Trivialisation." *Australian*, March 16, 2001, p. 39.

Weirick, J. "Landscape and Politics: The Museum and Its Site." *Architectural Review*, no. 75 (2001), p. 63.

Wilson A. "The Way Ahead"--"Garden as Theatre of Lights." *Landscape Design* (UK), June 1996, p. 12.

Young, C. "Czech Mate." *Garden Design Journal* (UK), October–November 2002, pp. 30–33.

INTERNET PUBLICATIONS

Weller, R. "Toward an Art of Infrastructure." *www.geocities.com/ateliermp/landscapeurbanism.html*

————. "Strange Parks: A Thousand Words on the Downsview Five" in *Juncus* (electronic journal – http://www.juncus.com/downsview, December 2000), no 1. *www.room413.com.au*

Interviews

Australian Broacasting Corporation (ABC). "Modern Gardens." "Gardening Australia" series, 2002.

"By Design." Foxtel Lifestyle Channel, "Future Gardens." July 31, 2000.

"By Design." Foxtel Lifestyle Channel, Episode 13. October 19, 1999.

"Der Garten als Buehne." Arte Television (European television channel), June 14, 2003.

"Search for Eden." Episode 6, ABC TV, 2002.

Shipp, A. "Pentagon Plans Crash Memorial." *West Australian*.

Sitta, V. Interview about design of Slavic Square in Brno, Czech Republic, Radio Praha, November 1992.

———. Interview with Michael Bates. "Paradise Transformed." *The Comfort Zone*, ABC Radio National, Canberra, May 1996.

———. Interview with Jirina Perinová, Czech Republic, Radio Praha, November 1995.

———. Interview with Alan Saunders. "Fire in the Garden." *The Comfort Zone*, ABC Radio National, Canberra, 1999.

———. Interview with Václav Starý. "National Museum Australia." SBS Radio, Czech broadcasting, 2001.

Weller, R. Interview with Michael Bates. "The National Museum of Australia." The Comfort Zone, ABC Radio National, Canberra, November 1997.

———. Interview with editors. "Room 4.1.3 – Interview with Richard Weller." *The Architect: Journal of the WA Chapter of the Royal Australian Institute of Architects* 2 (2003), pp. 34–35.

———. Interview with Kirsten McKenzie. "Education Forum." *Landscape Australia* 25, no. 2 (2003), pp. 8–12.

———. Interview with John McNamara. *The Pentagon Memorial*. Drive Time 7.20. ABC Radio

———. Interview with Natalie O'Brien. "Triumph Where a Legend Was Born." *Australian*, September 23, 1998, p. 14.

———. Interview with Alan Saunders. "The Garden of Intelligence." *The Comfort Zone*, ABC Radio National, November 19, 1998.

———. Interview with Alan Saunders. "The Ruins of the Pentagon." *The Comfort Zone*, ABC Radio, November 11, 2002.

———. Interview with Alan Saunders. "Wilderness and Western Australia." *The Comfort Zone*, ABC Radio National, June 15, 2002.

———. Interview with Frances Saunders. "An Interview with Richard Weller." *Landscape Australia* no. 3 (1999), pp. 259–263.

———. Interview with Alex Sloane. "Garden of Australian Dreams." ABC Radio, Canberra, November 22, 2003.

———. Interview with David Webber. "The Pentagon Memorial." AM 630 ABC Radio National, October 27, 2002.

———. Radio debate with Dr. John Carroll. "Garden of Australian Dreams." *The Comfort Zone*, ABC Radio National, Perth, July 19, 2003.

———. "The Rubric of Place." Eight-minute essay delivered on *Arts Today* (ABC Radio National, 24 September 1997). Responded to by Dr. Richard Read, UWA; Professor Emeritus George Seddon, UWA; & Professor Stephen Muecke, UTS.

Weller, R., and V. Sitta. Interview with editors of KERB. "The Room Replies." *KERB: Journal of Landscape Architecture*, no. 9 (2001).

———. Interview with Rhiannon Brown. "The Garden of Australian Dreams." *Arts Today*, ABC Radio National, December 4, 2000.

CONTRIBUTORS

ROD BARNETT is a Senior Lecturer in Landscape Architecture in the School of Landscape and Plant Science at UNITEC Institute of Technology, Auckland, New Zealand. He has a background in poetry and philosophy. His current research focuses on ideas of nature in contemporary urbanism, with particular emphasis on the application of nonlinear systems theory to landscape architectural design.

JACKY BOWRING is editor of *Landscape Review Journal* and senior lecturer in the Landscape Architecture Group, Lincoln University, New Zealand, with research interests in language and landscape, design theory and critique, and the cultural landscape. She maintains an active interest in design as a form of research.

PAUL CARTER, a Melbourne-based writer and artist, is the author of several significant postcolonial histories such as The Road to Botany Bay. His public art projects include Tracks (North Terrace, Adelaide) and Nearamnew (Federation Square, Melbourne). His most recent book is *Repressed Spaces: The Poetics of Agoraphobia* (London: Reaktion Books, 2002). He is professorial research fellow, the Australian Centre, University of Melbourne.

PETER CONNOLLY is senior lecturer at the Royal Melbourne Institute of Technology (RMIT). His research focuses on reconstructing the relation between aesthetics and design representation in landscape architecture. He played a leading role in the development of the design focus of the RMIT Landscape Architecture program during the nineties, was program director from 1997 to 2000, and founded and coordinated the Master's by Design project program.

DENIS COSGROVE is the Alexander von Humboldt Professor of Geography at the University of California at Los Angeles. His influential and interdisciplinary books include *Apollo's Eye: A Cartographic Genealogy of the Earth in the Western Imagination* (Baltimore: Johns Hopkins University Press, 2001) and *The Iconography of Landscape: Essays on the Symbolic Representation, Design and Use of Past Environments* (Cambridge: Cambridge University Press, 1988; ed. with S. Daniels), 2001. He edited a collection of essays entitled *Mappings* (London: Reaktion Books, 2001) and has contributed essays to James Corner's *Taking Measures Across the American Landscape* (New Haven: Yale University Press, 1996) and *Recovering Landscape: Essays in Contemporary Landscape Theory* (New York: Princeton Architectural Press, 1999).

GAVIN KEENEY is the author of *On the Nature of Things: Contemporary American Landscape Architecture* (Basel: Birkhauser, 2000) and director of Landscape Agency New York, a design, writing, and research office.

JULIAN RAXWORTHY is a landscape architect, lecturing at the Royal Melbourne Institute of Technology. He has worked for a range of design practices in Melbourne and Sydney, notably ASPECT, with whom he cofounded their Sydney office. He was one of the founders of KERB, an alternative Australian magazine of landscape architecture. His academic and professional research concerns contemporary design techniques and digital media.

VLADIMIR SITTA is director of Room 4.1.3 and also maintains a separate private practice in exclusive garden design. Australia's most distinguished international landscape architect, he is widely respected as a master craftsman. He received an Australian Institute of Landscape Architects award for lifelong achievement in 2002.

Index

Acknowledgments

Richard Weller and Vladimir Sitta wish to thank Elizabeth Burt, Karl Kullmann, Martin Musiatowicz, and particularly Thomas Griffiths for their consecutive efforts in the compilation and design of this book. Tatum Hands has been a shrewd in-house editor and provided constant encouragement. The office of Müller Knipschild Wehberg (now trading as Lutzow 7) deserves special mention, as they were instrumental collaborators in several significant projects.

We are also sincerely grateful to all the following individuals and organizations who have contributed in varying capacities to our work: Simon Anderson, Helen Armstrong, Constanza Bitzageo, Julien Bolleter, Victor and Cassandra Bossell, Veronica Brady, Craig Burton, Amanda Carol, Paul Carter, Dib Dib, Julie Dowling, Gerald Ekhart, Lutger Engel, Peter England, Robert Faber, Daniel Firns, Gary Ford, Luca Ginoulhiac, Simeon Glasson, Nathan Greenhill, Thomas Griffiths, Tatum Hands, Keli Harrison, Peter Ireland, Frank Kie ling, Connie Kolmann, Jo Law, Lorne Leonard, Geoff London, Kamel Louafi, Jenny Marschner, Joanna McNeal, Paul Moravcik, Elke Morneweg, Martin Musiatowicz, Andrew Nugent, Caroline Oldham, Pavol Pollak, Graham Pont, Oleg Putilin, Leon van Schaik, Lisa Shine, Eva Sitta, Des Smith, Sid Thoo, Jan Ûimek, Stephen Vigilante, Ian Weir, Nigel Westbrook, and Kevin Williams.

Creative Design and Technology; Lutzow 7; Studio Daniel Libeskind; Ashton Raggatt McDougall; Allen, Jack & Cottier; Faculty of Architecture, Landscape and Visual Arts at the University of Western Australia; Graduate Design School at the Royal Melbourne Institute of Technology; Museum of Contemporary Art, Sydney; Urban Contractors (ACT); Above the Earth–Landscape Constructions.

We wish also to thank the inspirational essayists, Rod Barnett, Jackie Bowring, Paul Carter, Peter Connolly, Denis Cosgrove, Gavin Keeney, Julian Raxworthy, and, of course, the team at the University of Pennsylvania Press and John Dixon Hunt, who first recognized, then risked this book.

Photography Credits
All photographs by Room 4.1.3 unless otherwise noted.

Walter Glover: pages 158, 159
John Gollings: pages 204, 209, 226, 227, 228, 229, 230 (bottom), 232–233
Heidrun Lohn: pages 107, 108, 109
Jurgen Wilhelm: page 145